HIST

07

D0438513

My Father's Secret War

JUL 2 4 2007

My Father's Secret War

A MEMOIR

Lucinda Franks

3 1336 07622 8825

miramax books

HYPERION

NEW YORK

Copyright © 2007 Lucinda Franks

All rights reserved. No part of this book may be used or reproduced in
any manner whatsoever without the written permission of the Publisher.
Printed in the United States of America. For information address
Hyperion, 77 West 66th Street, New York, NY 10023-6298

ISBN 1-4013-5226-X

First Edition
10 9 8 7 6 5 4 3 2 1

For Bob

Prologue

The hill is very long, but I'm taking it slowly, feet hard on the brakes. Below, our house is just a speck of red. I know my father is waiting for me in the driveway, straddling his bike. I know he's smiling.

As I pick up speed, I flatten my palms against the handlebars, steadying myself, just as Daddy has taught me. Gradually, calmly, I begin to lift them from the bars. Soon I'm soaring down the hill, arms raised to the sky, the hands of the wind holding me fast.

"Look, Daddy, look!"

I am at one with my beautiful bicycle. I am eight years old. I am queen of the wind, astride a panther's back, wheels growling, pebbles flying, swallowing up the black silky road.

But now I'm going so fast my feet can't find the brakes. I grab the bars but the panther bucks beneath me, roaring in my ears. The wheel goes this way, the wheel goes that way, and I'm heading straight for my father.

Daddy's arms fan out like wings. I cannot speak, cannot call out, cannot stop, faster and faster, closer and closer. Then I'm flying through space, over the handlebars. I'm going to die. My head meets his with a sickening crack, my foot twisted in the gears.

"Are you all right?" he shouts. "Are you all right?"

I open my eyes. Our tall red house is somersaulting over my body. I lift my head and see his face. Blood coats his teeth and trickles down his chin. My sweet, handsome Daddy, what have I done?

We are all tangled up, my father and I: arms spokes legs chains. My body hurts all over. But I can feel his breathing, in and out, in and out, gentle as the whisper of a butterfly. We are alive. And there is this peace, this tender happiness as I lie still upon his chest beneath the spinning wheel.

Chapter One

My father hadn't the pleasure of receiving his own eviction notice. It came to me instead, special delivery. "You will be forcibly removed from your apartment . . . ," it read, and for one cold moment I imagined that it was I who would be put out on the street. Then I saw the signature of my father's landlord, one of the world's most kindly souls. What horrors had driven him to this course of action? I could imagine his sympathy, his patience, hardening into desperation, the usual course of emotions that my father—a man so paradoxical he was almost an impossibility—induced in others. Rent unpaid, apartment overflowing with detritus, he had undoubtedly given the landlord my address and then run for cover. This was nothing new. Tom Franks had been a barnacle on my life for as long as I could remember.

It has never mattered what I do for my father: He sabotages it. I hire a cleaning lady; he fires her. I assemble the forms for veteran's benefits; he never files them. I ask him if he wants me to come up to Massachusetts and help him get organized, and—to my relief—he says no. Yet when things fall apart, I am the one he turns to.

For years, I'd closed my eyes. A respite. No cries of distress. No calls from creditors. Dared I hope that I might finally be free of him? But no, of course not. The eviction notice is followed by more warnings. His electricity, his phone, his gas are about to be cut off. He's been living in a firetrap, a health hazard, and an eyesore, and unless I come to the rescue, his next address—he, the perfect gentleman—will be a city shelter.

How can a man so vigorous he can still win state shooting championships in his eighties, fail to open his own mail? How can someone who so stubbornly dotes on his independence put himself in such jeopardy?

Furious, I take my six-year-old daughter, Amy, leaving my husband and son behind, and drive from New York City to my father's home in the little town of Milford, which lies forty miles northwest of Boston.

My father opens the door and gives us each a bear hug. Even though it's early afternoon, he's wearing a blue terrycloth bathrobe so full of holes it looks like it's been sprayed with a machine gun. Stubble sprouts from his chin, his fine brown hair sticks up at odd angles. I have to admit that even with his knobby knees peeking out from below his robe, there's something fortifying about my father. He's 6'3" and big-boned, with a big forehead and big chin, his moist blue eyes magnified by his glasses, and a Roman nose gone bumpy with age. His half-moon smile, topped by a frog-like upper lip, lights up his face and has inspired unbecoming behavior in even the most durable of women.

"Oh, you don't know how good it is to see you," he says. Then he ushers us into the kitchen with, under the circumstances, comical gallantry. I push past him into the next room, following a narrow path that winds from the study to the living room; it is essentially a canyon bordered by teetering towers of cardboard cartons. My heart sinks as I look at the piles of newspapers and flyers covering every available surface, save for a small space on the sofa reserved for his recalcitrant bottom.

He puts his hands on my shoulders and quickly guides me back into the kitchen, clearing a stack of Styrofoam takeout containers from a kitchen chair. "Won't you sit down?" he asks, pushing the chair right to the back of my knees.

I'd forgotten about this, his chivalrous persona. Even now, he hasn't lost it. He's always ceremoniously opened doors for women and rapidly surrendered his seat to them. "Please" and "thank you" fall frequently from his lips. It occurs to me now that these flourishes are a kind of salve, for he is exceedingly grateful for the attention they bring.

"Please," he entreats me, "let me offer you something to drink."

"No thanks, Dad," I say. What could we expect to find in his refrigerator? Sour milk? Rancid orange juice?

"Mom," Amy yells, holding out an open box of Wheaties she's found on the kitchen counter. "They're moving!" We proceed to unearth a half dozen other open boxes of cereal, all crawling with weevils. On top of the cartons there's a parade of plastic bags. Out of curiosity I open them. The first bag: flashlight, shaving cream, Tums. The second bag: flashlight, shaving cream, Tums. The third bag: flashlight, shaving cream, Tums. I'm in a movie that keeps rewinding.

"Dad," I sigh, turning to the man who stands there smiling obliviously, "what have you done here?" I'm about to cry. "Why do you do this? Just look! Look at this mess."

His neck comes out like a turtle's. He peers right, peers left, peers up. "Whatever do you mean?" he replies.

My father was born Thomas Edward Franks in Champaign, Illinois, an only child in a prosperous but unassuming family. His father, a morally erect man, owned an insurance firm and served as mayor of the city. His mother was an accomplished pianist who, when she found out her son was tone-deaf, lost interest in him. He seemed not to care. He was too busy teaching himself a multitude of skills. He perfected his marksmanship by shooting woodchucks and squirrels for local farmers. He built a chemistry lab in the cellar and set off explosions in a field on the edge of town until the Champaign police put an end to that. By the time he was nineteen, he was paying his way through the University of Illinois, majoring in chemistry and engineering. General Alloys, a specialized metal-casting firm in Chicago, recognized his gifts and hired him straight out of college.

My parents met sometime in 1940, when Tom walked up to the counter at Marshall Field's where Lorraine was selling silk stockings. Mother said that he was considered a great social catch: tall, handsome, clever, and aloof. Her roommates in Chicago all vowed to snag him, but she, who played hard to get, was the one who did. She'd been born into a prominent midwestern family, the Swannell-Leavitts, who had once all but owned the town of Kankakee, Illinois. Her antecedents included a lady-in-waiting to Queen Victoria, a Connecticut bishop, and a London hatmaker. People would describe her as pretty, with her full lips, large blue eyes, and lively personality. They would also say she was smart, merciless, and beneath her insouciance, possessed of a deadly wit.

They married on November 17, 1941. Tom entered the U.S. Navy in late 1942 as an officer candidate and was commissioned as an ensign a few months later. After the war, he worked his way up to first vice-president of General Alloys. Then, after years of pregnancies gone wrong, I was born. Six years later, they produced my sister, Barbara Penelope. Choosing a stylish suburb of Boston, my mother moved us into a sprawling Tudor home in Wellesley, Massachusetts.

Mother was the brains behind a half dozen charities. Gay and funny, she gave out gifts for no reason, offered help freely to friends in need, and was in general much admired. My father, by contrast, was considered a hermit, more comfortable puttering at his basement workbench than cruising the social circuit. However, he was an elegant dancer, did a mean Charleston, and squired Mother around town on demand. They swept into Valentine Balls and Boston Pops benefits in their chiffon ball gowns and white tie and tails, and graced dinner parties from Wellesley to Boston. My mother was head of the Boston Opera Guild under Sarah Caldwell and got her husband to act in several productions as an extra. She loved to tell the story of how, wearing a priest's hat and brocade robes and carrying a tall crucifix for a performance of *Boris Godunov*, he stumbled down some steps and nearly speared a bishop.

Years later, after Mother died, Dad, then in his sixties and unemployed, dropped a bomb on me and Penny: He was almost penniless. Our parents' finances were a mess, we'd known that, but not that the situation was so dire. We had to sell our beloved childhood home and we had to sell it in a hurry. Penny and I packed up some one hundred cartons that held not only the contents of the house, but the memorabilia of three generations of grandparents on both sides of the family. We saved every ivory button, every cracked ramekin. Over the years, Penny and I have emptied some of the cartons, but most of them accompanied my father first to his new little house in nearby Hopkinton and then, as his financial circumstances worsened still further, to this smaller apartment in Milford. As I squeeze past the cartons, it appears that he's never opened one of them.

After we arrive, I hire local boys to clean out the bulk of the spoiled food, scour the kitchen, and lug the newspapers out to the dumpster; my father follows them around, bellowing in protest, "I can do this myself!" That's always been his mantra. He's walled off almost everyone from his life with his obstinacy—his wife, his daughters, his friends, his co-workers. I've been forced into an impossible position, a nagging figure against whom he must play the game of deflect, hide, duck, and resist. I hate being the side of my own mother he and I both detested.

Since my son, Josh, was born thirteen years ago, my father and I have tried to reach some kind of accommodation, though every word we share feels forced. My husband, Bob, and I invite him often to come to our apple orchards in Fishkill, in the Hudson Valley in upstate New York. Yet he's always canceling at the last minute: He's sick, he's tired, he isn't up to the drive. Is the divide between us too painful for him? I'll never know, for he's certainly not going to admit to anything. He ducks Penny the same way, seldom flying out to California to visit her. I know that he'd rather be with us and his grandchildren than anyone on earth. But he's always been afraid of something; it makes him glue himself to his Queen Anne sofa, once my mother's pride, now torn, its velvet brocade worn smooth. It makes him open the door no more than a crack when the neighbors come to check on him, makes him quickly dispatch them with a nod and a smile.

After the initial cleaning frenzy, Amy and I begin coming up every weekend to work on my father's apartment. We want to make it more livable for him, and frankly, it's a relief to get away from home. It's the girls against the boys back in New York City. Josh and I have always been extremely close, but when he hit the age of thirteen, he made it clear that just talking to his mother was as much fun as having a Cambodian root canal. The strife between us has sent Bob in the other direction, but when pressed, he takes Josh's side. He's an older father, after all, and he loves to have his youngest son's approval. Amy, on the other hand, is my special pal. We've begun to rather enjoy our trips up to Milford. My father loves his quirky granddaughter, with her Alice-in-Wonderland hair and heart-shaped lips. This unsmiling man comes alive in her presence. Sometimes he'll make his hands into birds' wings and flap them at her. Sometimes he'll put his thumbs in his ears and wave. She rewards him by breaking out into giggles. Sometimes he'll just look at her and say, "My little princess."

I was his little princess once upon a time. Just he and I and a huge white telescope in the middle of the dew-soaked lawn. He bought it for me when I was five. Spring, summer, fall, winter, we would go stargazing, peering cheek to cheek through the large lens he had ground himself, like twin stars huddling in the Northern Crown.

January is our favorite month. Although the cold sometimes brings on my asthma, that's when my favorite constellation is high in the sky. He lifts me up, shivering under two blankets, my eyes widening at the wonder of the galaxy. "Look, Cindy, look to the left. Do you see the three bright stars? What are they?"

"Orion's belt, Daddy!" The Mighty Warrior slowly emerges as Daddy points out each star, giving life to the head, the bright knee, the red cloud of gas that is his tummy: Orion, sword drawn back, so tall he can wade through the deepest sea.

"Uh-oh, I think he's going to get Taurus the bull this time."

"No, Daddy, he's going after the rabbit, he's going to chop his head right off."

"What's the name of the rabbit, Cindy?"

"Lepus!" We tour the dancing Pleiades sisters, the scuttling Cancer, the Canis hunting in a pack of two.

Sometimes the stars, shimmering like the sequins on Mother's silk gown, make me short of breath. I try to muffle my wheezes, but Daddy always knows. He hears the cats meowing in my chest and carries me away, leaving our beloved galaxy for a bed clammy with steam.

By age nine or ten, I can stand on my own two feet and look through the lens. Bulls and swords give way to nebulae, asteroids, quasars, celestial explosions. "Dad, what's beyond the universe, what does it look like?" The thought obsesses me, makes me shiver. "What do you think nothingness is?"

"That's a very good question, and I just don't know the answer."

"Dad, I think maybe God is beyond there." I'm an Episcopalian, indoctrinated by Mother, and he's something she calls a "damned atheist."

He unscrews the lens. "Maybe you're right," he says gently.

As I grow older, we hurtle out of the orbit that held us together. He's away from home more and more, on mysterious business trips. The telescope slowly rusts in the garage. There are a few perfunctory kisses on the head as he goes down to his workbench. We play a board game or two, but he drifts off in the middle. He acts with me as he acts with all adults: remote, emotionally impenetrable, a voyager to places I cannot reach. I become caught in a conundrum: My father acts as though he loves me, but if this is so, why is he so far away? Like someone whose real self has been sucked up forever into the jaws of a big black hole.

Every carton I unpack now is a reminder of the puzzles and pleasures of my childhood. At the bottom of one, I find old records: Dixieland, Rag, the complete collection of Knuckles O'Toole albums.

I hear the rhythm of Daddy's footsteps as he comes home from the office, tossing off his hat, heading for the record player, which Mother had disguised as a French Provincial lowboy, taking off her Ezio Pinza LP, and dropping on Knuckles O'Toole. His favorite ragtime player could move his fingers up and down the keyboard as fast as a hummingbird's wings. Daddy would stand over the phonograph, tapping his foot and snapping his fingers. You always knew Daddy was taking a shower when you heard his sonorous bass booming "bum-bum, bum-bum." Unfortunately, he only had two good notes, which was why he confined his singing to the bathroom.

Sometimes, he'd take me to New York to hear bands like the Dukes of Dixieland. We'd sit in some smoky dive, my feet dangling from a barstool. The reticent father I knew from home would vanish, replaced by an animated man who joyfully beat his hands on the mahogany counter in time to the clarinets and saxophones and drums. Now he doesn't even listen to jazz. The phonograph is long gone, and he's never replaced it. If Knuckles still exists, he's somewhere in my father's head.

Another box contains a mishmash of chipped china wrapped in strips of pink insulation, decks of cards, papers, pennies, a butterfly net that my father had made out of green mesh, and a number of homemade bullets rolling around on the bottom. Bullets and butterflies, such a bizarre combination of hobbies. I let the lead slugs sift through my hand.

Smells of childhood: pea soup simmering on the stove, wet dog, hot radiators, sweaty socks, lilies in the living room. All the scents I never had. Instead, the warm, bitter odor of gunpowder and molten lead had wafted up from the cellar as Dad, in his murky lair, meticulously cast his ammunition. He melted old bullets on a special hotplate, slowly tapping the gunpowder into the rows of indentations in the mold. A champion marksman, he insisted that his homemade bullets shot more accurately. The acrid smell permeated everything, as my mother crossly strode about the house, squirting eau de cologne into the air in a futile attempt to mask it.

The carton bulges with evidence of his other hobbies. I find some old minutes of the meetings of the Cambridge Entomological Society. He used to be an officer of the society, an authority on insects, a tournament bridge player, and an authority on the Jazz Age. He had a pilot's license and flew planes, caught big swordfish that won prizes. He once had a collection of American Civil War tomes filling two wall-to-wall bookcases, many of them first editions. After he'd exhausted the subject, he'd given most of them to some library. Now his only hobbies are chain-smoking and reading gun magazines.

The next carton, stained and crumbling to the touch, is filled with delicious artifacts—old brocade napkins and lace doilies stained brown with age, baby dresses hand-smocked by my mother, skimpy negligees with gathered bosoms that she must have worn as a bride. I finger a disintegrating rose silk sweater that must have belonged to some distant granny. I love finding this stuff, the fusty smell, the miniature embroidery, the thought of careful, intent hands that worked the cloth under much dimmer lights.

The carton below it is labeled "Mother's BOTTOM Dresser Drawer." The secret drawer, where Penny and I knew that beneath her underwear she kept a box containing a pink plastic diaphragm and letters from an old flame named Jimmy Green. She spoke longingly of Green, who became a successful doctor; when I felt sorry for her, I would fantasize that she had married him. In the three decades since our mother's death, neither Penny nor I have had the courage to examine the contents of her drawer again. Inside the carton I find the satin nightgowns she liked so much. She bought them in different shades

of pastel. They're limp, sad, musty now. I lift out diamond-shaped bottles faintly redolent of her favorite Shalimar perfume, long white slips,
big bras with hooks crawling like centipedes down the back, huge girdles yellowed with age, the rubber brittle and cracking.

I turn to the next carton, which is filled with Mother's old files.
I'm tossing bunches of them into the mouth of a garbage bag, which
leans toward me like an eager lamprey.

I look over at my father, his big, veiny hand on Amy's shoulder.
They're sitting on the couch in the living room, watching westerns. He's
holding his usual cigarillo. There's a trail of ashes snaking down the
plaid flannel shirt beneath his ratty bathrobe. I'm embarrassed looking at him. This is the man who wore blue cashmere suits, real silk ties,
crisp white hankies peeking out of his pocket. The man who patted his
lips with a napkin, lit his cigarette with a flourish of silver, and wore
cheap English Leather cologne just because I gave it to him.

Suddenly I smell something. "Dad, look what you're doing!" I cry.
He is burning a hole in his pants. He looks at the cigarillo curiously
and then moves it away from his pants.

"You could have set yourself on fire!" I say.

"These pants aren't flammable," he replies in his deep, authori-
tative voice. "I don't wear flammable pants."

"What are you talking about? All pants are flammable! I mean, at
some point they're going to burn, they could go up in flames if you
doze off." I survey the room; the evidence of his carelessness is everywhere. "Look at all these burn holes, on your pants, on the rug, on the
sofa cover."

"I'm very careful, I know what I'm doing," he replies. He was always manic about fire when I was growing up; he would eye me after
I blew out a match to see if I would commit the uttermost crime of tossing it into the wastebasket before it stopped glowing.

"You don't put your cigarette down, that's the problem," I say, trying to get my voice under control. "Between puffs, you just hold it
between your fingers. You could set this house on fire and the people upstairs would never get out. They would scream and burn and

nobody would hear them!" His apartment occupies the bottom floor of a house, and a middle-aged woman and her adult daughter occupy the top.

"You're wildly exaggerating."

I whirl around and go off into the kitchen and start in on his refrigerator, throwing out all the expired food that has accumulated since last weekend. I stick my head back into the living room. "You're being irresponsible!" I shout, before returning to the icebox, where I drop a box of blueberries, sending them flying all over the place, pick them up and drop them again. I stomp back into the living room and shout some more.

"Look," he says, taking a long, deep draw from his cigarillo, "my landlord came to talk to me about my smoking and I gave him a tour of the house. This is what I showed him." He gets up and points out little fire extinguishers under the cedar chest, on the wall, next to the couch, everywhere. "He left without another word."

"Huh. This must be the same landlord who's about to evict you."

As usual with my father, there's no use arguing; it's like hitting a bulletproof wall. But I do manage a smile—my little helper Amy is writing notes in red marker and is taping them all over the place: "Put yr sigret down wen yr not smokin it." This he agrees to do, and does— for about two minutes before it begins to dangle from his hand again.

"I could use some fresh coffee," he says cheerily, coming into the kitchen for the fifth of his ten cups a day. He's apparently forgotten our spat over his smoking. But he's still wearing the blue terrycloth robe that he greeted us in when we arrived this morning, which I consider a hostile act. No amount of reasoning or even bribes have convinced him to put on a fresh shirt and a pair of pants so we can go out to his favorite restaurant, the Newport Creamery, whose name, for reasons I cannot imagine, he has somehow reinvented as the Herschel Creamery.

"Dad," I say, "why not just get in the car? You can make an appearance at the Newport or Herschel Creamery or whatever it's called in your nightclothes. You'd be a real hit."

"That's an idea," he says as he walks back into the living room, coffee cup held high.

"It's not as though I'm asking you to put on full tuxedo dress," I continue. "Just why are you doing this, Dad?"

"Damned if I know," he says, reaching for one of his many open packs of cigarillos. He taps the cigarillo down on the end table in front of him, takes a yellow Bic, and slowly lights it. "Okay, okay, just hold on a minute," he says. "I'd like to have another smoke first."

I give him a dirty look. Once again, I feel the old anger and with it the old pity. One moment, I'm sure he's refusing to dress just to torment me, and the next, I go cold and scare myself with absurd pictures: Has he forgotten how to dress himself? Is he worried he'll put his underpants on over his trousers? I wave the ridiculous thought away. My father is the sharpest man I know.

"Is there anything to eat here?" he asks plaintively, as though he were a guest in his own home. He has apparently forgotten about going out. I glance at the clock. It's three o'clock in the afternoon and he probably hasn't eaten since yesterday. I give up arguing with him and put a frying pan on his one-burner hot plate, melt butter, and tear up pieces of ham and cheese. Then I scramble in two eggs of unknown age that I find in the icebox. I'm no cook, so I lean over, nose to the bubbling mixture, to be sure the edges of the omelet curl up crisp and brown, which is how he likes it. I hear Amy's little voice, a diminutive version of mine in a sane moment, and peek into the living room. "Grandpop, come here. You have to get up and put on your pants," she says matter-of-factly, tugging at his hand. He smiles, holds onto the arm of the sofa, and allows her to think she's pulled him up. Then, uncannily, he goes into his bedroom. When he emerges fully clothed, in a faded short-sleeved shirt and wrinkled pants, with even his socks and shoes on, my daughter looks at me with sly pride.

"See, Mom," she says, quietly so he cannot hear, "if you scream for somebody to do something, they won't do it and then they feel terrible about not doing it and that makes them not want to do it even more." Thank you, my six-year-old daughter.

The eggs are ready and my father comes into the kitchen. I sit with him, watching him chew with an unnerving slowness, and I understand for the first time how frustrating my mother found this.

"Gee, look at that red bird pecking at the grass." Dad puts down his fork and peers out the window. He speaks in low tones, stretching out his vowels. Amy says he sounds like Eeyore. "I think it's a, oh, what's its name."

"A cardinal, Dad," I say. Funny that an avid birder would forget the name of such a common bird. The kindly women upstairs have put out a garden chair for him and spread seed on the lawn so he can sit outside and watch the birds when the weather's fine.

"Mmm, these are the best eggs I've ever had." I smile because this was what he always said when I used to cook him something, no matter how simple. Finally, after forty-five minutes, he folds his napkin and says, "I never eat like this when I'm by myself."

I sigh. I don't even want to think about what he feeds himself when I'm not around. I settle him back in front of the television again with Amy so I can get back to the chore of cleaning out Mother's old files.

Between a pile of them are two small boxes. One is a flat cardboard box sealed securely with layers of a kind of duct tape. I use a sharp knife to open it and find one empty, army-green film can and ten transparent envelopes with tiny rolls of negatives inside. I hold them up to the light; they're snapshots of distant ships, some aircraft, and blurred, factory-type buildings with smokestacks. Also a series of what look like some kind of machine and boiler. Boring pictures. Why were they taken?

Next I find a wooden cigar box whose latch is rusted out; inside are what appear to be old Navy pins and tiny bars of different colored ribbon. There's a smattering of foreign money: blue notes from New Caledonia, two large silver coins from Britain, French francs, a few Swedish kronor. And then a creased square of thin brown paper— it looks like the toilet paper I used when I was based in London— with three names on it: Bourbon, Granny, Alf. I also find a receipt from a restaurant or maybe it's a bar in Gotenborg, Sweden—I can't make out the name or date—and a carefully folded square of silky material. I open it to find a map written in fine black ink with the destination, X, in a circle. The street names are smeared, unreadable. What on earth do all these things mean?

I fish down to the bottom of the carton and suddenly I'm holding a military cap. It's grayish green with white trim and a sharp peak rising high above the brim and then sloping down at the back. At the top is the raised metal insignia of an eagle, and at the bottom a skull and crossbones. Now I find a threaded badge in the shape of a cross with flared sides and a thin white border. Was it what my mother had sewn on her Red Cross jacket during the war, when she drove trucks full of wounded soldiers? No, it seems too big.

Perhaps it's some kind of religious cross. During my childhood, my mother marched us off to St. Andrew's Episcopal Church each Sunday. My father was the only one of us who never went, he who had been an Episcopalian altar boy and once was so serious about his religion that he planned to go into a seminary. But by the time I was born, he had lost his faith. He scoffed at religion: "How can you believe in God after everything that's happened in the world?"

Anyway, this doesn't really look like a crucifix; it's too square. I turn the badge over and feel a chill. There's a swastika inside the middle of the cross, a symbol of the Nazi party. I examine the cap again, and sure enough, in a circle just below the aluminum eagle, is another raised swastika. An Iron Cross. A Nazi cap . . . in my father's house?

When I was growing up, all I ever knew about my father's military service was that he was a Navy lieutenant who wanted to go to sea but was instead assigned to be a liaison to the U.S. Marines in the Solomon Islands. He would divulge little more than that.

I feel a sudden wave of anxiety. Was my sphinx-like father presenting one character and living another? He was fluent in German. I knew that he was almost thirty when he joined the Navy. Was his history before that carefully constructed to obscure another life? Did he really go to the Pacific or was he at the Abwehr huddling over secret intelligence reports with Wilhelm Canaris? Was he an informer who went back and forth between America and Germany? Whose side was he really on?

Two years ago, Bob and I had convinced my father to give videotaped testimony about his war activities to the Museum of Jewish Heritage in New York. Even though he had never opened up for me, he had done so for the world, telling the story of one remarkable and grisly day in the European Theater. I had wanted to hear more. But after that day, every time I tried to pin his shadow to the events of World War II, tried to get behind his façade, I was met with his usual stony silence. He was still the Man Who Wasn't There. He probably always would be.

I look back down at the cap and Iron Cross in my hands, symbols of horror, buried beneath the files Mother kept while running charity drives, the epitome of suburban innocence.

Discovering them changes everything. What these odd things in the boxes add up to I don't know, but now I have visible evidence of something that even Dad cannot deny.

I walk into the living room holding what I want to know about most—the cap and cross. "Dad, what is this stuff?" I ask. "I found it in one of Mom's cartons."

He leans forward and squints. He looks at the cross and cap for a long time. "I don't know," he says blankly.

"You must know."

He takes the cap in his hands and turns it around. "Huh," he grunts. He doesn't touch the cross, in fact seems to recoil from it.

"Dad? What's a German cap and an Iron Cross doing in Mom's belongings?" I suddenly have an unpleasant thought. Could my mother have had an affair with a Nazi?

"It didn't belong to your mother," my father says. "It was mine, from the war. It's something I'd rather not talk about."

"It was yours? From the war? But I don't understand."

"I would rather not talk about it."

"I'd rather you did."

"Some other time, I'll tell you about it some other time."

I know that some other time will never come. I sit down and think about my father's attributes. He has a photographic memory and a face that he can keep absolutely deadpan in any circumstance. He is steel-willed. He is unflappable. He is a crack shot. And now the silk map and the foreign coins and the tiny negatives and the names written on toilet paper.

But it's the cross and cap that ignite a fuse, a sense of urgency about my dad that I've never felt before. I think about that bizarre story Lou Golden, then Dad's best friend, told me: the one that had led to Dad's museum testimony. And now I remember something else too: the hints Lou gave that Dad was a haunted man, that he had done some peculiar things during the war. Lou was a peculiar character himself and I had learned to tune out some of his more peppery monologues. Besides, life with my father had been too hard for too long. At the time, I simply didn't listen.

I pick up the cap and run my hands along the shiny, smooth brim. Perhaps now I had a reason to listen.

Chapter Two

It takes me a while to track down Lou's number, but I know that my pack-rat father will have it somewhere, even if he hasn't spoken to Lou for years. Finally I find it, written neatly on a napkin pressed between two gun magazines.

I dial the number on the kitchen phone and Lou's unmistakable voice answers. "Well, well," he says, "is this really *the* Lucinda Laura Franks Morgenthau? The one who writes for the great *New York Times*? Have you read your own newspaper lately? It really takes the cake, Cindy. Did you see that story last Sunday about a neo-Nazi demonstration in Skokie—the reporter was fairly leaking anti-Semitic—"

I cut him off. "Lou, remember about what Dad did in that restaurant and what he said to you afterward? Could you tell me that story again? Something's happened, and I need to know if I missed something." Perhaps I would hear the story with different ears, perhaps now it would yield some clues.

So Lou tells me about the night Tom and a few friends entered their favorite restaurant: The hostess is tossing her hair and giving Tom Franks a big smile as the men come through the door. She ushers them into the bar area. "Why don't you relax until we call your name?"

The atmosphere at the restaurant is warm and cozy, the low clinking of the crystal glasses a counterpoint to the high strains of Muzak. Patrons lean across little tables, enveloped in bourbon-laced bonhomie.

A loud voice cuts through the murmurings. A young man leans back in his chair and stabs the air with his finger. He shakes his head at his companions: "I tell you I was getting jewed at this kike store . . ."

One of Tom's friends rolls his eyes, looks behind him, and glares at the man. He turns back to Tom, "Can you believe this . . . ?" But Tom is gone.

In a blur of motion, he's knocked the man off his chair by slamming the heel of his palm into his chin. The man lays sprawled on the red carpet. Then Tom kneels on the young man's arms and coolly presses a thumb into the right side of his neck as he thrashes helplessly. It takes three men to pull Tom off.

Tom's friends are stunned. It's ludicrous to think that Tom Franks, a peace-loving man, would raise his fist, much less try to choke the life out of someone. How on earth did this septuagenarian lay out a man half his age on the floor of a cocktail lounge? They hustle Tom out the door, dinner forgotten. One of them calls Lou Golden.

The next day Lou is in Tom's kitchen in Hopkinton. Lou is head of the Massachusetts chapter of the Anti-Defamation League. Passionately pro-Israel, he is an intense man with eyes that shine ominously at the mention of anti-Semites; he caricatures them so virulently in a local Jewish newsletter that he seems to be employing a kind of reverse Protocols of the Elders of Zion. This has always attracted my father, ostensibly one of the world's most passionate Anglo-Saxon Zionists. But even Lou is shocked at Tom's reaction at the restaurant. He leans across the kitchen table and stares into his best friend's eyes.

"What the hell was going on in that bar, Tom?" he demands. "Tell me."

Tom lowers his head into his hands, balancing it on his finger-tips. "I took an oath," he says finally. "I swore I'd never tell anyone."

Lou says nothing, just waits patiently. He notices Tom's muscles are trembling.

A long pause, then the story slowly comes out, word by painful word. During World War II, Tom had been trained in special techniques; he'd learned how to eavesdrop on conversations, how to read lips, how to recognize the enemy and take them off guard. Skills long buried, or so he had thought. On one of his missions, in April 1945, he'd been sent into the first Nazi concentration camp discovered by Americans. "We were instructed to memorize everything we saw, turn in one hand-written report, and never to speak of it to anyone, ever," he tells Lou.

There was no time or place for him to understand what he'd seen, which was like nothing he'd ever seen before, but the images were blazed on his soul forever. Somehow he'd been able to push them down beyond conscious memory. They returned for the first time in half a century when he'd heard a man blithely slandering the Jews. "I couldn't help myself, Lou," he says. "I didn't even know what I was doing until I did it."

After Tom spilled his secret to Lou, he made his best friend swear he would never tell a soul. Within a week, Lou had told me.

When he found out, my father responded by abruptly ending the decades-long friendship. He never spoke to Lou again.

"Lou," I tell him now, "I found some stuff among Dad's belong-ings that worries me. A cap and an Iron Cross, the kind that was worn by—"

"The Nazis. Well, well. Surprised I am not," he says. "I guess it would fit."

"What do you mean? Fit what?"

"I don't know if I should be even talking to you about this. Look where it got me last time. There I was, simply trying to bring you and your father back together, give you something you could admire about him, and the next thing I know he's not taking my calls. And you haven't been either! But hell, I'm not one to hold a grudge. When he told me about the restaurant incident, he also let out he'd been in some kind of special outfit. That, I told you before. It did very out-of-the-ordinary things. He wouldn't go into it, but it obviously bothered him. I don't think Tom ever got over what happened while he was in that unit."

I go over every detail of the story with Lou, but he doesn't know anything about Dad's strange souvenirs. I hang up and sit there numb. Did the cap and cross have anything to do with Dad's "special techniques" training? Were they part of a disguise? Was Dad involved in some kind of undercover operation? For whom?

Daddy's stories about his tour in the Pacific always made it sound as if it was one big frat party. Ask him and he trotted out the same few yarns: They were desperately hungry in Guadalcanal and had stolen a buddy's pet pig and roasted it. Then he'd thrown a grenade in a lake and the natives thought he was a god because fish flew into the air and landed onshore. Was he in combat with the Japanese? He'd just give a cynical little laugh.

Why would Dad cut Lou off for revealing that he'd been to a concentration camp? What was so "secret" about that? Lou had been Dad's dearest friend and confidant since the seventies; he'd bailed him out when Dad ran into business trouble, stood by him through all his hard times. If my father was worried that, as an investigative reporter, I would dig further, he was mistaken. I'd long ago grown exhausted trying.

Fortunately, my husband hadn't.

Robert M. Morgenthau cared very deeply about a fact that seemed beyond dispute: Tom Franks had witnessed the liberation of a concentration camp. Bob was a founder of New York's Museum of Jewish Heritage: A Living Memorial to the Holocaust, and he was determined to get my father to talk about the camps. As I well knew, few people said no to Robert Morgenthau.

Heaven knows I'd tried to, twenty years before. When I first met Bob, I didn't want to fall in love with him, for though he was a man of grace and humor, he also happened to be about thirty years my senior, closer to my father's age than my own. He was also a widower with five children, two dogs, and a cat. I was a reporter for the *New York Times* and he, the District Attorney of New York County. I was looking for a good news source, not romance, while Bob claims he fell in love with me the first time I interviewed him. Those were the days when May–September weddings between professional people were uncommon, and no one in his family was pleased with our romance. In fact, when he announced our engagement, his cousins implored him to see a psychiatrist. My friends were also worried. We were quite badly smitten, however, and feeling like Romeo and Juliet, we were married in just over a year.

Lately, like many World War II veterans, Bob has become flooded with memories of a war that once he only wanted to forget. Having spent those years stashed away on two destroyers, in both the Mediterranean and the Pacific, Bob never really knew what was going on elsewhere on the war fronts. When the fighting was over, he had little interest in knowing. The hostilities had been so unbelievably bloody and the enemy so unimaginably evil that our soldiers came home in a fog, their world so altered that their survival depended on their determination to forget.

But time cleansed those years of the immediacy of their horror; books like Tom Brokaw's *The Greatest Generation* celebrated the veterans' unique modesty and courage. They began to remember and couldn't stop. In recent years, our home in New York has overflowed with books and videos about wartime naval battles, along with monographs and unbound testimonies from sailors who survived ships that sank.

It was only from others that I knew Bob was a war hero. I'd found a gold star, awarded in lieu of a second Bronze Star, tossed in the back of a bureau drawer. I knew that the second destroyer he was on, the USS *Lansdale*, was sunk in the Mediterranean by an aerial torpedo, but he refused to talk about it. It wasn't until we went to a reunion of his shipmates in Boston that I discovered what Bob had actually done on that day. Benny Montenegro, a gunner's mate, told me how Bob had given his life jacket to a sailor who was going under and had then proceeded to tread water for five hours, going from shipmate to shipmate, encouraging them to hang on. When Bob saw a ship in the distance, he swam to her, though it was at least a mile away. The Coast Guard finally picked up the survivors of the *Lansdale*. Later, when he was aboard the USS *Harry F. Bauer* off Okinawa, she took a torpedo in the bow and then was hit by a kamikaze, yet she stayed afloat, and Bob, the executive officer, directed the shooting down of seventeen kamikaze planes. The ship received the rare Presidential Unit Citation.

Mayor Ed Koch had charged Bob with establishing the museum back in the 1980s. He was a natural choice; he'd created a reputation as an indefatigable prosecutor of white-collar crime and a force to be reckoned with. He also was chairman of the board of the Police Athletic League, the city's largest organization for underprivileged children. He knew how to mobilize communities and get things done. Yet the museum languished in the world of ideas. The city's Jewish community was slow to provide funds; many wondered why New York needed a Holocaust museum when Washington already had one. It needed my husband's dynamism to get the museum literally off the ground. Bob had spent an entire weekend calling heads of corporations; by Sunday night he'd raised several million dollars.

In 1994 the museum was in its earliest stages. When it was completed, it would be a stunning hexagonal structure overlooking the Statue of Liberty and Ellis Island. It would have artifacts and special exhibits about the Jews in World War II and throughout the centuries, as well as recorded testimony of survivors and liberators of the concentration camps that visitors could access with the press of a button. But now all they had were offices. There, skilled interviewers were videotaping with a vengeance, and Bob, with the help of Steven Spielberg and others, was urgently trying to find survivors. Time was running out; some were in their eighties and nineties. Testimony by non-Jewish witnesses was also crucial.

Bob and my father, both Navy lieutenants in the war, had nurtured a close friendship, so my husband and I were natural co-conspirators. We began our campaign one day in Milford at the Newport Creamery. I had taken the first step, getting Dad to admit he'd been in a camp. Now I needed the details. I said, "Dad, there are people who are saying the Holocaust never happened, that the camps never existed."

"I'm well aware of that," he replied in his slow, heavy voice. "But I was told never to say anything about it."

"You know that Bob's museum is taking videotaped testimony from survivors and witnesses of the camps, and they're doing it so that in a hundred years, two hundred years, people can't try to prove that it didn't happen."

Bob reached over and forked up the last of my salad. I realized for the first time that Bob was almost as slow an eater as my father, especially since he likes to finish other people's meals as well.

"Where was this camp, Tom?" Bob asked.

"It was north of Frankfurt. It was called Ohrdruf," my father said.

"Or-derf?" I asked.

"Ohr-druf. It was the first camp we liberated, and I came in just after American soldiers had discovered it."

"What did you see, Dad?" I asked gently.

"I can't talk about it. I just can't."

I nudged Bob for help, but he ignored me and continued eating.

My husband believes that everything comes in its own time. For the next few months, he gently persuaded my father to bear testimony in front of a live camera, but he did it in his own way—by crafty indirection. He spent endless hours talking about the museum and the testimony that had already been collected. Finally, Dad, whose respect for Bob was enormous, got the point.

Chapter Three

It was 8 A.M. I opened the guest room door and walked into a burrow of bombinations: The three alarm clocks I had set were going off, not that this had any effect whatsoever on my father. He was in a twisted heap of pillow, sheet, and comforter, asleep on his good ear—he'd lost hearing in one during the war when the guns on his cruiser fired unexpectedly. His snoring was an extravaganza of sound: a long train of adenoidal reverberations, followed by a rush of cooing air, culminating in a ruckus of staccato snorts. I suddenly had great respect for my mother, who'd had to share his bed.

I saw a movement beneath his lids like the shuddering of a bird. I shook him gently. Then roughly. His eyes popped open. "Who? . . . what? . . . where?" He lifted his head and I saw that he had a shirt on. "You've been up?" I asked. "You've gotten dressed already?"

"Of course," he said, but his eyes were suspiciously puffy. And the pants he'd worn yesterday were slung over a chair. Of course. He'd gone to sleep in his shirt, just like my teenage son. "Get up, Dad, it's time to get up."

"Do I have to?" he asked in his mock put-upon voice.

"Yes, you don't want to be late." I turned off the alarms and took out a brown plaid shirt and the black polyester pants from off the chair. They were starting to pill at the seat, but it was the only pair he'd brought. He likes to shop at the big discount stores; they're near his house and have everything he needs. They're fine for decorating home interiors but less so for human exteriors. It's driven me crazy, especially when he was in his leisure-suit phase.

"I'd like you to wear these, Dad. You'll change into these, okay?"

I stood in the hall, waiting. I didn't know what he'd done to prepare his mind for this ordeal. I'd feared that at the last moment, he'd back out of it. But here he came, dressed, shaved, smiling down at me, patting me on the head, and turning to go out our front door.

When we arrived at the offices of the museum, we were met by the director and the woman who would interview my father, Bonnie Gurewitsch, a stolid, kind, but businesslike woman. Dad was visibly nervous. "I'd like to know who will see this tape recording we're going to do," he said, his arms folded, a cigarillo dangling from his fingers.

"Everyone. Anyone who comes to the museum," Bonnie replied.

"I want to know what it will be used for," my father asked.

"When we finally have the museum, there will be a room and in it your name will be displayed and your videotaped testimony will be able to be called up on a television screen."

My father took a drag on his cigarillo. "I won't have to talk about any other missions that I participated in, will I?" Bonnie shook her head. "And this won't be cut up or distributed or sent to anybody in particular?"

"It will stay right here in our museum archives," Bonnie replied.

"Dad," I took his arm as we walked down to the video room, "you know, don't be afraid to show emotion when you tell your story. In fact, it would serve a good purpose if you did break down."

"I will never break down," he said harshly.

"I mean just a little, you could."

"If I started, I would never stop."

My father paused at the door. "You know, Bonnie, I was told never to talk about this or anything else I did in this special outfit—"

"Mr. Franks, everything about the concentration camps is now public record," Bonnie said, ushering him gently through the door. "You probably would not be committing any breach of security. I really don't think you would be breaking any vows of silence at this point." She was used to reluctant witnesses. Most Holocaust survivors and witnesses want to do anything but give testimony. They have to be persuaded, sometimes over a long period of time. Most of them have remained silent about the horrors they experienced; they wanted to forget, and for a half-century after the war, the culture certainly didn't encourage them to talk. Survivors such as writer Elie Wiesel, with his early and vivid books on the Holocaust, were unusual—and unusually courageous. Despite popular documentaries like *Shoah* and movies like *Schindler's List*, the camps were still almost a taboo subject.

My father sat down in front of the camera. I watched him on a closed-circuit television. Bonnie asked first about his background, and he talked modestly about his career at General Alloys. I was reminded of the way he always understated his own importance. He said he'd never known any anti-Semitism growing up; out of about twenty-five people in his social group, three were Jewish, one of them his best friend.

Then he described Navy gunnery school, where he studied a variety of weapons, from the .45-caliber gun to the .30-caliber machine gun to the 16-inch guns of the Navy battleships. He learned how to fire these guns, to take them apart and put the pieces back together while blindfolded. He also taught others how to do the same thing. I wasn't surprised to hear this. Brass shooting trophies filled the glass cases in his den. Several years in a row, he had won first place in the Massachusetts pistol championship. It made sense that the Navy would want to make use of his expertise.

Bonnie asked Dad what he'd done in his special unit at the Navy Bureau of Ordnance. My father paused. Finally, he spoke. "The head of . . . Special Assignments sent me up to see the admiral and that was like going up to see God. The admiral gave me this assignment: 'I want you to go to a small base on the northeastern shore that trains sailors that are going to be operating machine guns on landing craft that land on enemy shores. I've gotten information that there's something wrong going on in that little base, that the CO and his assistant are spending Navy money on their own entertainment and doing many things out of order. We'll have papers made out that show you're a newly commissioned officer . . . wear that new uniform you have on. You're down there to learn how to teach sailors to operate machine guns. I'm putting a period of one month on it. If you think you've found out everything you can, call me, and I'll have you report to me everything you find.'

"I did spend a month . . . and they were doing things not proper to a Navy officer. So I left there and wrote up the report. [The admiral] said it was good."

When asked if he had served in the Pacific, Dad answered haltingly. "I was sent to the Pacific in '43 and the reason I was attached to the Marine Corps, which had been expanding and doing the fighting in the South Pacific, is that they had an awful lot of new Marines that had to handle machine guns and were not properly educated in handling them.

"They asked the Navy for half a dozen machine-gun experts . . . and they got in touch with . . . Special Assignments and they sent us right away to Guadalcanal. There was still a bit of fighting going on, but the battle had been won. It was being used as a base to assemble troops and send them on other island invasions."

"Were you training others in heavy ordnance?" Bonnie asked.

"I was supposed to be, except . . . I was moved out for invasions. I went to Bougainville and I had about twenty Marines under me, and we had a number of machine guns and we guarded a radio station and a radar outfit. After Bougainville . . . I was sent to an island called Emirau . . . and then to the island of Peleliu, which was a horrendous battle and a lot of resistance. It was necessary to go in and blast the Japanese out of their caves."

So my Dad had crouched and crept through the hills of the Solomon Islands, risking getting shot by the Japanese who had holed up all over the place. I'd discovered a World War II war map tucked in one of his books, and knew that Emirau was a tiny island in Papua New Guinea, north of Guadalcanal, and Peleliu was far away in the Palau Islands. He'd always refused to tell Penny and me about what he did during the war beyond cooking up that damn pig, and now he's notifying the public that he'd been in all these major battles in the Pacific Theater. I was impressed.

"What did you know about the German program to eliminate the Jews?" Bonnie asked. I leaned forward. This was what I'd been waiting to hear.

"Absolutely nothing. I don't think anything was known, certainly I knew nothing. I had never heard anything about it at all."

"What happened, Mr. Franks, in April of 1945? When you were chosen to go on special assignment to Germany?"

My father had his chin propped up with his thumb, his middle finger hiding his lips. It was an almost belligerent gesture. He didn't answer. He didn't move for what seemed like five minutes. Bonnie didn't push him. Finally he got out the words with difficulty. "We got in a troop vehicle and headed out, and two hours later over bad roads, we ended up in Ohrdruf . . . we were going into this place with some barracks and buildings.

"German troops had withdrawn, apparently within a day . . ." My father was swallowing. "We went into this hideous place where bodies were lying around on the street—one here, one there, eight or ten here, a dozen over there. We were sent into one of the buildings and there was a huge stack of bodies, six feet high, all nude, men as far as we could determine. We went into another building, there were more bodies stacked up.

"Then there was evidence of what had been a long bonfire . . ." he leaned over and raised his hand high. His face came looming large into the camera; he looked angry. ". . . where they lay cordwood down, big pieces of cordwood. Bodies, cordwood, bodies, cordwood." His mouth clenched and the muscles of his jaw worked in and out. "They probably poured gasoline over the whole thing and set it on fire because it had long ago gone out." My father took two quick breaths. "But you could see skulls sticking out, leg bones sticking out."

"How did you know it was a fire?" Bonnie asked.

"When you see burned wood like that, you know that there's been a fire and the flesh was all burned off of everything you could see, the skulls, the feet, the leg bones . . . ."

"Were there more bodies in the middle of the camp than in the sides?" Bonnie asked. "Photos of Ohrdruf show us large numbers of bodies in an open area, sort of a parade ground, like a square, and then individual bodies elsewhere in the camp."

My father could barely squeeze out a reply. "There were . . . hundreds of . . . individual bodies and bunches of them in the street out in the open, they all had clothes on. The bodies that were stacked in buildings were all nude . . . they all looked thin, unclothed bodies, looking thin and emaciated. And the bodies in the huge, long bonfire, you couldn't tell whether they were burned in their clothes or not because the clothes had all burned off."

"Was there any evidence that they'd been shot?" Bonnie asked matter-of-factly. She sounded so calm.

"Yes, you could see blood and bullet holes. Some of the bullet holes were in the head."

"Could you estimate how long the bodies had been there?"

"Not very long. They hadn't started to decay. There was an odor, but not a real bad odor as when you have a lot of rotting bodies, which I was familiar with."

So my father had seen decaying bodies. During combat, probably in the Pacific. His buddies, maybe, their eyes rolled back in their heads, their mouths open in ghastly surprise, maggots and flies feeding in the crevices of their skin, a sickening stench. Fifty years later, and he'd apparently never spoken of this.

"Did the troops tell you about how they discovered the camp?"

"American troops just overran the camps, the line moving forward overran the camps . . . We got out of our vehicle and we started looking around and it affected all of them. Several of them were crying. One officer ran over and started to go round the corner of a building and then vomited before he got around the corner." I sat there, amazed that my reticent father could remember so many details about something that happened half a century ago.

"What was your reaction?"

His eyebrows knit. "Mine? Sickening horror. Hideous. People, many, many people murdered. Some of them apparently were shot down at random by departing German troops. They were lying here and there, sprawled out, some with terrible expressions on their face of pain. It was sickening."

"Was there any conversation among the Army officers about what they were seeing?"

"They were saying . . . ." My father's forehead furrowed and he raised his voice until he was almost shouting. " 'Oh my God! Oh God! How could something like this happen!' . . . Just . . . everybody was astounded . . . shaken by it. You had seen dead bodies in combat, but not anything like this."

"Did all the officers have combat experience?"

"I would imagine so. Probably on ships if they had combat experience. Very rarely did naval officers have land combat like I did."

"How long did you spend in the camp?"

"Two or three hours and then we got the hell out."

"I guess you were eager to leave."

"Yes, very."

"On the way back, was there any conversation among the officers?"

" 'What the hell, who would do something like that? Why were they killed that way? Why were the bodies burned, why were some bodies clothed?' I handed in my report immediately when I got back. I was told to make a handwritten report only. I was given instructions not to talk about it at all, ever."

"What reaction did you have that the Jews had been killed?"

My father swallowed twice. He coughed. He looked down. I knew he was searching for a word that would tamp down his emotions. "Indignation. I developed a great hate for the Germans. Before the war, I had gotten intrigued by the German language. I loved the poets—Goethe, Heine—and I read German novels and lots of books in German." Perhaps only I could tell that the face my father was making, bringing up his bottom lip so his chin is crumpled, meant that he was having trouble controlling his emotions. "My library of German books. I tore them up one by one and threw them in the trash."

"How do you think you have influenced your children because of this?" Bonnie asked.

My father mumbled a response: ". . . conveyed my very strong feelings about anti-Semitism . . . and ethnic prejudice in general."

"Do you have any message you would like to give for future generations?"

He looked down and then spoke slowly, disconsolately. "Don't ever judge a person by his ethnic background."

After the interview, Bonnie told me that it had been tremendously helpful. "He was very articulate. It's one of the best interviews we've had."

Dad and I rode home in silence. I had to admit I was proud of him. He'd done it: drained the power away from a secret that had been festering inside him for more than half a century. I was sure that he had had many more "special assignments" than the two he had testified to, but little by little I would find out about them.

When we got home, I fixed him a steaming hot cup of coffee, black, the way he likes it.

"Dad," I began tentatively, "if the bodies you saw hadn't started to rot yet, you must have been in Ohrdruf right after liberation."

To my surprise, he began to talk—fluently, easily, without the hesitation I'd seen at the museum offices. "Yes, I believe I was. The bodies were not rotting. In fact, the blood coming out of the bullet holes in their throats, some had come right out the back of their necks, it was still moist. It had mixed with the dirt on the ground, it was fresh blood caking under the bodies." He swallowed. "What I could never figure out was that so many of the prisoners were naked from the waist down."

"Daddy, why do you think you were asked to make that report, really? I mean, there were American soldiers there already."

"I was told that our report was one of the things that persuaded Eisenhower to come to the camps," he said. "I think that Ike visited Ohrdruf, oh, something like a week later."

"It must have been so hard, Dad, seeing those horrors and then just being whisked off without any explanation. What you saw must have been terrifying and you were so young and naive."

"Huh," he grunted. He rubbed his forehead and looked out the window. "Body parts poking out of this sludge at the bottom, charred pieces of flesh, and then, what were they, long poles with hooks on them so the bodies could be turned while they burned. Next to the pit, I saw this one boot without laces. It was covered with ashes. Human ashes."

"What got to you most?"

"Oh," he let out a shuddering sigh. "I guess the ones who were still alive. There weren't many and they were wandering around with festering sores and bruises and scabs, looking dazed. There were some Russians and some Poles, I think I was told. Their skin was like parchment paper, you could see every manifestation of the skull." He put his hand over his mouth, then took it away. "This was a camp where there were mostly men but I saw a few kids there. There was a boy, he couldn't have been more than twelve. I think he was dressed in, oh, it looked like a dirty flour sack and this rag around his shoulders. He was so frail I thought at first he was an old man, but he had these big, shiny, black eyes sunk way back into his eye sockets. He was smiling at me or maybe he wasn't, maybe I just imagined that because his front teeth stuck out. His bicuspids were missing on both sides. He was trying to talk, and that I do remember, but it was like a baby talking, just sounds and grunts. I've always wondered, who was he? Who were his parents? Where had he lived? You couldn't tell anything about him the way he was, he was barely human."

"Oh Dad."

"I asked him, 'What can I do? What can I do for you?' I spoke German, but I don't know whether he understood or not, because he suddenly looked scared. Maybe he didn't understand. I had an American uniform on and I was speaking German, maybe he thought I was SS. So I held out my hand and he finally took it. His hand was cold and hard. To the best of my recollection, I offered him a box of nougats your mother had sent me. I had just taken some out of the box and he was biting into them when a medic came up and shouted for me to stop. Thank God he stopped me. Apparently the ones most starved couldn't digest regular food yet, and some had died from just being fed chocolate bars or even K-rations. Can you imagine trying to save someone from starvation and you watch him gobble up the food you've given him and then he dies because of it? This happened to several of the American soldiers. Someone survives by sheer will years and years of horrible abuse and then you come along, feed them, and," my father snapped his fingers, "they're gone."

"What happened to the boy? Did they get him medical help?"

"He died. I heard he died. He just was too far gone. I don't know if we could have helped him or not. The bit of candy didn't do him any good, that's for sure."

"But he never ate the candy."

"You know," he put his coffee cup down, "I'm not completely sure whether he ate my candy or someone else's or didn't eat any of it at all. I just know he died. It was kind of a blur then and it's a blur now."

"Well, even if he did, it wasn't your fault, Dad."

He began coughing.

"Did you see any German guards or had they all gone?" I asked quietly.

"There was one. He was lying on the ground with his face bashed in. Apparently, he had disguised himself as a prisoner and tried to attach himself to the Americans. But the real prisoners recognized him and took him over and beat him to death. . . . That was one corpse I wasn't in the least unhappy to see."

"But what was the reason you didn't tell Bonnie about what you've told me now, about the other prisoners and the boy and all?"

"I couldn't, I just couldn't." He had another coughing fit. "You see, I didn't really want to help. I just went through the motions because what else could you do? But I wanted to get away from that boy, from those people, I wanted to get away as fast as I could. I couldn't wait to get out of there."

"I would have too," I said. "Anything else you can remember, Dad?"

He pursed his lips. Then he nodded. "I can't talk about it. I can't talk about it."

"Dad, please."

He gave me a hard look. "I have always said that I was supposed to keep this whole thing secret."

I looked at him carefully. "And maybe you were afraid that if you told some things that you would break down?"

He wiped his forehead with the back of his hand. "I guess so," he said under his breath. He scraped back his chair, put down his napkin, and walked out of the kitchen.

I stayed behind nursing a now-cold cup of coffee. What else had he left out of his testimony?

He had talked incessantly about Israel when I was growing up. I'd thought he was ranting, a man obsessed. His words about the Jews came back to me now: "Cindy, you don't understand what they have been through, you can never understand." My father is a man who doesn't show it when he's hurting. But now I understood why I thought him near tears during those times when he talked about the beleaguered Israelis.

I was twelve when I found out about the Holocaust. "Want to see something really gross?" said my best friend. She took a book out from under her bed and made me promise not to tell a soul. I opened it and my eyes nearly popped out. There were these people who looked like the plastic skeleton in a science class, except they had skin and eyes and were walking around. Then she told me that the Germans had starved them, millions of them, back in the war before we were born. I'd felt sick. I'd shut myself in my room and cried for two weeks. No one could figure out what was wrong with me. My father would have understood, had I been able to tell him. But I never did.

The next morning he made small talk as though the videotaped session had never occurred.

"Dad, how are you feeling? Are you okay?"

He waved away all of my questions and turned to his paper. Why was I surprised? What did I think would happen? We had hid from each other most of our lives and were right back to where we'd started.

If he could shut down, so could I. After all, I still had a deeply seeded bitterness toward my father. I had had this for many years and for many reasons. Not the least of which was his role in systematically dismantling our family.

Chapter Four

A doll tree. I must have been about seven when I heard the words. "Tom is committing a doll tree," my mother was whispering over the phone to one of her girlfriends. She seemed beautiful to me, with her nipped-in waist that gave her ample flesh an hourglass figure. I can see her lying on her bedspread, sinking back into a meadow of giant blue flowers, combing her hand through her hair as she talked—unless, of course, it had been freshly puffed into a beehive by Alexandre, her beloved hairdresser, and then she wouldn't even let it touch the pillow. She and her friends loved to talk about everything, yakking and hooting it up. She was happier on the phone than she ever was off it. She could be in the depths of misery or screaming bloody murder at me, but let the phone ring and she would make a dash for it, trilling, "Hi, sweetcakes!" She relished flirting with Alexandre whenever he called her with his problems.

I regularly listened in on my mother's phone conversations, hoping to overhear something interesting. This time I'd hit the jackpot: a doll tree. Daddy was always making things, odd little machines and contraptions. Now he must be building me a special present. Doll babies swinging from little wooden limbs, maybe. I snuck down and searched his workbench in vain. Then my mother told me that there was no doll tree. He hadn't made me a gift; he had committed a sin. She spelled it for me: "a-d-u-l-t-e-r-y."

"It means that your father has betrayed his marriage vows, and you're old enough now to know that," she declared angrily.

"Marriage vows?" I asked. "What's that?"

"He won't get away with it, even if he only wanted her for those filthy things," she said distractedly. "The Ten Commandments says that if you do what he did, you can be struck dead."

I kept waiting for Daddy to die. I watched his every move, hoping to stop the lightning bolt.

I had long known there was something wrong between my parents. Mother was an accomplished nagger and could demolish you with a couple of words. The dining room table was her favorite battleground, in particular at Sunday noon dinner, a time when all my father wanted was to slowly savor his pork roast, bite by languorous bite. My mother, on the other hand, seemed to inhale her food and then was left with nothing to do. "When are you going to mow the lawn, Tom?" she might ask in a dozen different ways, citing the disgust of the neighbors, an infestation of ticks, the prospect of the town fathers wading through the towering grasses up to the front door. Her voice would grow sharper at his gritty resistance. Of course, we all knew he had no intention of mowing the lawn.

At the first sign of warfare, I would crawl under the table. I liked it down there because of the rich, red Oriental rug. In the corners, there were big triangular houses with roly-poly people trapped inside. They couldn't go outside because of the shoes that might drop on them, like the spike on the heel that was hanging off my mother's foot or Daddy's loafers, buffed to a shine. I would play down there until something happened: a glass of water knocked over in anger, dripping on my head through the table cracks, my father slamming down his fork, my mother ignoring his warnings that "I'm going to blow, Lorraine."

After one of their lawn battles, he took a can from his workbench, went into the garage, and squeezed a colorless liquid onto the blades of the despised hand mower. "This is something I got during the war," he told me. He let it dry for a minute and then said, "Now try to move the blades, carefully, so you don't cut yourself." The blades wouldn't budge. He'd invisibly cemented them in place. "Shhh," he grinned. "Don't tell your mother." What that magical substance was, I never did find out.

Sometimes, late at night, I'd wake to muffled voices, the sound of slapping, and my mother's cries: "Stop, stop it!" I would run to their room, fling open the door, and hug my father around the waist, begging, "Please stop, I love you, Daddy." I could barely get the words out. I hated that he'd made my mother cry. I hated the smell of the alcohol on his breath, which caused a violence in my father that I never saw outside our home. I hated too the feel of his belt buckle hard against my cheek. But then his body would go slack; I knew he wouldn't go after her any more that night.

Invariably, they'd fight when I had someone sleeping over. Cheeks burning, I would comfort my frightened friend. "Don't worry; it's just the television set. I'll go run and turn it off."

Their arguments often sent my father pounding down the basement stairs. He spent so much time deeply buried beneath the clatter of life above that I thought of him as a mole. "Do you have fun down there, Tom?" Mother would demand, raising the stakes. "What do you do that you don't want anyone to see?" Sometimes, however, she'd cry, "I think he's going to kill himself, Cindy, he's got all those guns down there!" at which point I'd head down after him and crouch behind the furnace. All I ever saw him do, though, was down a couple of bottles of airline whiskey and line up tools on his workbench. Later, I'd sneak back down to the basement, gather up all those rows of bottles under his workbench, and put them in the trash cans. More would reappear within days.

When I was much older, I snuck them into my school bag, went over to the home of another mutinous teen, and drank them between puffs of her mother's stolen cigarettes.

Maybe my mother diminished my father, baited him, forced him to engage with her, simply to get his attention. "All the other wives have husbands who buy them real gifts," she'd say, tossing the cheap necklace he'd given her for Christmas on the table. "They're real men." She would continue until, of course, he "blew." And then, to my amazement, she would just stand there and silently take whatever he doled out—a slap or a harsh word. I almost thought she wanted it.

Long after my mother's death in 1976, I found evidence of their dark dance in one of her beaded evening purses. Inside was a vellum place card; on the back was written: "You will pay for this." My parents' script was uncannily similar, but the other side of the card read "Thomas Franks," so there was no doubt who'd made a cutting remark about the other at a formal dinner table, and who then sat there, beneath the small talk, anticipating the payment she would eventually get.

I'd made a prayer book of blue construction paper yoked in red yarn. "Dear God," I'd scrawled in crayon, "I will be good forever if you keep Mother and Daddy together." As I lifted the mattress to hide the book, I noticed a bulk of black. I eased it out. A pistol. My palms got sweaty. Who would put a gun under my bed? Who . . . who, except for Dad. But why?

I searched the house. Sure enough, there was another gun under the mattress in the master bedroom, within easy reach. I went downstairs and poked underneath every piece of furniture. Nothing. Then I went into the den and stuck my hand behind the Civil War books in Dad's bookcase. There was a small gun behind a copy of *Andersonville*. I searched the cupboards in the kitchen and found another underneath the sink, behind a box of Brillo pads. I got a stool and felt around the shelves above the coat closet. On the top one, I found a big, black pistol underneath a brown-brimmed hat, the kind of hat—and the kind of gun, for that matter—that you only saw in old movies.

The next day I asked my mother about the guns. She looked cagey.

"Go ask your father," she told me. I never did. Nor did I find out what had possessed him to make me sleep on a loaded weapon. At night, I imagined I could feel its outline and wondered if it would go off and do me in.

Whatever his unseen enemy was, my father was watchful for it on every front. He'd look beneath the car before trips, explaining that he was checking for an oil leak while my mother looked on with a worried expression. One Christmas Eve, he took us to look at the big crèche in Boston. Afterward, we were walking down a dark path leading out of the Public Gardens when he suddenly waved us back and crept back up the path, arms out in a martial arts stance. He soon returned, apparently having vanquished our phantom enemy.

According to Ella Leavitt, my great-bosomed Victorian grandmother, her daughter had gained a hundred pounds after the war. Indeed, snapshots of Mother in 1946 show a plump, sexy, beaming woman and then, about four years later, an obese one, clearly unhappy. Mother always explained her weight away as a "glandular condition," but Penny and I thought that was an excuse (I once found a half dozen Heath Bar wrappers under her bed). Clearly, she was starved for something, probably love, maybe even sex. Perhaps my father didn't want to make love to her. Was the weight gain some act of revenge? Low self-esteem? Boredom? What happened after Daddy came home from battle, that made her stuff herself, day after day, even though she despised the betrayal of the bathroom scales?

I think about her vast girdles, rubber generously laced with little pinholes so the skin could breathe. I used to be ashamed of her weight, only faintly aware of how hard even the small tasks of daily life must have been for her.

"Cindy, I need your help!" came the plaintive call on the nights when my parents were stepping out to some event. ". . . and bring your muscle!"

It was a kind of ritual, wiggling Mom into her girdle. I'd grab the lip of rubber and pull while she pushed in the overflow, which I thought looked strangely sweet: dimpled white hillocks, delicately etched with veins. Her flesh so vulnerable. I didn't want to hurt her, so I'd loosen my grip. "Pull, pull harder!" she'd say. "I have nowhere to go." She'd shimmy her hips back and forth like a belly dancer. Then she'd begin to laugh and then so would I until we nearly collapsed and couldn't get the job done. She was half in and half out, and we'd have to call my father, who, with an avuncular air, accomplished the task with a couple of good shoves.

My father was too gentlemanly to comment on my mother's weight gain; I never heard him make a nasty crack about her size. But once, and only once, did he comment on mine. When I was a young woman and had gained a bit of weight, he approached me from behind and said, with a certain note of gravity, "You're a beautiful woman, Cindy. Don't ever let yourself go."

When I was sixteen, General Alloys, the company for which my father had toiled for more than three decades, went belly up, leaving him, at age sixty, with no income, no pension.

Daddy's boss, H.H. Harris, had died, double-crossing him. My father had spent half of his life trying to please this irascible, manipulative soul, a short, fat man who was never without his Chihuahua yapping away in a little basket. As far as Mother was concerned, H.H. was the Lord of Lords. Whenever he called, she put her hand over the receiver and said, "Quick! Go tell your father H.H. is on the phone!" Once when he invited himself to our home, my mother starched all the curtains and put Penny and me in matching crinoline dresses.

Much bigger companies had tried to lure my father away from Harris, but H.H. had pleaded with him to stay, insisting that upon his death Tom would inherit the company, whose profits he'd multiplied. When H.H. died of a heart attack, however, Mother was the only Franks mentioned in his will. She would get a small income only if my father died. To my father, H.H. left nothing. My mother was sick with disappointment.

The Harvard MBAs who took the company over after H.H.'s death fired everyone but Dad. H.H.'s betrayal had broken him, however, and he seldom went to the office. In any case, the company soon filed for bankruptcy. A gloom settled over our household. After school I would find Dad sleeping on his side, cheeks cradled in his hands, curled up like a baby in the tiny spare bedroom, withdrawing from everyone.

Dad's drinking, a constant source of worry to Mother, became an insidious presence after he lost his job. My sister and I, ignorant of that fact, thought our mother was a Prohibitionist reincarnated. Once he ordered a beer at a restaurant and a dirty look settled on my mother's face that lasted through dessert. Finally I said, "Why can't he have one lousy beer, Mom?" She just humphed, as though she knew a lot that we didn't.

"Poor Henry," Daddy told me that night, referring to my mother's father. His wife, Grandma Leavitt, often spoke longingly of the bygone Temperance movement. "She made him go down to the basement to have a drink. It's hard to believe, isn't it? I often wonder if the strain caused his heart attack."

I might have mocked my mother as a nagging teetotaler—my father never drank during the day, didn't slump down into a stupor—but certain incidents began to worry me. Once, after everyone was asleep, I heard my father talking to himself in the kitchen. I tiptoed down the stairs and stood at the door. I could smell the sweet, sharp scent of the Dewar's that sat before him on the table. He had a snarl on his face, but when he saw me, he softened and asked, "Would you like to sit down, or are you supposed to be in bed?"

"I heard something under my window . . . noises . . . like footsteps," I lied, knowing that he would be out there in a shot. When he left, I grabbed the bottle of scotch and poured out half, carefully refilled it with water to the previous level, and replaced it in the exact same spot on the table. When he returned, he poured himself another glass and began a long story about a ship called the SS *St. Louis*.

"She was full of Jewish refugees fleeing the Nazis," he said bitterly. "We wouldn't let her dock and sent her back to Germany. They went to port after port, country after country. It didn't matter where they went. Nobody would let them in. They sent them back to their death." He never seemed to notice that he was drinking whisky-flavored water.

The war. Whatever happened between my parents clearly started with the war.

Mother once told me that she married very young and that Tom, three years older, never gave her a chance. I imagine her as rather gullible then, anxious to please. She probably felt self-conscious in the face of her husband's intellect.

I can see her in her Chicago apartment as if she were in front of me, with the kitchen clock ticking, the restful sound of Vaughn Monroe on the big mahogany radio. It's the fall of 1943, perhaps, and her husband is still stationed in the United States.

She turns one of those tall, thin, cut-glass bottles upside down and sprinkles starch and water onto her husband's shirt. Then she lifts the heavy iron and runs it as smoothly as she can up the sleeve. The shirt is already pressed, but she's pressing it again because Tom has been gone for six months now and it's his favorite shirt and she wants it shipshape when he comes home on leave. He could just appear at any time, without warning, because he's doing something for the Navy that he cannot reveal, and that takes him all around the country. She wishes she knew what it was, but he can only hint at secret activities in his letters. Whatever it is, it's sure to be dangerous, though she knows he always plays down the danger. Sometimes she wakes up at night breathless.

It's the ironing that she loves best. To run the iron down the arm, seeing the wrinkles disappear. It's kind of sensuous, slapping the damp shirt, feeling the swoosh of steam rise up and moisten her skin. The drops of warm water on her face feel beautifying.

She wishes she had been born beautiful. Perhaps then Tom wouldn't chide her so about this and that. He's always teasing her for being foolish. One Christmas, he got up on a ladder to put on the ornaments while she held the tree, but then the phone rang and she ran to get it. Yes, the tree fell and he almost tumbled off the ladder, but she just forgot, that's all. Then she'd rolled up one brown sock with a gray one. It was that kind of thing. Her absentmindedness was funny, she had to admit. But sometimes her follies would become his favorite stories. Like the artichokes. She'd clogged up the sink with the leaves. He'd gotten down and opened up the pipe and cleaned out the gunk and put it in a bucket. He'd handed her up the bucket and without thinking, she'd emptied it into the sink, and it had sloshed down all over his head.

She finishes the shirt and hangs it up in his closet, making sure that it's carefully buttoned up so it won't fall off the hanger and wrinkle up on the floor. Like it had when he was home before.

Of course, if she were thin, she would be beautiful. But she's not thin, though God knows she's trying. It's that she's hungry. All the time. Chocolate candy, fried chicken, mashed potatoes puddled with butter, spaghetti glinting with oil, peanut brittle, oh yes, and éclairs, thick creamy custard and frosting so sweet you think you're going to die. She baked a loaf of anadama bread this morning, and now she cuts a thick slice, but because of her diet, she doesn't slather on the butter, she just spreads it thinly. She likes to eat when there are no suspicious eyes pinning her, because when you eat alone you can cuddle right up with your food. She tries to get rid of thoughts that spoil the experience, like the thought that her mouth is a vacuum, sucking up everything in sight.

One thing is good. She's kind of fat, but not so fat that her husband doesn't take his pleasure with her every chance he gets. As soon as she gets into bed, he's on her. Poking, prodding, just like her mother had warned. Her mother had told her this was a woman's greatest cross to bear. She'd said that what you were to do was lie there and take yourself to Tahiti or ride a gondola in Venice until it was all over. When she walked down the aisle in her wedding gown, she'd earned the right to wear white, so just the thought had been terrifying. But really, it isn't so bad when she dares to give herself up to it. Of course, she needs all the chances she can get for a baby. She wants a baby more than anything.

Now the Ink Spots are singing "I'll Be Seeing You." The song makes her cry, the words are so sad: "I'll be looking at the moon/But I'll be seeing you." It makes her think about all the boys she knows who won't be coming home, all the mothers and wives who will get that dreaded telegram, whose lives will crumble in a moment. Her life could crumble in a moment.

Years after the war is over, she realized her heart's desire: her husband safe by her side, a comfortable home. Thick, lustrous curls tickle her forehead as she bends over the cradle and looks at me. My father holds her hand. I can hear her voice. "Look, Tom, isn't she the most beautiful thing?" It's the voice of a woman in love. She's struggling with her weight, with her imperfections, fearing, perhaps, that she will lose him. But for now, she's given him what they've both wanted for so long: a baby.

From the moment I was born, my mother acted as though I'd been personally mailed to her by the Almighty. My earliest memories of her are of our morning routine. "Come into my office," she'd call to me when I woke up. I'd climb into her bed and we would cuddle and giggle and tickle each other, sometimes for the whole morning.

My mother adored babies in general; she regularly volunteered in the delivery room of Newton-Wellesley Hospital even though her feet ached so much afterward that she would pay me a quarter to rub them. (Still, her position had its perks: as my father humorously told it, she would speed through town at 80 miles an hour, waving at the local policemen whose babies she'd helped deliver.) If she gloried in parenthood in my early years, however, she soon tired of its novelty, was worn down by its cares. "I own and operate you," she once said out of the blue. When I came home from school, I'd never know whether she would be inexplicably warm, full of surprises to delight me, or frosty, with a sting to every word. She'd refuse to tell me whether or not she'd pick me up from school, and I'd stand there, anxiously peering down the street, watching for her new, silvery Edsel, until the playground was empty.

Mother sat in back on the first day of church choir practice. I was singing away, my heart swelling with the beauty of "Jesu, Joy of Man's Desiring." At the end of it, I had tears in my eyes. I expected Mother to have them too, but when I looked over at her, she was sitting in the back pew, rigid with embarrassment. "You were swaying when you were singing," she told me as she ushered me out the door. "You were the only one."

When my mother's moods were good, they were incomparably good. I was the youngest and most spurned child in the neighborhood, and God help her if she couldn't change that. She sewed curtains, hooked rugs, and bought little rocking chairs for my playhouse, and the neighborhood came in droves. "Children, it's time," she'd call from the back door and then distribute glasses of juice and fresh-baked sugar cookies on Howdy Doody napkins. She'd stay all morning at the window, making sure I wasn't left out of the neighborhood games. We'd go shopping and she'd sit patiently while I tried on a dozen dresses. She could make anything an adventure. We'd ride the bus just so we could guess what kind of lives the passengers lived. A Renoir at the Boston Museum of Fine Arts was a rhapsody of milky faces. A woman's frumpy housecoat would be an opportunity to study a stunning pattern. She was full of cozy homilies; "Cast your bread upon the waters and it will come back to you" was my favorite, imagining as I did a pond full of loaves floating towards me like little boats.

Once, my friend Diane and I were playing a game of tag, crawling under the doors we'd locked in the girl's bathroom. Suddenly, she pushed my face onto the hard tiled floor and broke my front tooth in half. I expected my mother to be livid and she was, but not at me. She picked me up from school, gave the teacher a talking-to, and then bought me a dozen powdered donuts. We ate them sitting on stools at the kitchen counter. The red linoleum, the red poppies of the wall-paper wavered in front of my eyes. She wiped the tears away with her matching poppy apron, excoriated Diane, and absolved me.

"I'm going to look like a Halloween pumpkin the rest of my life," I wept.

"Do you think I'd let that happen to you? Listen, we're going to go to the dentist tomorrow and he'll put a cap on it and nobody will know the difference," she soothed, putting another donut in my hand. "And you don't have to go back to school until the cap is on." She stroked my cheek tenderly. The next week, the cap fell off just before my poster presentation. The class tittered. When I told her about it, so did Mother, who became fond ever after of calling me "Snaggletooth."

I was six when my sister Penelope came along. We would kneel by the bed, Mother and I, and pray for a healthy baby. I adored Penny. When at last she arrived, I carried her around everywhere. Later, she became my pupil. If my mother started in on one of us, I would whisk her away to our secret place, Daddy's empty bathroom. We would turn on the shower and crouch on the tile floor, where I would weave a sequel to the enduring story that we were orphans lost in the rain forest.

My sister was a rather precocious child and she lost no time in re-taliating against my mother's disparagements. When she was about three or four, she would regularly empty out the dresser drawers in the house, cheerfully endure a spanking, and proceed to empty them out all over again.

My mother hardly needed a reason to suck Penny and me into her inner storm. She would often inexplicably wake me up by screaming, "Get out of bed, you lazy, selfish brat!" Once in a while, my father would come in and wearily say, "La-raine, La-raine," but mostly he withdrew from the battlefield.

One day, at the age of eleven, I rose up and chased her out of the room, spitting, "You! I hate you!"

"You're going to send me to my grave!" she screamed, in shock.

"I'll be happy if you're in the grave!" I cried, barely believing what I'd said. After slinking about remorsefully, I finally came and put my arms around her waist. "I'm sorry, Mom, I'm really sorry," I said, tucking my head into the crook of her neck. She pried my arms off and pushed me away. A sensation of doom came over me, the same one I'd had in nursery school when I cried so hard for my mother that she'd had to come pick me up. The fourth time the school called her, she'd shaken her finger at me. "This is the last time I'm coming to get you, sister." I never cried in school again.

Now her voice was much cooler: "Don't think you can get back with me so easily, sister." She turned her back on me, made for the telephone, and picked it up. That was the last time Mother touched me.

Only now do I understand that my mother must have suffered from a bipolar mood disorder. Back then, manic depression was a disease that was only whispered about in corked-up towns like Wellesley, Massachusetts. I knew only that she had a ferocious need to control me. She didn't want me near her, but she didn't want me out of her sight. Even when I was a teenager, she barely let me out of the house.

Then I discovered that I could outwit her. One day, when she had her weekly cut 'n' style with Alexandre, I slipped into the back of the car and lay on the floor. By the time she was in the salon, I was on my way to the movies. Sure, I chewed my fingernails through the broomstick antics of Mary Poppins, but it became easier with time. I would steal into my father's room while he was asleep, ease his wallet out of his pants, and relieve him of ten or twenty dollars. I began to sneak out at night, and though I came close, never get caught.

My first undiscovered crime filled me with happiness. From then on, I knew I could get away with anything. I had earned my freedom.

My father refused to be conscripted into my combat with Mother, even though I'd always turned to him for the affection and attention I craved.

I am three. His big hands are under my arms and up I go; his fingers play piano on my shoulders, making me giggle. I like to run my hand up his cheek, feeling the roughness, and down again, all smooth, like a blanket of mohair. I wear a coat with muttonchop sleeves and a matching brimmed hat. We're standing in front of our old, round-topped Lincoln, squinting in the sun. I ruffle his hair, fine threads of gold. "Give me a kiss," he says, and I kiss him on his ear.

I am four, in bed, blinking to keep my eyes open so I won't miss him when he comes upstairs. At last, the door opens and a long shadow stands in the shaft of light. He enters, tall, with a slight smile, wearing his smoking jacket, holding my glass of water. He sits on my bed while I drink it to the bottom. I take little sips because then he'll stay longer.

I am eight. He goes away a lot, so it's a festival when he comes home. He carries presents, four or five, wrapped in gold paper. "Here," he says, holding his fingers around a tin top with candy cane stripes. "You spin it like this." It whirls off across the floor, finally falling over like a fat clown. He takes out pink pens, huge balloons, sometimes a teddy bear, and once a squirrel leaning on its elbow. I didn't know a squirrel could lean on its elbow.

I am eleven. One day he takes me out on our boat and moors it in a little cove near Falmouth Harbor. It's empty; only he knows about it. There's just the two of us.

"We're going scalloping," he announces as we swim to the beach. "Wiggle your toes into the sand wherever you see a hole," he tells me, and to my delight, I unearth one scallop after another. The shells are beautiful, with their russet streaks and deep ridges, like ruffled dancers. We cook them in a hot copper pan with butter and white wine, and eat them on the deck, watching streaks of violet fill the sky. They are tiny and succulent, and we just keep smiling at each other and saying how delicious they are.

* * *

I loved my father's attention, but I yearned for a real family, the kind where Mommy and Daddy tell their daughter, "I love you"—words I never heard from my parents' lips. The older Penny got, the more I craved it. A family outing to Ken's Steakhouse would fill me with happiness, the four of us sitting together, munching our hamburgers. My parents would register a kind of satisfaction with each other: My mother would start joking, they'd tell tales about each other's foibles. This was love, I told myself, until some years later, when I knew it wasn't.

I developed a fondness for retreating into my own world, devouring Victorian novels by female authors, imagining myself inside each joyously perfect family. I would repeatedly sing, or rather shout, "I Feel Pretty, Oh So Pretty" to the thunderous applause of a Broadway audience, until my father came to the door and asked in a pitiful voice if I could sing something else.

I never stopped believing that my own family could be transformed, and I was always plotting how to do it. This involved telling a mountain of lies. One day I decided to break a freeze, so I went to Dad and told him that Mom said he was "the most adorable man." This obvious fiction got me laughed out of the room. So I begged my mother to give me a joke to pass on to Daddy. "Go tell him he's an icklebick," she said. I would browbeat my father into returning the compliment, and he would come up with something like, "Tell her she's a picklepuss." I would never tire of running back and forth ferrying these nicknames, and when my parents next came face to face, there would likely be a friendly truce—for a while.

Inevitably, however, warfare would break out again. Sometimes Mother would pack up her gray Samsonite luggage and matching overnight case, call the babysitter, squeeze into her Lincoln, and drive the three days and three nights to get to her mother's house in Kankakee.

Soon my parents were encased in separate rooms. "It's his godawful snoring," Mother told me. "I just can't take it anymore."

* * *

After I first found out about the Adultery, I kept listening to Mother's phone conversations for more news of it. For a while there was nothing. Then came the calls. "Hello . . . hello?" she would say, and then she would look at me. "There's nothing but a dial tone." Eventually, panic crept into her voice whenever she answered the phone. I knew from the movies that an adulteress would call her boyfriend and hang up if he didn't answer. Sometimes, with good luck, I answered the ring first. If my mother was there, I would nervously chat to the dial tone for a minute. "Wrong number," I would say brightly. "I don't believe you," she would reply, arms folded but eyes wet. One day, after the fourth call came in the space of an hour, I ran to the bathroom and threw up.

When Daddy called from a business trip, I'd listen on the other extension. "Business is so good I won't be home for another two or three days," he'd tell her. "Uh-huh, uh-huh, sure," Mother would reply, not in the least fooled. She had, you see, once called his hotel in Detroit; they'd never heard of him. Then a friend told her she saw him talking to a woman at the Swan Boats on the Boston Commons. A few days later the front door would fly open. "I'm home," he'd shout as Penny and I ran down the stairs. But Mother would turn her back on him.

I think that as we make our way to adulthood, we keep inside us the people we were. Like Russian dolls, we can be taken apart until the smallest is revealed; each one holds dreams and desires that do not perish with time.

As a child, I'd been sure that someday the power of my prayers would unite my parents. Sunday school had washed right over me, but I loved the candlelit theater that was our church. I wore a cross around my neck, dreamed I'd be a nun, and bowed low as the glinting gold crucifix passed by me. I craved the minister's blessing, the unexpected warmth of a hand on my head. When I knelt at the rail, his brocade robes brushing my face, his soft voice murmuring, "The blood of Christ," as he lifted the chalice to the lips of the grown-ups—I felt like I was sitting at the feet of holiness.

But by the age of eighteen, I was embarrassed by it all. My hypo-critical mother, who had reddened at the way I sang hymns, belted out the processional so loudly that the kids in front of us peeked back to see who it was. I had pretty much given up on God, who had failed to bring my parents together. But I felt no loss. I was, to be frank, terribly unconcerned. Thus, nothing prepared me for my reaction when my father made his confession to me.

I had come up from Vassar to meet him for dinner at Mama Leone's, a tourist trap Penny and I insisted on because we loved the kitschy statues and stained glass. Dad and I ordered our favorite pasta, with garlic and oil. This was our usual at Stella's, an Italian eatery up in the North End of Boston that was a favorite of the locals. Stella's was Daddy's and my little secret, our refuge when Mother was in one of her rages.

Now, at Mama Leone's, Dad had procured a prime table nestled against a fancy plaster railing. "O Sole Mio" was wafting through the air. My father cleared his throat. Then he said: "I've loved another woman since you were born." My forkful of pasta halted in midair. "Her name is Pat," he continued, "and I'd like very much for you to meet her."

I couldn't speak. Finally I managed, "Don't you love Mother?"

"No," he said, a little reluctantly.

"You don't feel anything for her?"

"Um, well, when you've lived together for that long, there's, well, a certain camaraderie."

I burst into tears, surprising both my father and myself. All those prayers were for nothing. They never had stood a chance. I had failed and it was irretrievable.

"What can I do?" he said, reaching for my hand, still holding the pasta twirled around my fork.

"I think I want to leave," I said, putting the fork down. He quickly got the check.

We didn't speak about his affair, his adultery, again until almost two decades later. Meanwhile, I would receive the occasional raft of handwritten poetry, mailed without a note or explanation, from "Pat." I would toss the poems in the wastebasket without reading a word.

I could never forgive my father for destroying once and for all my childhood dream of family happiness.

Chapter Five

"O ne day my daughter went into her room," my father would tell people, "and the next, she came out a monster."

Mother, with her rages and restrictions, was the main target of the myopic misery that was my adolescence. During our ear-piercing fights, I taught her words she never even knew, four-letter ones, sure, but also the polysyllabic gems. "Cocksucker! Motherfucker!" I'd yell in her astonished face. My epithets propelled her home again to Kankakee, this time to sob to her mother not about Dad, but about me.

As the first child, I had many years to be grandly spoiled before my sister's debut. My parents called me the "Queen Bee." In time, my moniker became "Black Sheep." "Every family has one," said Mother tartly. She and Penny, who had fought for years, now clung to each other to defend themselves against me.

I upped the ante by becoming more and more disagreeable. I had developed nicely in my role as the family felon. Penny would regularly run into my bedroom yelling that I'd stolen her stuff. There was some truth in this: With Mother having placed herself squarely at Penny's side, it was easy to hate my sister, to pluck up one of her records, or swipe the beloved stuffed animals that huddled on her bed as spoils of war. By the time I was fourteen, I was regularly tormenting her, that is, when I wasn't busy flipping off my mother. (In this, I was actually encouraged by my father, who, when he saw my middle finger pop up, would stifle a smile.)

My father's antisocial inclinations initially saved him from my antipathy, for I too loathed Wellesley. I'd become a lefty Democrat in a hateful town full of men in yellow pants and red jackets who belonged to the John Birch Society and housewives who planted themselves in garden clubs—a town with no blacks, only one family of Jews, and girls whose motto was "Wear bobby sox or die."

Daddy might have shared my scorn for the town we lived in, but eventually even he turned against me. He seemed to like it when I made a fool of myself. I was clumsy, I'll admit it, but simple gaffes, like walking into the woodwork or struggling to screw a cap on the wrong way, made him chortle conspicuously. Even my mother was more temperate.

After my father was fired from General Alloys, Penny alone managed to penetrate his inaccessibility. She would boldly wake him from his frequent naps, sit on his bed, and they would talk conspiratorially for hours. They went deeply into intellectual science fiction, discussing such writers as Heinlein and Asimov. They achieved a closeness that I could not duplicate.

At the age of nine, she began pestering him to teach her how to shoot: "At first he just laughed at me, I was the little squirt of the family and I didn't have any claim to fame." Finally, he relented and attached a cut-out target to a sheet metal contraption in the cellar that he had rigged up to stop the bullets. "Now first you're going to learn the safe way to handle a gun," he said. "See this safety? You always keep it on. You never point the gun, you don't wave it around, you only aim it if you intend to use it." He put a small gun in her hand and he let her feel, very delicately, the magazine, the safety, the trigger. Then he stood behind her, helped her line up the sights, and told her not to flinch. She pulled the trigger several times, not only flinching but rearing back as she heard a 'blam, blam, blam.' He yelled, "Hold on, hold on, put on the safety!" and went charging over to the target. Then, chuckling, he brought it over to Penny. Every shot had hit the bullseye. He told this story countless times and Penny went on to become his favorite shooting partner.

One day, to my dismay, he decided to try me: "You should learn how to protect yourself. It might be necessary when you least expect it." He chose an unnecessarily large gun, which felt like a lead brick. My hand shook at the thought of having a gunfight with some rapist, not to speak of the loaded pistol that lay under me as I slept. "Go ahead, fire!" he said and I did, shooting several holes in the ceiling. They happened to whiz through the kitchen floor where Mother was making a baked Alaska. "Oh no," said Dad, retrieving the gun from the floor and slipping it into his vest. We quickly ducked under the stairs, and sure enough, Mother came cascading down them. When she saw the mutilated ceiling, she let out such a wail that my father had to put his hand over his mouth to keep from laughing.

By the age of fifteen, I was so impossible that my mother decided to send me to Beaver Country Day School, a prestigious private school in nearby Brookline, to "knock the rough edges off." Instead, the edges were all over the place just waiting for me. A dozen Alices from the artsy town of Cambridge took me under their wings, and down the rabbit hole I went. I was soon playing folk guitar, wearing Marimekko dresses and peace amulets, parting my long hair in the middle, smoking dope in people's cellars, and lighting incense to hide the smell. I had become my parents' worst nightmare: a seditious hippy.

I was soon so far left I thought of myself as a Kropotkinite, and this drove a bigger wedge between me and my father. He was at heart a Republican, and had I been older during the 1960 presidential elections, I would have realized it. We'd gathered around the television set, and everyone inside the ballroom on the screen was roaring for the winner, Jack Kennedy. I, of course, began cheering too. My father gave me a dirty look and I noticed my parents had both fallen silent. Mother said, "Well, there's nothing we can do now. He's our president." My father replied, "Just watch the world go to hell in a handbasket."

In a bizarre role reversal between parent and teen, he'd often come into my room to pick a fight, clearly just so he could rail against the Russians. His belief in Richard Nixon, a man I thought evil and a liar, was obsessive, as was his paranoia about the perils of creeping Communism.

"Cindy, the Russians have a five-year plan to take over the free world. If we don't stop them in Vietnam, they'll keep going, one country after another." Then he would pound on about the beauty of the domino theory.

I talked right back. Read *The Communist Manifesto* in his face. Waxed poetic about the joys of the political anarchists who broke from the Bolsheviks to espouse a more radical form of Communism. By the time I was through, I thought, I'd have him begging me to be a Bolshevik.

One day I told my father that I intended to go to London after I graduated from college and live in this anarchist commune I'd heard about, a place where they put a bowl in the hall under the sign "Give What You Can. Take What You Need."

"Oh, Cindy, where is your common sense," he said dismissively. "Do you really think that a bowl like that is ever full?"

"I know it is. Some people are devoted to a just and fair society, Dad, not a competitive one. Don't you have any ideals?"

"No, I don't. They died at the hands of something called reality."

"Well, I can understand that. Especially if your whole reality is lying in bed."

I usually saved my insults for my mother, so the fact that I'd lowered our discourse to such a spiteful level surprised me. But I was even more surprised at his uncharacteristic reply. "You can be a bitch," he said thinly, "just like your mother."

Despite my prickliness, Mother seemed determined to mold me in her image and groom me for the social circuit. When I was eighteen, she talked me into "coming out" and attending cotillions and debutante balls, all of which I suffered with great eye-rolling. In truth, I was afraid of what defying her would mean. All my life, at the least hint of misbehavior, she'd threatened, "I have high blood pressure and I can't take this anymore! The doctors say it could kill me."

The summer before I was to go off to college, my poor mother came up with another plan to civilize me: She enrolled me in the young people's section of the Junior League, an endeavor that back-fired mightily. It happened that the League, a fashionable volunteer organization, sponsored a program they knew little about except that it was run by Phillips Brooks House of Harvard. The name Harvard was all Mother apparently needed to know.

The program was Welmet, an experimental residence in Cambridge for volunteer students and mental patients recently discharged from state hospitals. I moved into Welmet in a flash. It was a Valhalla of funky patients, who were amusing and challenging to work with, and earnest undergrads who stayed up late at night smoking Gauloises, dis-cussing the theories of Erik Erikson and Noam Chomsky, and sleep-ing with each other. I'd found my new family.

I also acquired my first boyfriend there, a Harvard senior named Steve, who happened to come from an Orthodox Jewish family in Queens. I was rather proud of him. One day, after Easter lunch, I arranged for him to pick me up at home on his Harley-Davidson. My parents were about as warm as a blast of arctic air. My mother, who didn't know any Jews but secretly disliked them anyway (though she was careful not to reveal this to my father), was offended because Steve wore sneakers to her door on Easter, a fact my father couldn't have cared less about. But as soon as he saw me roar away on Steve's bike, he got in his car and roared after us. He swerved right in front of us and we nearly crashed into him. That, I thought, would have been some sort of justice.

Dad calmly ushered me into the passenger seat. As we drove home, I turned to him and said icily, "You just did that because he's a Jew!"

"What?" he piped, so shocked by my accusation that he couldn't get out another word.

At the end of the summer, I finally went home to pack up to go to Vassar. The college had something for everyone: social cachet for my mother and left-wing politics for me. I lived in Cushing, the dorm reserved for individualists, loners, and weirdos. I went to every anti–Vietnam War march, joined agitprop demonstrations, threw blood on draft files, and attempted to put LSD in the coffee at a DAR luncheon.

When I phoned to tell my parents I was going to march with Martin Luther King in Selma, Alabama, I'd hoped for the approval of my father, so like me in his support of civil rights, of the Jewish minority. Instead, with visions of high-powered hoses dancing in his head, he broke the speed limit to get to Vassar before the bus left. He didn't make it, much to my glee. Then, approaching the Tappan Zee Bridge, we began to hear a persistent honking. I watched as a depressingly familiar salmon Buick, lights flashing, signaled the bus to pull over. For me, the march was over before it had begun.

As I approached adulthood, Dad became ever more fixated on the family's safety. He cleaned and oiled the guns in his cabinet more obsessively. I once came down to the basement to find him crouched low, aiming a pistol at an invisible attacker. He began to issue devastating life warnings to all of us, but mostly to me: "Cindy, you never know who's going to be behind you." He described in vivid detail the horrors that befell other hapless young women. Life was a death trap. "You drive a car on the highway, you take a risk of being crushed under a truck that jackknifes, and on back roads, if you get a flat, you're defenseless against any shady fellow who passes by." His opinion of mass transit was no rosier. "Trains are dangerous. You go through one car to get to the next one and you can fall right through the spaces between them. And that would be that."

I considered this all as pure malice; he was going to thwart me for my politics. I felt like a political prisoner. I couldn't even get my driver's license until long after everyone else had theirs. He and Mother were pathetic. Really, what was there to be afraid of?

While I was off at college, life at home was grim. My father was spending more time away from home. Why was he still taking all these business trips when he was barely working at all? Where he was going no one really knew. Mother phoned me at Vassar. "Did you know your father's getting mail at a special post office box?" Penny and Mother were now at odds constantly. My mother kept a keen watch over her, sending her to a private girl's school less than a mile from home.

By the time I graduated from Vassar, I was tired of being anchored to my shipwrecked family. That June, I took the money I'd saved working, rather ironically, in summer programs for the emotionally disturbed, and sailed away to London on a battered old student ship. I got a job rewriting cables at United Press International's London bureau that fall, and reveled in my independence and the miles of water I'd put between myself and the family Franks.

After General Alloys finally let my father go, money began to be tight for my parents. "Your father's run through almost all our savings," my mother told me, her panic crackling down the phone line. "I don't know what we're going to do. Your grandmother uses her income for her travels, I can't take money from her." But apparently she had no compunctions about taking it from me. Of course, I offered it gladly. How easy it was to be noble—the sacrifice being only half my weekly paycheck—now that I'd left all of them behind. And how much I enjoyed my mother's gratitude, her newfound respect for me.

Besides, I thought I was getting off cheap. I didn't really need the money anyway—I was the only woman at UPI London, and after work "the boys" would repair to the Tipperary Pub and buy me round after round of Guinnesses with Paddy whiskey chasers, a combination that provided more than enough nutrition. Then I began taking up my guitar and singing folk songs at the Tip and soon found pound notes tossed at my feet. My dates would buy me noshes, and my apartment was a steal. I lived in a big room that contained a bed, a gas fireplace, cumbrous Jacobean furniture, and a claw-foot bathtub with a tank whose flames blasted out around the bottom and kept me warm on the dampest English days. My landlady was a lonely, housebound soul and every day I brought her a Bakewell tart; she'd often wave away my rent, and when she died, she left me her big, rococo, leather-topped desk.

In spite of the excitement of being on my own, I was actually rather dejected and—though I wouldn't admit it at the time—homesick. I wrote my father a fervently nihilistic epistle. I wanted his comfort—and I wanted to impress him with my existential agility. It took me four hours to write. "What did life mean?" I asked. Who was I, really? Who was he? What was my purpose? "What was the use in living? How does one go on?"

I knew my father was the only one smart enough to understand these heavy questions. But I got no answer. I waited and waited. Months went by. And I got no answer. Not even a scribbled "I understand." Years later, my mother told me that he'd given her the letter. "You handle this," he'd said, which she never did.

When I went home on vacation that summer, I walked into a deathly quiet house. I went upstairs to her bedroom and there was the shocking sight of Mother, crouching on the floor in a blue satin nightie. She looked up at me, her face blotchy. "Your father told me about Pat." I froze. I knew that she'd always suspected his infidelity, and it had made her angry. But this was something different. This was making her sick. "I didn't know there was only one," she said. "I thought he used other women so he could . . . you know . . . do those things nice women don't do. I never dreamed there was just one." I helped her up onto the bed. "He told me he didn't love me," she wept. "He told me he loved this Pat."

She spent the next few days in her room. It was a large room, with twin beds and an Art Deco dressing table with a chaos of perfume bottles scattered over the marble top. She stared into its big, round mirror as though she would find enlightenment in it. Then she walked up and down the room, crying. She'd lived within the same fantasy I had: in spite of everything, she believed, or at least hoped, that Tom had really loved only her.

"What am I going to do?" she said. She had a raft of social engagements coming up. "How can I go alone?" How, she sobbed, could she *be* alone?

"You can find someone else," I lied.

"Just look at me. Old and fat."

"Mom, you're beautiful. You could find someone. We'll find him together. I'll help you."

I thought of her generosity last Christmas. Both parents had implored me to come home, and fresh into a new relationship, I'd reluctantly taken a few days' leave. No sooner had I landed in the States than I got the news that my boyfriend in London had been kissing another girl at the Tipperary Pub. I took my father's Jack Daniels from its hiding spot and guzzled it from the neck of the bottle. My mother sat quietly by my side. It was almost a provocation, since she was such a rabid teetotaler. She didn't say a word about my drinking, however. "Go back early," she urged me. "Go wherever they are—into the Tipperary if you have to—and just let him see your face. He'll drop the other girl." And she was right.

I wanted desperately to comfort her now. Tell her how to get Daddy back. But I, the wordsmith, couldn't conjure up a single thing to say.

I finally had to go back to my job in London. I loved my work at UPI, even though I was assigned to beauty contests and donkey shows, the hazard of being the only woman in the bureau. One weekend in Northern Ireland changed my beat forever. I decided to go to the British province (considered England's Vietnam by young English radicals) with a bunch of anarchist students supporting Catholic civil rights and a united Ireland. I was hoping to find a story, and I did. We were attacked by Protestant bullyboys and I sustained a photogenic scalp wound that sent blood running down my face. When my editor saw the shot, he ordered me back to London. UPI had a rule: no women in war zones. I reminded him that the battle would be over by the time he flew a man in; besides, I knew that UPI, which we cognoscenti called Under Paid International, wouldn't shell out for the flight. So, to my happiness, I was allowed to file stories from there for several weeks.

Then, a fancy townhouse in New York City's Greenwich Village mysteriously blew up, killing three young people, including a Bryn Mawr graduate, Diana Oughton. They were members of a radical anti-war group called Weatherman. The country was stunned; for the first time in modern history, political violence had issued not from the underclass, but from the sons and daughters of the privileged.

My mother's best friend knew the Oughtons, who lived near Kankakee, and convinced them to talk to me. I was whisked back to New York to do the story. I talked to Diana's parents, slept in her room, read her letters. I entered the radical underground and followed her footsteps, met her comrades, hid out in the cellars of "safe houses," and once got put up against the wall by White Panthers suspicious that I was an agent provocateur sent by the "pigs."

I became engrossed in Diana's story. I understood the reasons for her downward spiral, felt the power of the era's intellectual hysteria that had put her hand on a stick of dynamite she hardly knew how to use. I went back to UPI New York to write the story and was assigned an assistant, Thomas Powers, who was writing a book about the anti-war movement and understood its background. He provided context for the story, and before I knew it, I was asking Roger Tatarian, UPI editor-in-chief, to give us a double byline. We wrote a five-part story that was printed in hundreds of newspapers around the world. Much to our amazement, it won the Pulitzer Prize. Powers went on to write a book based on the articles, *Diana: The Making of a Terrorist*, and I went back to London to face an office full of jealous men who literally turned their heads and refused to talk to me. Some had worked their whole lives hoping for a Pulitzer, and here I was, the youngest person to collect the prize, and the only woman to win it for national reporting. Who could blame them for shunning me? This torture ended fairly soon, however, for I was sent to Northern Ireland again to cover the escalating war.

Meanwhile, my mother was in a state of excitement over the Pulitzer. "Your poems!" she'd said when I was young and had regularly written ditties for her friends' birthdays. "You have a marvelous way with words. You're going to be a writer." When I'd been hired by UPI, she'd gone to Boston to buy every newspaper from every city to see if she could find an article with my byline. She'd watched for story possibilities for me. She bragged that I'd had tea with the queen and had my toe shot off in Belfast. (It was actually my toenail. I'd dived under a car when snipers began firing at each other and my sneaker took a ricocheting bullet.) Now, she hung copies of the prize declaration in three rooms and began to introduce herself as "the mother of the Pulitzer Prize winner."

This helped cushion another blow: Dad had made good on Mother's worst fear, moving in with his mistress, Pat Rosenfield.

Not long afterward, Mother began to have debilitating pains in her abdomen. Her voice sounded so weak on the telephone that I flew home and took her for X rays. They showed a suspicious mass in her colon. Penny immediately came home from college. We somehow managed to get Pat Rosenfield's phone number and told Daddy that if he didn't come home right then, that very night, we would never speak to him again. He was home within an hour—and never left again.

Mother languished for months with what the doctors at a leading Boston hospital diagnosed as diverticulitis. Finally they operated and promptly sewed her back up, declaring the "mass" inoperable cancer. UPI was primed to send me to the Paris bureau, but Daddy called and begged me to come home. In those days, it was customary for the doctor to break the news of a terminal illness to the spouse, who then broke it to the victim. My father, who was paralyzed by the news, couldn't bring himself to tell Mother, nor could he seem to handle her medical situation. So I declined the Paris transfer and asked for one to New York instead. ("Can't you get one to Boston?" my father asked, as though transfers grew on trees. It was a suggestion that made me tremble.)

When I came home, my mother was understandably distraught—and bitter. She pointed to the stress of my father's affair. "He knows exactly why I got sick," she told me, and I agreed with her.

In spite of his forlorn look, I could hardly meet my father's eyes. I brusquely took charge. I wasn't going to let my mother die. I took her medical records to New York and ended up at Memorial Sloan-Kettering Cancer Center. There I found an aggressive and audacious specialist who proceeded to take out the tumor, gave her heavy chemotherapy—and three more good years of life.

Much to my surprise, my father cared for Mother heroically. He was there throughout her surgery. He took her to doctors' appointments, cooked her meals, swept the floor, made her bed . . . and changed her colostomy bag. A colostomy is an opening in the abdomen out of which pokes the end of a severed intestine. A rubber bag, where feces collect, fits over it. Nobody who hears that description would think that a colostomy could be a lovely thing. But to my father, it apparently was. A little, pink mound of flesh, it folded over like a flower. He called it a rosebud. Three times a day, my mother would lie down and Daddy would empty the bag. Then, leaning down over the rosebud, he would meticulously clean it with an alcohol-soaked Q-Tip. Then he would dab it dry with a little cloth. Last, he would put the bag back on and, with several gentle strokes, smooth it down so it wouldn't show under her clothes. It was the first time I'd ever seen my parents touch each other tenderly. My mother was so proud of this that she asked Penny and me to watch him do it. He did it with a little smile. He hadn't had such a sense of importance for a very long time.

The three years Mother lived after her diagnosis were rich. Her husband was finally by her side, tending her rosebud. She spent a few weekends in Cape Cod with her girlfriends; her children visited often.

Meanwhile I'd been hired as a reporter by the *New York Times*. My mother would come down to New York by train and I would take her to her chemotherapy sessions. She was eager to see the *Times*, so I took her there one day after chemo, making sure it was when most people were out to lunch. She hoisted her large body up onto one of the waist-high file cabinets and crossed her ankles. I flinched at the sight of her legs, thick as tree trunks. She was probably feeling, for one moment, young and healthy, thrilled with where she was, who she was: the peppy mom of a *New York Times* girl who could swing her legs on a file cabinet with the best of them. She got down off the cabinet fairly quickly. I wondered if she'd read the embarrassment on my face. When we walked out of the building, my cheeks were burning, not because I was ashamed of her but because I was ashamed of myself.

During the last weeks of her life, Mother slept in a hospital bed in the den, where she could watch her beloved birds; Daddy had put a feeder up outside the window. He'd made it himself, soldering the contraption together from homemade bullets he'd melted down. He slept on the couch in the next room to be near her. She called him often, sometimes for water, sometimes to hold her head while she threw up.

A week after my mother died, in January 1976, we finally found her will folded up in the pocket of a bathrobe. The onionskin pages, in a baby blue cover, left everything to Penny and me, including bankbooks in our name containing $6,000 each. There was nothing for my father, not even a good-bye.

Chapter Six

Three days after Mother's death, my father told us he'd mortgaged and remortgaged our beloved childhood home, and now the house would have to go.

My career was blossoming: I was in the middle of covering the 1976 U.S. presidential campaign, a plum assignment. But that would have to come to an abrupt end because I—along with Penny, who was now working in New York City—would have to take leaves in order to help Dad sell, pack up, and move to a smaller house. We'd chosen the quaint town of Hopkinton because it was close to Wellesley and the birds and butterflies had not yet been decimated by DDT; Dad could pursue his beloved hobbies. During the day, Penny and I poured everything into cartons while my father wandered around helplessly, peering inside them. After everyone was in bed, I found myself drinking wine spritzers while hurling pillows across the room. For the second time, Dad was asking me to give up my life for his.

Penny and I pestered Dad to get some kind, any kind of job. He finally was hired by a management recruiting firm. It was then that he began his friendship with Lou Golden. When Dad was fired for not producing, Lou set up a partnership with him in his new house. But

Dad spent too much time with his head on his desk, sleeping. Lou dissolved the partnership, and once again, my father was unemployed.

Then Penny took pity on him and went to live in Hopkinton for a time. They'd watch endless episodes of *Star Trek*, and she became his captive audience as he expostulated about world events; she wouldn't interrupt him for fear of hurting his feelings. She'd hoped to accompany him on job interviews, but no white collar firm would hire a man over sixty. "Be a driver, a mailman, anything!" we urged him. But he was too proud. Besides, why should he begin driving taxis when he had me footing the bill?

Then Dad began to drink more heavily and go off on abusive tirades. He cast Penny in the same hectoring role of wife that had stifled me. Exhausted, she packed her bags one night and set off for New York to seek out her big sister, the one she both admired and disliked. I tried to discourage her from coming; in addition to my job at the *Times*, I was frantically trying to complete my overdue book about former Vietnam army deserters, *Waiting Out a War*. In researching the book, I'd met a draft resister, Roger, with whom I was now living. Much to my surprise, my father, the war supporter, had helped Roger cross the border illegally from Canada and, out of loyalty to me, had even hidden him for a time in his underground preserve.

Penny came to New York anyway and took a vacant apartment directly above me. Roger the Dodger, a protective and possessive young man, did his best to keep her away from me. And as soon as I heard her voice, I would scurry into our bedroom and softly close the door. I could have taken an hour here and there to see her, to advise her, to be the big sister she wanted me to be, but I told myself I simply didn't have the time. In truth, I wanted to avoid the familial Sturm und Drang.

Finally, Penny left for good. She left New York, she left the East, she left Daddy, she left me. California became her new home, as far away from her daft relatives as she could go. She called Dad often; even at their lowest points, they still remained attached. But she left the financial support of our father to me, as I was in a better position to absorb it. Eventually, she developed such an aversion to flying that it constrained her from coming back home.

Now that I was in New York City, giving Daddy money really did begin to hurt. No shopping. No theater. I once overheard a male *Times* reporter ask my deskmate why I looked like a refugee from a thrift shop. I wore my one pair of boots so often that eventually I felt icy water seeping through one of the soles.

Had my father ever broken down, asked for advice, comfort, or even just company, I wouldn't have been so distressed. But as it was, I felt used—and unloved. I would pay his rent. I always paid. But I hated him for it.

I watched as my peers sailed blithely through their twenties, losing boyfriends, acquiring others, dancing, living dangerously. I, on the other hand, was stuck down in the mud with my father. It wasn't enough that I should pay for him; I had to *be* him too. If he was depressed, so was I. If I should have a happy moment, I couldn't enjoy it unless I first called to make sure that his sentences didn't have that telltale plunge. A girl was supposed to have a father to turn to in a crisis, but what if the crises were all his?

My wedding to Bob Morgenthau in 1977 took some of the chill out of Dad's and my relationship. My father was pleased to be asked to walk me down the aisle. Bob and I had bought an eccentric Federal house in Greenwich Village with a sunken garden and French doors that led nowhere. My image of a marriage ceremony included descending a sweeping staircase, so the day before the wedding, bare wooden stairs were still being nailed into place between the French doors and the garden. As the music boomed forth and some two hundred people fixed their eyes upon me, I started down the steps arm in arm with Dad. Halfway down, I suddenly felt my pump begin to slip between the boards. My father quickly clasped my hand and tensed his arm hard, lifting me back up so I could continue down the rickety bridal stairs. I was profoundly grateful; for once, my father was supporting *me*. Until that moment, I hadn't realized how deeply I'd been yearning for the nurturing father of my childhood.

Such tender moments, however, were too often buried by his maddening behavior. Pat, who had come back into his life after Mother's death, had for some reason temporarily removed herself from it. He was a walking paradox. Tall and looking as impressive as ever, with not a gray strand in his light brown hair, he appeared to be utterly in control. But in reality he was paralyzed within the four walls of his home.

Bob had more empathy for my father than I did. My husband had had great success in his career and marriages; my father had stumbled seriously in both. Nevertheless, they were very much alike: reticent and reserved, both were storytellers who had a dry sense of humor. Men of a time when commitments were kept, standards observed, and self-congratulation spurned. Both have taken the high road with an inner dignity that can't be shaken.

Bob, with his multitude of connections, tried to get my father a job in Boston. My father, probably numb with fear, didn't even show up at the first interview my husband arranged. Finally, we thought we had the perfect solution: Give him work that he could really love.

My family had spent many blissful hours on the *Pencilot* (named for Penny, Cindy, Lorraine, and Tom), a big wooden fishing boat that Dad had used to take us miles out to sea on swordfish expeditions. These were daring trips, and several times we got caught in swells that clapped the boat down so hard we were thrown around the deck. My father had become famous around Falmouth Harbor for bringing in swordfish weighing several hundred pounds. So Bob and I had the idea of sending him to a course that would license him as a boat captain. Bob offered him the use of his own thirty-two-foot Brownell fishing boat so he could take tourists out on fishing trips in the warm seasons. But he never ended up running the boat, claiming that there wasn't enough business on the Vineyard. I assumed he never even bothered to take the course. Then one day as I was cleaning out his clothes closet, I found a new, uncreased captain's license tucked in a jacket pocket. He had done it after all. Done it and then walked away, for reasons I would never know.

My father's first grandchild, Joshua Franks Morgenthau, was born in March 1984. In classic fashion, I gave him the freedom that my parents had never given me. I helped him decorate his walls in crayon, let his toilet paper sculptures block the hall for weeks, and, to the disapproval of other mothers, allowed him to crawl away down the beach unimpeded. But in this perfect world, there had to be a grandparent. Bob, whose parents were long gone, urged me to invite my father often to our apple farm in the Hudson Valley. He and Josh grew to adore each other and I encouraged the relationship, although I kept my distance.

Four months after Josh was born, Penny had her firstborn, Luke. Though he seldom saw her, my father bragged to everyone about Penny and how skillfully she could finesse the giant egos of Hollywood. She'd grown up to be a pretty, tenacious woman who had worked as an executive assistant to studio heads and major actors. She later took a fascinating top-secret assignment at a jet propulsion aeronautics company in Los Angeles. Then she settled into the quieter and more rewarding job of working with special needs children.

Dad was thrilled with his second grandchild. When Josh was born, he had wryly remarked, "He looks exactly like Henry Leavitt," my mother's father, a Kankakee patrician who was stout and round-faced. But Luke looked just like him—thin lips, fine blond hair, and mischievous eyes.

Despite some reconnection with his family through his grandchildren, Daddy still kept to himself. By 1985, though he didn't drink by day, I knew that my father had become an accomplished alcoholic. A night owl like him, I saw what happened after midnight. Sometimes he would lurch around the kitchen, swearing, clenching his fists, and kicking chairs. One day I discovered where he hid his cache. Carrying a stack of blankets, I opened our guest-room cupboard and yelped at the vision of men inside. But it was only Dad's shirts, with bottles of vermouth and Beefeater gin stuffed into the sleeves, the cuffs knotted.

One night I got a call from my father's friend Doug Haward. "I went to your Dad's and I called but he didn't answer, so I went in. He wasn't there, but the place was in chaos. Suits from the thirties and forties were lying over the couch, the chairs, the tables. Garbage bags stuck under the dining table. A real foul odor. I was concerned, so I looked in the oven. It was filled with dirty dishes. You don't put dirty dishes in your oven. That's what alarmed me most of all, Cindy."

What alarmed *me* most were the suits. They could hardly have fit him anymore. Was he trying them on, imagining himself setting off to meet a General Alloys client? Penny always claimed that he still thought of himself as a vice-president. He carried himself like an executive, talked like an executive, and spent money like one—buying his umpteenth gun, for instance. The only thing missing from the equation was the job itself.

I'd written about alcoholism for the *New York Times Magazine* and learned that crisis interventions were often successful. I made a plan, and Dr. Nicholas Pace, an expert on alcoholism and my chief source for the story, was my ally. I rounded up a group of Dad's closest friends, including Doug, Bob, and Lou Golden. Our job was to convince Daddy that he was an alcoholic and harangue him into going into treatment. We were to use reason, histrionics, and even threats to accomplish this task. I brought along his treasured grandson, Josh, now eighteen months old, as extra ammunition.

On a hot day in August, we arrived without warning at his house. My father blinked several times when he saw all of us. His eyes were bloodshot and his pants unzipped. I wanted to run from the door.

But I stepped into the living room, where every surface was covered in a layer of dust. Everyone sat down; apparently reluctant to brush off their seats, they perched on the edge of them. I sat on the floor, while Dad gingerly poured coffee into paper cups and delivered them to his uninvited guests. He sat down and we stared at him. "Daddy, we're here because we love you," I said, as Josh tried to wriggle out of my arms into his grandfather's. "You look awful. We think that your disease is alcoholism."

"I can understand your concern," he said. "But all I have is the flu."

"Tom, you've begun to cheat at chess," Doug said softly. He was a tall, red-faced man with a toothy grin, and I couldn't help but notice he was squirming uncomfortably. Doug was my father's drinking buddy.

My father looked hard at him but said nothing.

"I can smell alcohol on your breath," Lou remarked, rather weakly. He kept smoothing down his hair and looking around the room as though for evidence. He didn't have to look for very long. Curtains were falling off the rods, the rug was grimy.

"Look, can't you understand?" Daddy glared at us. "I'm sick, yes; depressed, yes; getting old, yes. But that's all."

"Tom, it sounds like you'd rather be anything at all but an alcoholic," Bob said.

"I'm not an alcoholic," Daddy said urbanely, his legs crossed and hands folded. "I never have a drink before the evening, and when I do consume alcohol, I can still talk, drive, and walk a straight line with no trouble at all."

My father was so convincing that I could see the group weakening, weighing whether he might be right, after all.

We kept at him for three hours and then finally my father lost his cool. "Geez, if I couldn't go down to the club and have a few drinks, I think I'd go nuts!"

"Daddy," I pounced, "you just admitted it. You can't live without booze. Look what your grandson is doing." I pulled Josh away from an open bag of garbage spilled across the floor. "Do it for him. He needs you. Please don't die. Choose life, for us."

"Tom, why don't we go down to the hospital and have a doctor examine you and let him decide," Bob said. He got up and put a hand on Daddy's arm.

My father balanced his face, which was the color of gravel, in his fingers. No one spoke. He finally looked up. "Okay, okay," he said.

So at 10 o'clock that night we went to the emergency room at a hospital in Worcester. The intern declared he wouldn't touch my father. "An alcoholic won't stop drinking unless he wants to, and I've got dying patients here."

"But if we don't get him help, my father *is* going to die," I replied.

"You can always bring him back when he starts hemorrhaging," he said.

We called Dr. Pace, who persuaded the intern to check my father's blood for elevated liver function. I begged the intern to say the tests showed liver damage from alcohol, even if they didn't. He just stared at me. Two hours later, he came back holding a sheet of paper and said, "These are the test results and they do show extensive liver damage."

"It must be my diet," my father said stonily.

The doctor shook his head. "It can only be caused by one thing: alcohol. And you're well on your way to sclerosis of the liver. I'd do what your family wants you to do." Then he strode away.

"Dad, what about it? Will you go into a rehab facility?" I asked.

My father was silent for several minutes, and then he said, "All right, all right. I'll go."

The next day, we drove him to Edgehill Newport Treatment Center, in Newport, Rhode Island. After several weeks, he emerged looking considerably better. His skin was a healthy color, his eyes clear. The rehab center, however, gave him a poor prognosis. Dad had despised group therapy. He'd boycotted shuffleboard. And worst of all, he'd called the twelve-step recovery program of Alcoholics Anonymous hooey.

Afterward, I worriedly searched his closet and suitcase whenever he came to visit us. I never found any alcohol there. One time he caught me in mid-search. He knew exactly what I was doing. "I have stopped drinking," he said through gritted teeth. "My training in chemistry has convinced me that I could further harm my liver if I ever drink again." And he never did.

But he was, as they say, a "dry alcoholic," someone who still denies he ever had a problem—"I stopped just to show you all I could"—and refuses to take full responsibility for his own life.

Unquenchable, he continued to drain my emotional and financial reservoirs. As a last resort, I went to a support group for children of alcoholics. There I learned the word "enabler" and was told that my father and I were in a kind of morbid collusion. If it wasn't a revelation, it was a relief. I was reminded that I didn't have to do what I was doing; I wasn't even *supposed* to do it. The world was full of sisters stupidly sacrificing themselves for their addict brothers, mothers for sons, fathers for daughters, daughters for fathers. I'd always been the rescuer. But if I was stifling, so was Dad, for I was taking away his dignity and the self-reliance he had so prized earlier in his life. If he was depending on me, I also depended on him to provide the emotional attachment—or what passed for it—that I so craved. Gradually I found the determination to unglue myself from him, and the conviction that it was right to do so.

Daddy had been clanking around like Jacob Marley's ghost in the Hopkinton house he had bought for the three of us. But Penny and I had married and settled elsewhere and our bedrooms lay empty. Bob and I stopped paying the mortgage and we urged him to sell it. "I don't like that idea one bit," he growled, but to our surprise, he did it—on his own. He also found the rental apartment in nearby Milford, comfortable though a step down for him—the first floor of a rather ramshackle clapboard house in a somewhat meager part of town. Bob invested most of the money from the sale of the house so that Dad could receive a modest monthly income of his own. After that, I left him alone to fend for himself. Miraculously, for awhile anyway, he did. There were even signs that Pat had come back on the scene, but I didn't ask and he didn't tell.

I imagined that after I stopped being a codependent with Dad, our relationship would improve. But that didn't happen. If I had been continually angry at him since my teens, his anger at me now was palpable. After all, I'd stripped him down in front of his friends, forced him out of his house, taken away his meal ticket, taken away his control over the capital he did have. Our phone calls got further apart, shorter. His visits to us were less frequent.

One day, however, Dad asked if he could bring Pat for a weekend visit. My mother had been dead for a decade; I took a deep breath and said yes. Having my father near me was so painful, how could I refuse a ready-made buffer?

Pat had never stopped sending me poems over the years; they fell unexplained out of envelopes with no return address, as if she were some close personal friend. Shortly after I'd written the Diana Oughton story, she'd sent me a twenty-page poem entitled "Diana." I'd thrown that in the trash too. I had no idea whether she was a good poet or not and I didn't care. The sight of her spindly cursive on a letter sent a wash of fear through me, as though I were hearing the tread of a stalker.

When she walked into our home, however, I was startled. She had a beaked nose, thin lips, and hair bleached a bit too yellow. Her skin was so white she looked like she'd been born in a flour barrel. This was the love of my father's life?

I considered Pat's unremarkable looks a count in her favor—my mother had been far more beautiful—along with the fact that she never reminded me that she'd sent me a single poem. Then there was her warmth and helpfulness; she chopped carrots with me and scrubbed pots and pans while Bob and Dad sat sprawled on the couch. She wasn't the least pushy but kept an appropriate distance. Yet she treated me with unabashed affection. I considered this commendable given that she must have known I'd always hated her.

A high school teacher at the time, she played with little Joshua, and my father reported that she thought him exceptionally brilliant. To my amazement, I began to become fond of this woman. It didn't hurt that Bob, the most discerning judge of people I know, immediately thought she had character.

I even felt friendlier toward Dad when Pat was there. But she was forbidden territory. This was because I felt the presence of the Great Mother in the Sky, the demand for retribution still unanswered. I avoided being alone with Pat. I was willing to entertain a guarded peace with her but didn't want her to sneak in any heart-to-heart talks.

Over the next few years, I continued to find it hard to be around my father. The barrier he'd erected all my life had now become mine. I respected him for only one thing: the rugged will he'd shown when he'd stopped drinking on his own.

I would tolerate family get-togethers. But the minute Dad and I were alone in a room, I'd make excuses to drift away. To my surprise, he noticed my distance and would look pained when I avoided him. He would drift after me from room to room until I felt forced to sit down and make awkward small talk.

Bob and Josh, on the other hand, made up for my coolness. In the morning, when he heard that Joshua was awake, Dad, in mock agony, would call, "Coffee, coffee, coffee!" This was the signal for a delighted six-year-old Josh to take up a steaming mug to him. Dad and Bob would have bacon and scrambled egg whites together and chat. Inevitably and to my great irritation, he would ask, "Is Sleeping Beauty up?" I would stay in bed until I was sure he'd gone upstairs to dress.

When Amy was born in August 1990, she quickly became as precious to Dad as Josh, but he and I did not budge from our wintry deadlock. I never could figure out why it was me he wanted to be with more than Josh or Amy or Bob or anyone else. During one visit, some months after his Holocaust testimony, he found me sitting alone in the kitchen. He sat down across from me and without preamble said, "Pat thinks you don't like me because I loved her instead of your mother." Flabbergasted by this sudden intimacy, I mumbled something about how I'd wanted the family to stay together. He mumbled something like an apology. Then he took a section of the newspaper, got up, and left the room.

Chapter Seven

He was right; I didn't like him. It had nothing to do with Pat, of course, and everything to do with us—our emotional stalemate. Holding myself back from him was hard work but I didn't know how not to. An idea began to nag at me—what if I tried to find out not *who* he was but who he *had* been? What if I tried to find out what it meant for Dad to see a concentration camp?

I wanted to see what he saw in Ohrdruf. I wanted to walk with that skinny lieutenant with the crew cut and the smooth baby skin, follow him into that apocalyptic place. I wanted to watch him put pencil to paper and document the scene as he'd been told to do, as though it were as routine as taking an inventory of warehouses filled with ordnance, counting stacks of rifles and guns and grenades.

I went down to the library at the Museum of Jewish Heritage. An hour later, I was sitting in a cubicle filled with old newspaper articles and the written and audio- and videotaped testimony on Ohrdruf given by other soldiers and survivors.

Ohrdruf. Bach composed some of his most sacred works there. The name sounded strange to me, like an imaginary land of moats and milkweed and talking trees. In reality, it was a satellite of the

Buchenwald death camp, originally established in June 1944 to provide labor in the surrounding hills. The prisoners dug tunnels for gun emplacements and laid railroad tracks that would carry Hitler and his aides into an underground headquarters. The retreat was to be the Führer's birthday present, but he killed himself in his Berlin bunker before it could be given to him.

About a thousand men began the work on that particular project; soon only two hundred remained. As men collapsed, they were put on the bare floor of the "infirmary," where their wounds remained undressed and they were given neither blankets nor medicine, and only half the food rations the other inmates got. When they died, they were piled in trains called "death transports" and sent to Buchenwald for cremation, and more slave laborers were brought in. All told, an estimated ten thousand prisoners died at Ohrdruf, and some nine thousand had been evacuated from the camp, bound for Buchenwald, a mere two days before the American soldiers raided the camp. The men my father had witnessed lying all around the courtyard had somehow escaped transport and returned to the camp. They'd been shot by SS guards at the last moment before they fled approaching American troops.

The American soldiers liberated the camp on April 4, 1945. This was the first time any Allied forces had witnessed an occupied camp; the previous September, American troops had entered the Natzweiler camp in Alsace, but it had been abandoned. Now they were seeing the survivors of incredible atrocities firsthand.

When he received early eyewitness reports from the soldiers, Eisenhower, the supreme commander of the Allied forces in Europe, said he was too busy to visit the camp. The Allies were closing in on Germany, and at the time, the American High Command was also engaged in tracking Jewish gold and artworks worth millions of dollars that had been seized by the Nazis. Lieutenant Colonel Lewis Weinstein, chief of the Liaison Section of the European Theater of Operations, urged Eisenhower to go to Ohrdruf. Ike responded by telling the Jewish officer, "I know that it's especially important to you personally, but I just can't."

Weinstein replied, "It's not that it's important to me, General. The issue is that the world must know about the atrocities; the world won't believe them if they come secondhand, but if General Eisenhower and others like him are there on the scene and can relate exactly what happened, that will make a great deal of difference." When Ike continued to stonewall him, Weinstein pleaded with him a second time.

"Weinstein," the general said in dismay, "I told you I'm busy. There's the door. Now get!"

Finally, eight days later, on April 12, 1945, Eisenhower visited Ohrdruf, or North Stalag III, as the Germans called it. General Omar Bradley, Army Group commander, and General George Patton, Third Army commander, accompanied him. The scenes of devastation were undisturbed. The bodies that had been shot still lay exactly where they'd been found when a battalion of the Fourth Armored Division of Patton's U.S. Third Army had broken through the iron and barbed-wire gates. Only now there was an odor, a strong one, and flies and lice swarmed the corpses. General Patton, a battle-hardened warrior who'd witnessed countless human atrocities, refused to look into the "punishment shed" stacked with naked, emaciated bodies whose skulls had been bashed in, explaining that he didn't want to become ill. But then he did anyway. He went behind a barracks afterward and vomited.

Eisenhower's face "whitened into a mask," according to General Bradley, as he deliberately inspected every corner of the camp: the gallows, the whipping block, and the block used to smash the gold out of the mouths of prisoners. He wanted to be able to say that he'd personally investigated every inch so he could counter "the belief or assumption that the stories of Nazi brutality were just propaganda . . . I can state unequivocally that all written statements up to now do not paint the full horrors."

Ohrdruf has been largely eclipsed by larger camps like Auschwitz and Buchenwald, camps more fervently devoted to the extinction of as many people in as little time as possible. But as the first camp to be liberated, Ohrdruf represented the world's loss of innocence. Its place in history would have been far more prominent had not a much bigger news story captured the world on the very day of Eisenhower's visit: the death of Franklin Delano Roosevelt.

When American troops converged on Ohrdruf on April 4, they also included battalions of the 89th Infantry divisions. I turned on the tape recorder to listen to the testimony of witnesses.

"There were no birds flying, no animals, it was misty dark air like the gates of hell, as if nature knew what was ahead," recalled GI Sol Tannenbaum, who spoke Yiddish to the few survivors they found. Still, the prisoners were terrified. "They acted like cornered wild animals until finally Sol's words penetrated," reported another GI, Jack Coulston. The survivors did not understand that the Germans were gone, that they were now free.

One liberated prisoner said that the bodies that were stacked up in the "punishment shed" were men who had died after they'd received 115 strokes on the naked back with a cudgel or a sharp-bladed shovel for minor infractions. One of the bodies inside was of an American flyer.

As I listened to these accounts, I learned the answer to a question that had plagued my father. According to one of the surviving prisoners, the Germans had ordered the prisoners to drop their pants so that they wouldn't run away before they could shoot them. That was why my father had seen all those corpses in the courtyard with their trousers around their ankles. "But there was this one man with a crumpled hat, black trousers, hands gripping a rope belt, pulling it upward," recounted Coulston. "He was on his back, eyes to heaven. He had challenged the SS and died a free man."

The pit my father had described must have been the largest one, in back of the camp, near the woods. It was about a quarter of a mile long. According to an eyewitness account in the *San Francisco Chronicle*, charred scraps of human bodies and gray ashes of bone littered the pits. Cadavers were stacked on a grill of logs and rails, and a detail of firemen were charged with keeping the flames hot enough. I thought of my father describing the sticks used to turn the bodies.

Untold thousands of bodies were disposed of in pits around the camp. Before they left, the guards had hurriedly tried to cover the pits with dirt, but they hadn't done a very good job.

I wondered how my father reacted when he saw the heap of disjointed limbs, hands dangling, the fine outline of scapulas, cheekbones, ribs, leg bones, jawbones jumbled together in a monstrous collage. I wondered whether he was one of the ones who cried. Perhaps he had, and perhaps that was why he'd never cried again.

Immediately after his visit to Ohrdruf, my father said he'd been shuttled away, stunned and disoriented; he thought it was probably so that he wouldn't talk about what he'd seen. I think he was right. As I paged through the first-person accounts of soldiers and survivors, I received confirmation that, unbelievably, in the days after the camps were first discovered, those who spoke of them rarely did so above a whisper. No one could quite comprehend the extent of the genocidal atrocities, and those who did felt a sense not only of outrage but of shame. The official tendency was not only to doubt the reports, but to keep them secret from the public at large. The brass regularly had what Milton Bracker, then a *New York Times* correspondent, called "double vision." American officers in France infuriated the local citizenry by scoffing at reports of the atrocities. The older generals were perhaps skeptical because they'd heard propaganda about German atrocities during World War I that had turned out to be untrue. But more likely, the disbelief was due to the inability to process the magnitude and detail of what the Nazis had done. "I wrote to my parents describing the experience, which was read at a local gathering of businessmen," said Bruce Nickols, a member of the 89th Infantry Division. "It was widely disbelieved."

"We all heard rumors, stories, but too incredible to be believed. I thought maybe a few thousand Jews had been murdered, but six million?" Lieutenant Colonel Weinstein said. "There was a great feeling of guilt when we actually found out what happened in these camps."

This double vision was probably why, with hundreds of American soldiers witnessing that first concentration camp liberation, they sent my father and a special team to confirm the findings. My father was a precise, meticulous man. He was strong, tough-minded, and prone to understatement. He was just the kind of officer who would send back facts instead of sentiments, who would tell what was really there in exacting, painstaking detail.

After his harrowing visit, Eisenhower brought in newsmen from around the world and delegates from Washington. "We are told that the American soldier does not know what he is fighting for," he said, "Now, at least, he will know what he is fighting against." He ordered every American unit nearby that wasn't in the front lines to tour Ohrdruf. As a result, the camp, its pits of skeletons, its piles of bodies in the courtyard, remained untouched until the first week in May.

As I listened to the audio testimony, watched video testimony, and read transcripts of survivors, liberators, and witnesses, I found that while each man had a slightly different version of events, there was a similarity of aspect. The eyewitnesses told their stories the way my father told his. The videotaped testimonies were especially powerful: The men, in their seventies and eighties, were straightforward, businesslike in their descriptions, but inevitably some little gesture—the quivering of an eyebrow, the licking of lips, the revealingly timed cough—betrayed a lifetime of repression.

Bonnie Gurewitsch, the woman who had interviewed my father, didn't find these telltale signs at all surprising.

"They all suffered a major psychological trauma, and they had all tried very hard to forget it," she told me. For most witnesses, the horror forever divided their lives into Before and After.

"Everybody that saw what was going on there was literally stunned into silence . . . ," said Paul P. Lenger, a Jewish GI and a military intelligence agent. "At night, I could see the faces of the people in the camp in front of my eyes . . . the camp was something completely outside the war. I can see shooting somebody in a war, but the technical and completely inhuman way of handling people, reducing them to an 'it,' disturbed me quite a lot . . . I had to force myself to 'daven' every day," he said, referring to the Jewish recitation of prayers.

John Searle, now a clergyman, testified that he nearly didn't enter the ministry after seeing Ohrdruf: "How could you talk about a Prince of Peace?"

Dr. Lloyd Kalugin, who was with the Fourth Armored Division, testified that he'd heard rumors of concentration camps but couldn't understand what they were talking about. Then he saw it for himself. "For fifty years, I had no emotion. I blocked it out of my mind. I would take out some of the pictures and look at them, but I was numb, I had no feelings. Then, a few years ago, I went to the Holocaust Museum in Washington, D.C., and on the fourth floor they had a big picture of Ohrdruf." When he saw it, he began to cry and couldn't stop.

Ernest Koller, of the 89th Infantry Division, which followed the Fourth Armored Division into the camp, "knew how bad the Nazis were, but even I couldn't comprehend it. We were in a state of shock. I didn't talk to anyone, we hardly talked to each other, even after we had seen it."

The videotaped testimony of Lieutenant Colonel Lewis Weinstein, the man who had done so much to insist that General Eisenhower visit Ohrdruf in person, was especially unforgettable. He'd gone in with the 89th on the day of liberation and entered the office of the camp commanding officer. He'd found the remnants of papers that had been hastily burned, a book with a list of names in it, and then he came upon a storage place for personal belongings. "There was hair tied up, flesh around rings rotting, earrings torn off, notebooks, papers, diaries. There were boxes marked 'Human Soap' and they were yellowish brown squares, about six or eight inches thick, irregular shapes, twelve by ten. They might have been melted down from larger quantities. There weren't many people left. One man told me about some things, we talked in a mixture of German and Yiddish, he was extremely emaciated, no flesh on his bones. He died in front of me.

"I had been prepared for horror but not prepared for this," Weinstein's voice began to quaver. "I couldn't believe what I saw. I was feeling sick, but I mustn't vomit, I said. I was arguing with myself about whether this was happening. I had to keep telling myself, this is real, what I'm seeing is real . . . one guy says to me, 'Can you believe anything like this is possible?' Then he threw up. Under the pile of bodies, someone moved. We dug down but nobody was alive. But one person must have been alive underneath."

"It was the most horrible thing I have ever seen in my life," testified G.I. Roland Perske. "When I think of the number of years I couldn't have talked about this for my life . . . I would have such terrible nightmares. At night, I couldn't sleep. I probably won't be able to sleep tonight."

Reading Perske's testimony made me think of the nightmares my father had had throughout my childhood. He would cry out in his sleep, "No, no, no!" or "Oh, oh!" in a deep voice that resonated through the house. My room was next to his, so it always woke me. Sometimes I would go into his room to see if he was all right and find him with his blanket pulled up over his head, his feet sticking out beneath. Now I understood what had stalked his dreams.

Meyer Birnbaum, another American soldier, was likewise haunted by stories from the survivors he met at Ohrdruf. He reported that he couldn't stop thinking about the unique ways the SS guards had dreamed up to torture and intimidate. One survivor had witnessed the guards making a little boy, whose father had a noose around his neck, kick the bench out from under him.

John Ehrman, of the Fourth Armored Division, said, "There were corpses piled like storage, and there was this one [survivor] named Wallach walking around with a blanket over his head, and he was mentally pretty much deranged. People who saw this couldn't understand, they couldn't, couldn't just live with it." Ehrman was in charge of interrogating German prisoners. "We said to the inmates about a few guards we found, 'Go ahead and do something with them, do whatever you want to them.' The guards were crying and saying, 'We were good to you!' The inmates wouldn't do anything to them, they had no strength, they had nothing left."

"We fed them sugar and water but they were too weak to hold the spoons. They could not speak. They could not hold up their heads," recalled G.I. Joe Cone. "The scene of these combat-hardened GIs openly weeping . . . my brief touch with suffering, pain, dehumanization, and death will forever remain with me."

"The smell of death is still in my dreams," Jack Coulston testified. "In just five months here, they exterminated ten thousand people. That's one hundred percent of my town of Manhasset."

As with all the camps, the heartbreaking question was: How could the German citizens have allowed the massacres to go on? Could they really have known nothing about Ohrdruf? The Germans in the nearby town routinely said exactly that; even when they were downwind of the burning bodies, they claimed they hadn't smelled anything. Yet in his testimony, Bernbaum remembered commandeering German homes and finding that the owners had confiscated and displayed Jewish souvenirs: "In one there was a drinking cup, a becher [Kiddush cup] to sanctify the Sabbath. They knew!"

I looked up accounts about Colonel Haydon Sears, the commanding officer of Combat B, the Fourth Armored Division, who had entered Ohrdruf on April 5, the day after liberation. His visit confirmed the willful denial of the local Germans regarding the carnage right under their noses. Colonel Sears ordered the mayor and the townspeople to come to the camp. Observers said that about thirty leading citizens, well-dressed burghers, walked gingerly around the bodies with expressions of distaste. The Germans protested that this was the work of a few and that they couldn't be held responsible for it. But Sears made them tour every last part of the camp. He spoke to them in perfect German and his voice was severe and ringing: "This is why Americans cannot be your friends." Showing a German medical officer ten bodies readied for cremation, he asked him, "Does this meet with your conception of the German master race?" The bürgermeister's wife wept hysterically and the bürgermeister kept mumbling, "I didn't know anything about this, nothing at all."

Later that night, they both hanged themselves.

Sears ordered the citizens of the town to clean the filthy barracks, dig holes to bury the dead, and attend the funeral services. The military newspaper *Stars and Stripes* described them as trudging up the street "leading to and from the camp, their women in whispery knots behind them, and now there was mud on their shining shoes."

These citizens, good Nazi sympathizers, now became stolid anti-Hitlerites. So compliant with the victorious American military were they that their women enthusiastically offered to sleep with the GIs. They allowed their homes to be requisitioned with the greatest of sycophancy. They were good followers, the Germans, only now the ones who gave the orders had changed. Secretly, however, many were unrepentant. In the files of the museum, I came across a document in German, a memo that deplored the American occupation of Germany. It complained bitterly about the "noise of U.S. military exercises, the helicopters, the shooting . . . immune to time, day, Sunday, or holidays . . . this is deeply engraved in the memory of the people."

Out of all these testimonies of horror, I was cheered to find some uplifting stories. The museum had put out a book called *Ours to Fight For: American Jewish Voices from the Second World War*, which included the experiences of American soldiers working with men and women from Ohrdruf and other camps who'd been put in displaced persons camps. The soldiers became emotionally involved with the survivors and tried to help them, sometimes against the orders of their superiors. Some conducted Shabbat services in various camps, allowing survivors to express their Jewish identity for the first time in years.

Victor B. Geller, a Jewish army chaplain, compiled descriptions of the relatives of girls in a work camp near where he was stationed. He sent it to his mother in New York, who turned it over to a Yiddish newspaper, which published the information. "You know, some of them made contact with their families," Geller said.

Jack Scharf, an intelligence agent with the 42nd Infantry, wrote his mother asking her to send nylons, lipstick, and food. Without his knowledge, his mother put the letter in the Jewish newspaper *The Forward* and "the packages started coming from all over the country. They had to go to a local synagogue, and they actually set up a special post office for us."

Many organizations had asked Scharf to speak, but he'd refused, sounding a familiar note of anguish. "I just can't do it. I'm afraid I would crack. I have guilt . . . I suffer nightmares every night of my life."

So many of these soldiers had no authority to help the survivors, but they just did so anyway. My poor father; if only he'd been one of them, had been able to nurse a survivor back to health, to send home to my mother asking for clothes and toiletries and food, to see life emerge from the death and destruction that he'd witnessed. Perhaps, if he'd stayed there long enough to save another human being, he wouldn't have had to stay there for the rest of his life.

Chapter Eight

D addy, naturally, continued to deflect my questions about the war, so I wrote away for his military records. I also dipped into a few accounts of espionage organizations, but found nothing that applied to my father's service. Then it hit me: Pat Rosenfield had been Tom Franks's lifelong confidante.

Pat had now become a regular fixture in my father's life, and, increasingly, in my own. She chatted cheerfully about everything except my father, giving gentle advice on child-rearing, house decorating, and good living. She especially touched me by quoting the things she loved in my articles (a writer's delight, hating as we do the thudding "I liked it"). But I continued to struggle against caring for her too much. She was, after all, the woman who'd ruined our family. How could I ever forget that? Was I supposed to kill my mother all over again?

Also, I entertained fleeting suspicions that perhaps Pat was just using me, hoping that through my connections, I would help get her poetry published. At least now I understood why my father loved Pat more than Mother. She had the talent of listening intently. It must have been a refreshing change from his wife's petty disregard. If Pat lacked my mother's Waspish breeding and social polish, she possessed more

intellectual depth. She talked of the miniaturist painters of the Otto-
man Empire, the logical fallacies relating to our time, the literary
dicta in Gabriela Mistral's *Decalogue of the Artist*. She ruminated over
ontology and the nature of man, topics my mother would not have
known how to access. True, I would sometimes tune out her arcane
carrying-on, but she could also be down to earth like my father. In point
of fact, it seemed that she could be anything you wanted her to be.

I began to see that Pat was actually quite pretty, not at all the plain
woman I saw when we first met. There was something about her
jaunty self-confidence, her twinkling, blue Irish eyes, her easy laugh,
and her penchant for taking people off guard. I took her to a New
York gala once and introduced her to the writer Dominick Dunne,
who hates party small talk even though he does it well. Within minutes, I heard her asking him, "What is the most important thing in
your life?" By the end of the evening, she'd charmed not only Nick,
but the likes of Kitty Carlisle Hart and Wayne Lawson, executive editor of *Vanity Fair*, who offered to read her poetry. One well-known
politician even slipped his card into her bag.

Pat also had a loopy side, writing quixotic notes to me in syntax I
could barely understand. She continued to send me poems, which were
actually quite good, but never expected me to praise them. In fact, unlike my own mother, she never expected anything from me. She
dubbed herself my kids' "honorary grandmother," or "HG." I began to
miss her the times she couldn't accompany Dad to see us.

I could see that my father, in his courtliness, held himself back
from her when he was in our presence. But I would peek at them
when they were alone. They talked in low, intimate tones. She relaxed
him; he was more personal than I'd ever seen him, affectionate and
even fascinated by her after all these years. How different he had been
with my mother, most of the time so stiff and evasive.

It was early May, and Pat and I were taking a stroll through the apple
orchards at our country house in Fishkill. The trees were an explosion

of fragrant, velvety white blossoms, each bud curled up as sweetly as a baby's hand.

"Well," she sighed, "I never thought I'd see anything like this when I was growing up in Lower Mills in Dorchester, Mass."

A world away from Wellesley. "Um, you know, Pat, I was wondering. When or how *did* you meet my father?"

"Well, it was just after the war. I was a lowly secretary at General Alloys and he was vice-president," she said with a little smile. "And I asked him out."

"You asked him out?"

"Your father was a good-looking, worldly man and I was in trouble. I was a waif. I didn't know anything."

But she knew enough, I thought, to set her sights on my father. A married man.

"I wanted someone to help me get a lawyer so my small son, Peter, and I could escape my abusive husband," Pat said. "He suggested we meet at the Copley Plaza in Boston. He was the most gallant man I'd ever met though he didn't seem to take a lot of pleasure in things. We sat at a table in the Carousel Room where you go round and round and if you have more than one drink, you'd get dizzy. He ordered shrimp. I had never had shrimp before. Then he called your mother, told her he wouldn't be home for dinner, and took me into the next room, and I had a meal like I've never had before!"

All those sad little dinners at the kitchen table. Mother, Penny, and I eating silently, the fourth chair empty.

A breeze blew through the trees. Pat stooped to pick up a fallen blossom and twirled its petals. "You can see through them," she smiled. "Do you know you can see through a piglet's ear?" She sighed. "Your father had this mythical power . . . Ernest Hemingway, that was Tom Franks. A man who could and did do anything and everything. I suppose I was his Galatea. You know, my Catholic upbringing was really holding me back and he broke that hold it had. He whetted my appetite for knowledge. He encouraged me to get a hobby, a craft, so I took up poetry. He urged me to go back to school, which I did. I finally got my college degree and ended up teaching poetry at Harvard.

"He loves my poems, but he's a very tough critic. He'll lean over them and say, 'I don't really understand why you have this diversion. Maybe it belongs somewhere else.' And you know, he's generally right."

My father, who never read my book, *Wild Apples*, criticized Pat's poetry?

She must have seen the dismay on my face. "Are you thinking about your novel, Cindy? I read it and I thought it was wonderful. But there was a reason Dad didn't read it." She took my hand. "He was afraid he would find himself inside it. I told him the father was a very nice person, but still, he was afraid. Really afraid."

Why didn't he just tell me that instead of fibbing that his eyes were bothering him? I surveyed the orchards around us. They were the setting for the novel, which had been published a year after Amy was born. It revolved around two grown sisters who return home after their mother's death, ignore their alcoholic father, and try to unearth the family secrets that will help them come to terms with their unhappy childhood. Yes, the broad plotlines sounded like our family, but the characters and the dramatic arc were very different. In all honesty, it had occurred to me earlier that my father might confuse reality with fiction, but I preferred to nurse my grievance against him.

"Cindy, don't look so serious. Smell," Pat said, breathing in the scent of the silky blossoms on either side of us. "You want to know about your Dad, well, I can tell you he is the most laissez-faire man I know. Once, he took me to Provincetown and my eyes almost fell out of my head, but he talked respectfully about the transvestites we saw. He wasn't prejudiced about gay people, the way everyone was in those days; he was more like a student of them."

Her eyes lit up. "Oh, I will never forget when he took me on the boat he kept in Falmouth. We went blue fishing with Doug Haward."

My father, sharing our boat, our friend, our family recreation, with his mistress?

"Afterward I wrote about it. I wrote a poem about my catching a bluefish and hauling it into the boat. I compare it to pulling your father out of the depths of the sea and onto the shoals."

"You caught him?" I asked. "Or you rescued him?"

"Cindy, he was a different person with me than he was in Wellesley. He could let down his guard; he didn't have to be fancy or smart or witty. He walked into my home in Newton and he could breathe. He was a ruined man—the war did that, I think—but he knew he could get some tenderness, some acceptance from me."

We crossed the road. The tractors were at the top of the hill, moving along the rows, spraying the trees. I guided us downhill to avoid them.

"You know," she said, "not all of our moments were pleasant. Before he stopped drinking, he would get drunk sometimes. Once, when we were first going out, he took me to a lot of bars, ordering one drink after another, and I kept telling him I wanted to eat, but he ignored me until I was completely starving. The next morning I told him I was upset with him. I told him I was defenseless and in his care and he abused that trust. He looked at me like I'd slapped him. He never did that to me again."

"He didn't get angry at you for criticizing his drinking?"

"Cindy, he's *never* gotten angry at me."

I stared at Pat in disbelief.

We walked a little farther. A bride's veil of Queen Anne's lace covered the face of the hill. I stopped then, folded my arms, and took a deep breath. "When I was a kid, my mom got a lot of hang-up calls. I was just wondering, do you know who might have made them?"

She started. "Not me, I never called your house. There was no reason to. I knew where he was most of the time."

I looked Pat in the eye. "I wonder who it was, then."

"I don't really know," she said, looking right back at me. "But something . . . there's something that comes to mind . . . a signal of some kind, a signal from a group of people he might have worked for."

I tripped on a branch that had been pruned to the ground. She caught me. "Careful now, this is the type of rough ground you can turn your ankle on."

"Pat," I asked carefully, "was my father a spy?"

"You know that your father plays things very close to the chest," she said. "Even after the war, it was a mystery where he would go when he went on trips without me. I know it wasn't client business, but he wouldn't tell me what it was. Sometimes I wonder whether he was reporting into the FBI or the CIA or some official agency right through the fifties. I guessed that, but what it was he never shared with me."

I told her that I'd learned from my research that the FBI and CIA tapped the phones of many intelligence agents after the war. Had those agencies made the hang-up calls? Both had failed to answer my repeated requests for my father's files. "I know he made several trips to Germany after the war, and he was supposed to be there on business, but now I don't know. Pat, I found an envelope addressed to my father. It had these surveillance reports dated May 1951, on a guy named Edward Connolly. Every time Connolly made a move, somebody, a detective or an intelligence agent—they only used their initials—wrote down the time. They knew stuff like when Connolly went up and down the same elevator at his office within the same five minutes, when he met with a man at a trucking firm, when he went to the park to write notes in a black book, when he left town without notice."

"Hmm. You know, I always wondered about those telephone calls your father made when we were having dinner," Pat said. "He would get up to make a telephone call in the booth at the back. He had this thing about checking in with his family—but then a half hour later he would get up again and make another call. He would never call from hotel rooms, only from restaurants, and he never told me who he was calling. I think he could well have been doing something sub rosa. We would go out to dinner, we always went to Little Italy in Boston, usually to this dark little dive called Stella's—"

"Stella's!" I cried. "That's where Dad and I used to go! We always had spaghetti with garlic and olive oil."

"And don't forget the garlic bread!"

"Or the Chianti," I said bitterly. "Our own little place," that was how Daddy had described Stella's. It had belonged to us. Or so I thought.

"He didn't mean any harm," Pat said, reading my mind again. "Your dad has always tried to make everyone feel special. Maybe he failed with those that he loved most, but at least he tried."

"Ha. Tried to double-deal, you mean."

"Cindy, he's a good man! Did he ever tell you how many people he's helped? He's always doing things for the underdog, you know."

"Huh. He's a hermit, except apparently when he's with you," I said. "My mother, she was the one always doing things for everyone. Charity drives, soup for sick neighbors."

"I don't mean those kind of people. I mean the ones he meets in the coffee shop, the ones with frayed collars and soiled caps: the down-and-outers, the retired policemen he taught to shoot who can't make ends meet now. Not that he has a dollar for a donut, but he always has time for people, Cindy. One of them was an alcoholic and he helped him stop drinking. Another one had Alzheimer's and he talked to the wife and got him help. He was a devoted friend. He was there when both of them died. Once he sat down at a counter where the waitress had ignored a black man who was there first, and your father wouldn't order until that man had been served."

I didn't know any of this. For so long I'd seen my father as a some-times likable leech, a hard-nosed recluse. Who was this man who de-fended the destitute and downtrodden?

The sun had set long ago. It was getting dark, and the petals on the apple trees had begun to glow like stars. "Let's turn back now," I said to Pat. "Dad will wonder what's happened to us."

Pat visited for two more apple blossom seasons. One day Dad and I were sitting on the couch. I was reading; he was packing the pipe he smoked occasionally. But most of the tobacco was fluttering to the floor. I looked over at him.

"Pat's married another man," he said.

His voice was matter-of-fact, but his forehead was creased and his eyes were locked on the ground. He got up and walked out of the room.

"Shit!" I said, flinging a magazine to the floor. No explanation to me. No good-bye to her "honorary grandchildren."

And there went Pat, out of our lives.

Chapter Nine

A ll this has brought me to where I am now, in my father's apartment in Milford, where I've discovered the Iron Cross and Nazi cap. If I'm going to put this puzzle together—the mistress's hints, the wartime artifacts, the "special assignments"—I'm going to need some help.

I have appointed the housekeeper I've hired to look after Dad as my accomplice. Ironically, her name is Pat, and she's a gritty, funny, and feisty Yankee who gives my dad hell and somehow cheerfully bullies him into getting dressed in the morning. Excited to be my sidekick, she's also cleaning out drawers and cabinets, knowing I'm eager for anything remotely related to Dad's World War II duty.

I've sent away for more books: histories of secret organizations during the war, including the OSS, Bill Donovan's famous and flamboyant Office of Strategic Services. I've written away to the Naval Institute for books on wartime spies and combed vintage bookstores like the Argosy and the Strand. I've put ads asking for information on a spy ring at the Bureau of Ordnance in two naval history magazines. I've surfed the Internet endlessly and gotten swept up in its undertow. I type in "U.S. Naval Intelligence," and three hours later I'm downstream on some home page with a recipe for boeuf bourguignon.

When Amy and I arrived last night, Dad opened the door and looked stricken at the very sight of us. "My nose is running like a faucet," he complained. It seemed less like a warning than an invitation to turn around and go back where we came from. "Oh, then we'll make you feel better," I said, brazening my way inside.

This morning I look around with satisfaction. It's been six months since we began digging Dad out. Now you can see that this is a real apartment: three good-sized, connecting rooms—kitchen, study, and living room—with a small bedroom and workroom off the study. I sit down and admire it. Pat and I have mined K-Mart for new shades and lace curtains and throw rugs, giving each room a different color theme. I've covered the tables and chests with old pictures—my father as a Navy lieutenant, my mother as a bride, my sister and I as toddlers. We bought Martha Stewart towels, a kitchen tablecloth with little blue Dutch girls on it, and other girlish odds and ends. We've created a dollhouse out of my father's manly chaos.

Today I'm going through the cartons again, looking for more wartime clues. Instead, I find dozens of little notes he's written to himself. Some are about visiting us in Fishkill or Martha's Vineyard: "Things To Do—get anal and nasal relief medications, find suitcase, take money out of savings." But others are less innocent:

Call Cindy
1) *I've been glued to the weather channel*
2) *Heavy rain forecast through most of today into evening. Plus Severe Storms will occur.*
3) *** *I had a slight cold yesterday. Now I have a severe cold, I'm sneezing, wheezing, and coughing. I don't think you would want me around.*

He's written one note on how to deal with the driver whom we'd hired to pick him up:

> *I have a case of diarrhea*
> *I have a temperature of 102+*
> *I have lung congestion*
> *I have sinus congestion*
> *Doctor at Walk-in clinic said I was undoubtedly contagious—*
>   *probably flu possibly the viral flu. Advised to go to bed and*
>   *stay there.*

In another note, he's apparently devised a way to blame his car:

> *I started out when I got my car from the shop around noon. On*
> *the Mass Pike around Palmer the front end started to shimmy—*
> *I headed back slowly. The car is now in the shop again. I'm not*
> *sure when I will get it.*

I think back to all the times he's called to stall my visits to see him or cancel plans to see us. The excuses are right here on pen and paper. He's had to write down his fibs in order to remember them.

Among the notes, I find evidence of another of his betrayals: copies of my *New York Times* articles that I'd sent him, crisp and un-folded. He's never read them. There was a time when he read every one of my pieces. When had he stopped? If I confront him, I imag-ine he'll say his eyes were bugging him again, or he was waiting un-til he had time. Or maybe he has some other excuse written down, waiting in the wings. I wad the articles up and throw them in the wastebasket. It's just more of the same, I remind myself, like my books he's never read. He brags to everyone about my accomplish-ments, yet spurns me in the privacy of his own mind.

*   *   *

I'm so put off by what I found that it's two months before I can make myself return to Milford. Finally, I relent. Pat lures me back with the prospect of one of my favorite activities: further redecorating of Dad's home. Tonight, after the three-hour drive from New York, Amy and I step up to his apartment in the dark and find the door unlocked. Inside, the place is like London on a foggy day, dense with smoke from my father's cigarillos. All the lights are on, but he's nowhere to be found. He can't have left more than a few minutes ago—the smoke is fresh—and he knew we were to arrive at 10 P.M. Amy and I fling our bags down. This is typical of him. God forbid that he should ever be where he says he's going to be.

"Where's Grandpop?" Amy asks.

That's a good question. "I guess he had something he had to do," I say. Still, in spite of his absence, I'm happy to be here. The atmosphere is warm and cozy. The smell is so familiar, so Daddy. I think I got hooked on it when I was little and had earaches; he used to take his pack of Pall Malls out of his shirt pocket, light one, and blow smoke in my ear. He thought the heat would help, and maybe it did; the pain always decreased. He gave up cigarettes ages ago in favor of these little miniature cigars, which he's under the illusion are better for you.

In Dad's absence, I start putting up the "Buy War Bonds" vintage posters I brought from the city. They belonged to my husband's father, Henry Morgenthau, who, as secretary of the Treasury during World War II, had commissioned and distributed them to the public. There's a poster of the taking of the hill at Iwo Jima, one of a mother in a blue dress holding a baby, and one with a woman going through the pants pockets of a man in bed; his head is lifted as he winks: "Just Give 10% to War Bonds." My father, who has a rather ribald sense of humor, will like that.

Amy has been feeding cereal to her pet rats. They're the love of her life: Pepper, a gray rat, and Sugar, a white one. Now they're running around on top of Dad's desk. They stand up on their hind legs and sniff all around, crawl up her arm, get lost in her hair. "Grand-pop's going to love Pepper and Sugar," Amy says, returning them to their cage.

By 11 P.M., it's clear that my father hasn't simply run out for a quick errand. We decide to go to bed. Amy, who manages to make a nest out of anything anywhere, has pushed two easy chairs together and lies sound asleep with her blankie tucked under her chin and her stuffed animals sprawled on her head. I'm on the living room couch with a pillow and blanket.

My father finally comes home at midnight. I can hear him making his way in the dark, looking for us. "Oh, I'm sorry, I'm sorry," he says after I hug him hello, "I didn't realize the time, I didn't realize you were here." He seems genuinely apologetic, really distressed, and I can't help but feel sorry for him. But I'm not going to reward his behavior.

"We'll talk in the morning, Dad. Amy's already asleep. We need to sleep."

"It's much too early to sleep," he says. During our last visits he's carried his preference for the night to ridiculous limits, putting on his bedroom light and then prowling around the house at all hours.

He sits down at the end of the couch, almost on my toes. "You would not believe those idiots who want to banish guns," he begins.

"Dad," I say, "I'm tired. Can we talk in the morning?" He seems not to hear me and continues railing about unfair gun laws. "Dad! It's midnight! I am tired. You're making me tireder."

He blows his nose in his characteristic rhythmic way, first one nostril and then the second. "I'm sorry I'm such a burden," he says, and my stomach clenches. But I remind myself that I'm a grown-up now, and I have a right to be firm and to sleep when it's time for people to sleep. I yawn and close my eyes and begin to fake a snore. But through my lashes, I watch him standing in the slice of light from the other room, looking at me.

* * *

The next morning I'm woken by a howl. "What the bejesus are these?" My father is peering down at the two little animals on his desk, out on furlough from their cage.

"They're rats, Grandpop." Amy, grinning, runs over to him.

"Rats! You mean R-A-T-S?"

"The white one is Sugar and the gray one is named Pepper. Here, Grandpop, you can hold them if you want."

"You let her have rats in the house?" Dad asks, incredulous.

"They're pets, Grandpop. They don't come from the sewer," Amy reassures him.

"Oh," he says and reaches out to Sugar, who crawls into the palm of his hand. He smiles and pets her: "Cute, cute, cute."

He gives Sugar back to Amy and makes for the couch. He seems to have difficulty standing upright, shuffles a bit to regain his balance.

"Are you okay?" I say, sitting up.

"No," he replies, "and I never have been." This is a standard quip of his. He always follows it with a deadpan expression, and if you don't chuckle, he chuckles for you.

"Really, Dad, is everything all right?"

"Sure, just fine." He wouldn't confess if it were otherwise. I'm sure he has aches and pains and a great deal of loneliness, yet he's always stoical, never complaining. This is probably the reason he's always waited until the last minute to make the calls we both dread. The ones that go like this:

"Cindy, several months ago, I had to have all my teeth pulled. The dentist gave me dentures, but now he wants his bills paid. I have a lot of expenses."

"Are you asking me for money again, Dad?" I'd say coldly.

Silence, and then: "You don't know how much I hate to ask you for help," he'd say heavily. "You just don't know."

Now he looks up and says, "I want to tell you who's not okay. Marion Mustard. She has multiple sclerosis."

"Oh no," I say. I love Marion. She's the daughter of Bob and Barb Mustard, who were great friends of my parents. Our two families would go to baseball games and never fail to get ourselves in the newspaper. "The Franks and the Mustards enjoy Fenway Park's finest," it would read, beneath a photo of us stuffing hot dogs into our mouths.

Marion Mustard is about the same age as my sister. My father is shaking his head as he describes Marion's complex of symptoms. "It's a terrible shame. What a beautiful girl she's always been and now she is remarkably courageous." I think of my father and mother and Barb and Bob and all the other friends who once zipped around Wellesley and Boston, going to charity balls and bridge tournaments. They're in their eighties now and I imagine them hobbling about, confined to their homes.

My father always seems to be drawn to stories of disaster. His face is expressionless now, but his blue eyes seem to swim as he tells me about Marion's plight.

"Dad, I have a surprise for you," I say, hoping to cheer him up. I give him a tape that I found in a used music store. Dad breaks out in a smile. "Knuckles O'Toole! Oh, my favorite!" He puts the ragtime king on the tape player I bought for him and slaps his knees in rhythm to the beat. Then, to my surprise, he struggles up and takes Amy's hands, swinging them back and forth as he sings, off-key, "My Gal Sal" to Knuckles' sprinting piano.

"You know that Knuckles was not his real name," he says, collapsing on the couch. "He was Billy Rowland, born in England. He got his big break on *The Perry Como Show* and then played with Perry Como and all of the fifties big bands. He was one of the inventors of honky-tonk piano. You know how he did it?"

"How, Dad?"

He grins. "By putting thumbtacks on the hammers of the piano. That made that great tinkly sound."

"Wow," I say, appreciating my Dad's total recall of the most arcane particulars of the past. I have to tell Pat the housekeeper how Dad came alive when he heard his jazz. She should put it on when she's around the house.

After tidying up the breakfast dishes, I try again to ask Dad about the Nazi artifacts, but he waves me off. "Just a minute, I want to tell Amy a story about my old dog Bing." He motions for her to come to the couch. I must know every amazing feat that Dad's dog ever did. "Guess what happened to me when I was your age? I was playing on the rail-road tracks and . . . ."

I waft away, slipping into his workroom to look for more war stuff. I try the gun cabinet. Locked. Just like it was when it was in the cellar in Wellesley. I find the key on the top of his dresser. I can guess what I'll find inside: his Colt .45s, Browning automatics, the usual pistols. When I was young, he used to test me to see if I knew just about every type of gun there was. But when I open the cabinet, a combat-green holster with pouches and straps falls out into my hands. Shoved in back is a gleaming, stiletto-like knife and another double-edged, flat knife. A Glock and a lot of other pistols. Some of them look old, some new. This one is a German Luger. And that one a purse-size Italian Beretta, or at least I think it is. I don't know what the rest are, in this veritable United Nations of weaponry. Then I see a slim, rectangular case. Inside is a black metal tube, about 6 inches long. My hands go cold. I look at it for a minute and then fit it onto a Colt .45. It's a silencer. Why would Dad need a silencer? Certainly not for pistol-shooting contests.

Why did he have all these strange weapons? Were they spoils of war? Or had he bought them from the ads in one of his gun magazines?

I go into the living room and poke around in a cedar chest that I haven't plumbed yet. It's crammed with dozens of flashlights, new memo pads, unused address books. There's also the old Minox cam-era from our youth. I remember Dad snapping pictures of me and Penny on the beach, the sleek lozenge, not much bigger than a ciga-rette lighter, disappearing inside his hand.

I also find some brittle, age-darkened manila envelopes stacked on one side of the chest. I look over at Dad and find him absorbed in regaling a spellbound Amy with stories about President Abraham Lincoln's quirky habits. I open another brown folder and am excited to find old military orders. Perhaps they'll tell me if he was in some kind of spy unit.

The orders confirm that he was assigned to the Navy's Bureau of Ordnance, which designed and produced the Navy's weaponry for the war. I flip through order after order. It's confusing. He'd been sent to so many places, given a bewildering array of assignments.

He began as a commissioned officer, an ensign, in December 1942, entered the Naval Training School at Fort Schuyler in the Bronx the next month, then moved on to Ordnance School in the Washington Navy Yard. Throughout early 1943, he seemed to be sent all over the place for short periods of time, always as part of the Bureau of Ordnance. To the Naval Operating Base in Norfolk, Virginia, where he had permission "to carry all and any photographic equipment" and did something at the Amphibious Force of the Atlantic Fleet. Then on to Pontiac, Michigan, where he went through antiaircraft artillery school. Next to Port Hueneme in California, where several times he was detached from the bureau on "temporary" assignments. But no mention of what those assignments were.

My father seems to have spent a lot of time around Washington. Had he been sent to one of those confidential "country clubs" outside the city that made you into a spying machine? Did the Bureau of Ordnance have its own pod of spies? Did he run and jump barbed-wire hurdles and scramble up hills till he dropped? Did he learn how to act German? How to pass messages under café tables? I picture him penetrating enemy lines, parachuting behind them, landing in the middle of a fan of resistance fighters surrounding him from out of a dark wood. I smile at myself, cooking up this romanticized vision of my father as a swashbuckling spy, when he's spent so much of his life so buttoned up, so dependent on me.

His orders for Port Hueneme say he's an "Officer in Charge of a Group" in an "Argus Unit." There's no explanation of what Argus is. After Port Hueneme, he did a long tour of duty with these Argus units in the South and Central Pacific from October 1943 to December 1944. In 1944 he was with the Marines when they captured Emirau Island in March and the Ulithi Atoll in September, and then fought in the bloody battle for Peleliu.

This all fits with what Dad told Bonnie when he was giving his testimony: MacArthur's strategy had been to route the Japanese in the Pacific Theater by "island hopping." The plan was to move ships, planes, and troops from one Japanese island to the other, starting at Guadalcanal, selecting only the ones that were vitally important to the enemy. The invasions of Emirau, Ulithi, and Peleliu were all part of this approach of staging surprise attacks.

But what was this Argus? I skim over the hundreds of books on my father's shelves until I find one on Greek mythology. Argus is listed under a chapter on the god Hermes, who slew the mythological monster; Argus was a giant, an all-seeing, never-sleeping watchman who had a hundred eyes. One hundred eyes. To see what?

When I return to open up more service records, a bunch of cards spill out. These give my father entry into the officers' clubs in Ulithi and Espiritu Santo. A humorous one says he is "a duly accredited member of the Talamanca Tourists, having made a wartime cruise on the USS *Talamanca*." It's signed by "W. T. Hatch (Ship's Spirit)."

Among the orders are wills or "beneficiary slips" written every few months, naming my mother as next of kin and inheritor. There's one that he signed, rather strangely, right after he got back from the Pacific in December 1944. What did he do then—after his tour of duty in a battle theater was over—that was so dangerous that he needed to make another will? Then, on March 9, 1945, his classification was changed, from Lt. (junior grade) Thomas E. Franks, O-V(S) to Lt. (junior grade) Thomas E. Franks (SO). Could it have been Special Operations? My father had visited Ohrdruf in April 1945. Why, a month before he visited that camp, would his designation have been changed? A document said he was promoted to full lieutenant a few months later.

Curiously, there are no orders for several months. Then a document dated July 17, 1945, sends my father to the naval base in Norfolk as a liaison officer from the Bureau of Ordnance "until at least one combat mission has been completed." He's to be part of an amphibious warfare unit.

The orders describe his unit as "one of the first groups of its kind to report to the forward area with a number of new developments in the use of rockets and rocket launchers." Wow. Dad was at the cutting edge of work with some of the first rockets; the only "forward area" left was the Pacific.

The orders give my father permission to "vary his itinerary as may be deemed necessary" and authorize him to "carry and use such photographic instruments and films as may be necessary." What was Daddy photographing in the middle of the ocean, and what was he doing that he could go wherever he wanted whenever he wanted? Did those photos of ships I'd found have anything to do with this?

I close the chest. It's time to get some answers—or at least give it a try. "Dad," I say, going to him with the sheaf of thin paper, "I found your military orders from the war."

"Let me see," he says. He leafs through them. "Huh."

"There are so many orders that say you're assigned for temporary duty here or there. And you spent a lot of time in Washington. What did you do there?"

"Oh, I had a lot of training."

"What sort of training?"

"Ha," he laughs. "Just about every kind of training you could think of. And some you couldn't. "

"Name some things you did."

"I did a lot of things, assignments that were poles apart. Wherever they wanted me to go, that's where I went."

"Did you see combat in the Pacific?"

He gives a cynical snort. "You could say so."

"You fought the Japanese?"

He pauses. "Did I ever tell you about the pet pig we roasted in Guadalcanal?"

"Daddy, I've heard about the pig. I've heard about the pig so many times my head is full of the pig. I want to know what you did in the war. I mean, what you really did. I want to know about this secret unit you were in."

He leans back and folds his hands. "I don't think you fully appreciate how delicious that pig was."

"Dad."

"Somebody got some palm oil and I think another chap had some salt and we put together a spit over the fire. We all wanted to turn it because most of us, we'd gotten so little to eat for so long, our pants were falling down. After K-rations, that smell was—"

"Daddy, will you be serious?"

"I couldn't be more serious. We had great difficulty in pretending to Jack Steele that we didn't know what had happened to his pig. We had to bury the carcass and there was virtually nothing left on the bones."

"What was your job in Guadalcanal?"

"I watched for planes and would radio back whether they were enemy aircraft."

"Really?" I sit up.

Just then the doorbell rings. I flinch at the interruption, but it turns out to be Bob, on his way back from a reunion at his alma mater, Amherst College. Amy runs, jumps up into his arms, and wraps her legs around his waist. My dad gets up and gives him a hearty handshake.

Oh well, I think, as we all pile into Bob's car for a drive, at least I gleaned a clue or two. I slip the orders into my bag.

She's back. I walk into my apartment one day and nearly trip over a big box full of Christmas gifts: holiday finger towels, a superannuated tome on the history of locks, a snow globe featuring Santa with his hands on his belly. From Pat. Cartons of See's candy follow on Valentine's Day. Birthday cards for everyone. I'm puzzled, and skeptical. Pat vanished almost two years ago without a word, and now she's reaching out to us? Why?

Whatever the reason, manners dictate that I write her a thank-you note and we're soon corresponding regularly. I'm impressed that her first volume of poems has been accepted for publication. Eventually, she asks me to write the foreword to the book, *Always Being Born*, released under her new married name, Patricia B. Cosentino. I discover Dad is seeing her again, first with her husband, David, and then, I suspect, without him. He's happy, and so am I. The two lovers have been playing a game of hide and seek ever since I can remember. But I decide not to question him. Like my father, I'm laissez-faire.

After my mother died, I'd found a box of her correspondence, that I'd never had the courage to look at until now. I open the box and find a letter that piques my interest. It's from her father, Henry Leavitt, dated June 1943: "I heard from Tom," he writes, "but he won't talk about his work. Something very hush-hush, I think."

I suspect that my father didn't tell my mother everything either, but surely he told Pat more. I'd only gotten intimations from her during our talk in the orchard, but now, through our emails, our level of trust had grown. I call her up and ask if I can visit her in western Massachusetts where she now lives.

"Cindy!" she cries when I walk into the hotel lobby where we've agreed to meet. "I'm so happy to see you," she hugs me. "Too long, it's been too long." We chitchat at first—about the kids, my writing, her writing—for I want to get into this slowly. If Daddy told her anything, he'd surely exacted a promise of silence.

"Pat, we talked about the possibility that Daddy was spying in the fifties, and you didn't know. But what about during the war? Do you know whether he was a secret agent then?"

Pat clears her throat, brushes something invisible off her sleeve and finally nods. "He was. He definitely was. But you must never tell him that I told you."

I hold my hand up. "Not a word."

"I know that during the war your father made dangerous missions, both inside America and outside. He told me that when he got assignments to spy on other Navy officers, he *hated* it. We were staying at the

Sheraton in Cleveland when he told me about this one assignment. It was at a base in Texas, I think. I know it was more sensitive than anything he had done, and he was known to be very discreet."

"What did he do there?"

"Espionage, Cindy, real espionage. He was sent in to infiltrate a ring of Navy officers who were selling weapons to middlemen in Mexico. Selling them to the enemy. The big shots in the Navy in Washington wanted to know about it. He told me, 'Pat, I thought on that one I might have conveniently ended up in a motor accident.'

"I don't know what happened to these traitors, whether they were secretly court-martialed or something else happened to them, but I know that he said the whole thing was done clandestinely. It never reached the public."

Pat glances around at the other visitors milling in the lobby. "I wanted him to talk more about it, but he wouldn't. You know, generally I succeeded in getting beneath that crust he has. After the war, I would question him until he told me what was on his mind. He had to talk, I knew that, or he was going to explode inside."

We look up. A man is peering down at us from the balcony.

"Who is that?" I ask.

Pat shrugs. "Well, he gives me the willies," I say, inching toward her on the couch and lowering my voice.

"What about Europe? Did he tell you about Europe? It's not on his military records, no orders to Ohrdruf, no trace that he ever set foot there."

"Well, he did go to Europe. I know that. He told me about it. Some of the things, anyway. Not all, I don't think. He was trained for those missions in a couple of places out in the country, away from Washington. He learned disabling body chops, you know that? But he said the worst was the psychological torture. He said, 'Pat, you can't imagine how terrible it is, what they put these guys through.'

"Oh, Cindy," she says. "I know. Ask him about Scandinavia. Ask him about that, he'll tell you. He trusts you. There was something about picking up enemy battle information or targets for sabotage. He had to get the intelligence to a commando group or some agent.

"I think he also had some attachment to foreign navies. And in France, he went underground . . . and then, oh yes, he was attached to the U.S. Army when they overran Germany. He said he wore the uniform of every different outfit he was put with, whether it was the Army or the French or the Swedish, whatever." Pat pauses. "But he always played everything down. He'd describe a covert mission and he'd be pulled out before he knew what the results of his work were, and he'd say, 'Oh, I don't think it was anything of consequence.' But I knew it was. Nothing your dad did was without consequence."

Chapter Ten

"H is old car was shot, so I took your dad to a Toyota dealership to buy a new one," Benny Montenegro tells me.

I smile into the receiver. Benny, Bob's old Navy buddy, a short, compact vet with a broad Yankee accent, lives near my father and has befriended him. He's been generous with his time, helping Dad with errands great and small. Now he's putting up with my friendly interrogation.

"So Tom pretended to examine several models, but I could tell he wasn't taking it seriously," Benny continues. "After a while, he turned to me and said, 'I won't buy a Japanese car. In fact, I won't buy a Japanese *anything*.'

"I asked him why. He wouldn't say anything till we were back at his house. Then he told me, 'I just don't like the Japanese. In fact, I hate them.' He's something else. He carries a lot inside, you know, except for sometimes, us being two veterans together, he'll just come out with these stories.

"There was a Christian mission somewhere on the Solomons, and he told me about something horrible that the Japanese did to some nuns. He told me not to tell anyone, don't know why. Go ahead, ask him what happened."

Not long afterward, I do just that. I've come to Milford to pick Dad up for the Thanksgiving weekend in Fishkill. We're sitting in his kitchen and he looks relaxed, pleased that I'm there. I take a breath and use the old reporter's ploy of pretending to know more than I do.

"Dad, it must have been really horrible seeing what the Japs did to those nuns in the South Pacific. Terrible torture, really terrible."

Dad frowns at me. "Who told you about that?"

"Huh," I say, knitting my brow. "Can't remember."

"It's got to have been Benny. Why is it that everybody who's supposed to keep my affairs confidential feels compelled not to?" he grunts.

Now I'm worried that Dad will cut Benny off like he did Lou Golden. "Why is it you can tell someone else about something so important and not your own daughter?"

"Benny's a toughened veteran. He's a man and he's seen what happens in wartime."

"You know, you'll feel so much better if you tell me. You carry these things around and they eat at you. You can get rid of them by talking about them." I hope.

Dad stares down at the table. "There are some things you can't ever get rid of."

I've done some research and I've guessed that the incident happened in Bougainville, where the Japanese fought on after the Marine invasion of October 1943 and held parts of the island until the end of the next year. One of my father's Argus units, 14, had been in Bougainville at some point in 1944. European, Chinese, and other foreign refugees, including missionaries, hid in the hills; Japanese patrols would seek them out for torture.

"Dad, it's hard to believe the Japanese would do such a terrible thing. The Germans were so much worse."

"Huh!" my father sits up in his chair. "Huh, huh, huh. You don't know *what* you're talking about. The Japanese were bloodthirsty and ruthless. There's nothing they wouldn't do to anybody."

I ask him to give me an example, and he begins to speak in a deep, unsettling monotone. "I was with a reconnaissance group deep in jungle occupied by the Japanese. We were patrolling and . . . ." He puts his cigarillo out. He coughs. "We heard what sounded like the banzai cheers and then some terrible screaming. It wasn't very close by, maybe a few miles away, but we'd learned that there was a village in the direction that the screaming was coming from. If you've ever been in the jungle, you know how far voices can carry. The closer we got to the village, the louder the screams got. It was bloodcurdling. We bushwhacked through the undergrowth as fast as we could, and when we got near the village, we stopped and we saw what was happening. These Japs were using two nuns and a priest for bayonet practice. They had stripped them naked and tied them to trees. They had holes up and down their bodies and blood was running down their bodies."

"Was there anything you could do?"

My father leans over, balancing his forehead on his fingers. "There was nothing we could do. We were just a few men and there was a whole company of Japs. We couldn't give away our position . . . we had to just stay watching them . . . laughing, hollering, taking their time." He looks up at me, beseechingly. "They executed innocent people . . . and they did it with bayonets! The Japs pulled quite a few stunts like that. They were worse than the Germans."

"Your patrol, was it advanced recon? What else did it do?"

"I dunno. I went out with the Marines a good bit of the time . . . ." His voice trails off, then he says abruptly, "I have to go to the bathroom." He puts his glass down and walks quickly out of the kitchen.

I stare at his linoleum floor, colored olive with yellow specks, and I feel like being sick. Maybe that's what Dad's doing right now. No more questions. For today.

However, when he comes back, he seems calm, matter-of-fact. "You'll never know what seeing something like that does to you. . . . you want to kill somebody."

"Kill the enemy," I say.

"Yes. At the time, yes."

"So what did you do?"

He sits down, shakes his head, pauses, shakes his head again. "Something very stupid. We set out looking for this outfit, the ones who had used the missionaries for bayonet practice. Of course, we had to go deeper into territory held by the enemy."

"Weren't you afraid?"

"Huh, we were too mad to be afraid. We wanted to find these dirty Japs and tie them to trees and machine gun them, starting with their toes. We hadn't gotten very far before we began getting shot at." Dad gets up, runs the faucet, takes a glass from the sink, rinses it out, and pours himself a glass of water. All in slow motion. I try to say nothing for fear of breaking the spell, but finally I can't stand it.

"So then what happened, Dad?"

He sits down and leisurely sips his water, ignoring me.

"You can't just say you were shot at and then stop in the middle of the story!"

"It's not a very pretty one."

"Look, Dad, I don't care if you found those Japanese soldiers and shot them in the back while they were sleeping. You picked off the enemy any way you could. What's so wrong about that?"

"The way it makes you feel," he says quietly.

I look at him closely. "How, Dad, how did it make you feel?"

"The Japanese were very tricky," he barks, back to business. "They had the habit of creating decoy positions with mounds of foliage, bamboo, sandbags, other things they'd find, and we kept getting fooled by them. We crept up on one of these positions and all of a sudden bullets went zinging past us from another direction.

"The Japs would tunnel right through cliffs and mountains. This is what made them so difficult to fight—you never knew where they were."

"So, Dad, you were tramping through the jungle and you began to get shot at—"

"Not tramping. More like tiptoeing. You didn't want to give away your location. The fire was coming at us from above. Everybody went down on their bellies and slithered to cover, except for me. I saw these palm fronds moving and I figured: This is where the Jap spiderhole is. Then I did something real stupid. Instead of plotting out a strategy with the other men, I went off half-cocked and zigzagged up the hill until I got near their position. Then I threw a grenade into their hole."

"Did they get you? Were you wounded?"

"Oh, just nicked. But those Japs bought it." His face clouds. "All twelve of them, slumped together. They were only kids."

We're quiet for a little while. Then I break the silence. "What did the rest of the unit do? Did they back you up?"

"No. They ceased fire. There was some reluctance to blow me up, in spite of my stupidity." There are beads of perspiration on his forehead.

"Wait," I say. "Were these the same troops that tortured the missionaries?"

"Hard to tell. But I'm not sure it mattered. One Jap was as bad as another."

"Did you get a medal? Did someone put you in for a medal?"

"Ha! You didn't get medals for doing the kind of things I did. You couldn't even talk about the things I did."

"You mean because you were in a secret unit or you were doing secret stuff?"

Dad's eyes slide away. "Something like that. But anyway, what I did was damn imprudent. There are better ways to annihilate the enemy without taking off on your own, forgetting you're part of a team, leaving your men."

But his actions had been tremendously courageous; didn't he understand that? Surely as worthy of a commendation as some of Bob's heroic acts had been. But he had been left with only the horror—killing twelve men—with none of the praise and perspective that might have come with recognition of his heroism. Though I'm afraid to do it, I really just want to hug my father.

He rubs his midsection gingerly. "Talking about this gives me a burning in my stomach, Cindy. I'm going to take some Maalox and lie down."

"Dad, you gotta get ready. We have to be in Fishkill by dinner-time."

He takes out one of the linen handkerchiefs Pat bought him and wipes his head. "I don't think I can go. I'm feeling a bit sick."

"Dad, that was an awful story. That's what made you sick."

"Maybe it did. But I'm still sick. I feel very sick."

"Look, Dad, I came all the way from New York to pick you up. It wouldn't be Thanksgiving without you. You love the farm. You love being with us."

"Of course I do, but I don't want to infect anyone." He goes into the living room and I follow him.

"Daddy, you can't do this to us!" All those little notes full of ex-cuses—the weather, his health—that he wrote to himself so he wouldn't forget what he needed to say to avoid leaving his comfortable little nest. I'm wise to his game. I'm also confused. On the phone, Pat the housekeeper told me how much he'd been looking forward to be-ing with us at Thanksgiving.

"You do this all the time," I tell him. "You want to be with us, see your grandchildren, don't you?"

"Oh yes, I do, I do. And you!"

"I know you want to go, but then you won't let yourself do it! You turn into a coward." Here the poor man has just confessed an incred-ible act of heroism and I can't stop myself from calling him a coward.

"If I am, I'm a sick one." He reaches for a Kleenex and wipes his nose. "I just can't go, Cindy."

Damn, I think, I spoiled the weekend. Maybe I really did make him sick. I take several deep breaths. "Would you like something to eat?" I ask, switching tactics.

"Why, that would be nice," he replies.

I go into his room and fetch his suitcase. I pack clothes, his vanity case, his medicines—blood pressure pills, six-pack of Tums, milk of magnesia, vitamins. I toss in a carton of cigarillos with reluctance; if I leave them out, he'll just buy more. Then I tiptoe quietly outside, put the suitcase in the trunk of my car, and go back into the living room.

"Okay, let's go, Dad," I say, pulling him up from the kitchen chair.

"I thought you were going to make me something to eat. Go where?"

"Off to the Herschel Creamery."

"Oh, that's a good idea." And so we go out the door and don't return until the end of the Thanksgiving holiday.

Having bypassed the "Herschel" Creamery, I get on the Mass Pike, and head for the Hudson Valley. Our home is among 150 acres of apple orchards that have been in Bob's family for two generations. It is isolated and geese and deer are regular squatters on our front lawn. A decade earlier, we would have been spending the Thanksgiving holiday in the old Morgenthau homestead across the road. A big, white Georgian house with high-ceilinged rooms, it had belonged to Bob's late parents and we used to spend nearly every weekend there. It had been graced by furnishings from another era—overstuffed couches and pastoral wall murals hand-painted by a WPA artist, canopy beds with ivory popcorn bedspreads, and monogrammed linen sheets that had grown yellowed and frayed. In 1984 Bob and his brother and sister had divided up the orchards and sold the house. Bob, a farmer at heart, kept the working operation—the tractors and the cider press and the apple graders, the flaking red barns, and the farm store, which sold the apples and barely broke even.

For the next ten years, we were tucked away in a far corner of our part of the orchards, in a small, dung-colored mobile home. I struggled through my pregnancy with Joshua in the baking trailer heat, but six years later, when Amy was born, I lobbied for a real house. With Amy in a sling on my hip, I worked with the contractor every day, putting in wainscoting and bay windows and other touches that would remind Bob of the old house where he grew up. The edifice was also faintly Victorian, to remind me of my own grandparents' home, a turreted, nineteenth-century gem in Kankakee, Illinois, where I'd spent many happy hours as Rapunzel.

But nothing could replace the old Morgenthau estate. It brought to mind Franklin Roosevelt's mansion in Hyde Park, whose shabby elegance I have always loved. The Roosevelts had been such close friends of Henry and Elinor Morgenthau that when he became president, FDR made Bob's father Secretary of the Treasury. One time, while I was in the attic, I came across a dollar bill with Henry Morgenthau's name engraved on it as well as his childhood stamp collection.

My husband worships his father. Sometimes, when he talks of him, you can detect a slight waver in his voice. We never speak of it, but I think a desire has taken hold of both of us to explain our fathers, perhaps to ease the discomfort of having, in certain ways, surpassed them. Though Tom's obscurity cannot be measured against Henry's fame, fate had dealt them comparable blows. They were both paladins of a sort, who had gone mostly unrewarded for their considerable contributions to the war effort.

As I was discovering what the war had done to my father, an ordinary Navy lieutenant who had acted alone and behind the scenes, I was learning from Bob what his late father, a public figure, had tried to do in the Roosevelt war administration, likewise often alone and behind the scenes. In the face of an angrily isolationist country, he'd helped Britain and France buy planes and other weapons of war in early 1939 and went on to support the Lend-Lease program. He'd established the War Refugee Board and helped Jews to escape the Nazis. He'd pressed for the United States to accept more Jewish immigrants, winning the enmity of the Wasps in Roosevelt's cabinet and irritating the majority of congressmen who wanted to limit the flow. He'd supported the establishment of a colony on Lake Ontario for Jews who'd escaped from the occupied zones, and he had been excoriated for it when Capitol Hill found out. And after the war, he'd been derided for advancing a plan to turn Germany, which had instigated two world wars in the space of twenty years, into an agricultural state. Lately, criticism had again been leveled against him for failing to convince Roosevelt to bomb the concentration camps and to let more Jews into the country. I knew that the Museum of Jewish Heritage was not only a memorial to the Jews who died during the war, but a very private memorial by Bob, who has won nothing but honor, to his father, who died unappreciated by many. It was a way of finishing what his father had tried to do a half-century before.

"Dad, what do you think, about whether Grandpop was a spy in the war?" Josh asks. Bob, Josh, Amy, and I are in the living room in Fishkill while my Dad rests up from the shock of having been abducted from his home.

"I'm not sure. I'm not really sure at all," Bob says, surprising me.

"What do you mean, you're not sure?" I raise my head.

"I'm just not so sure."

"Bob, I did find that Nazi cross and a military cap in his stuff," I remind him, "and he refused to talk about it. He says he watched for incoming Japanese bombers and warned the right people about them. Benny says he went into enemy territory and spied on the Japanese before the main convoys went in. Pat says he did all these missions behind enemy lines, that he had all these uniforms. And he blew up all those Japanese soldiers and no one else ever found out about it."

"I don't see how he could have done all those things," Bob says.

"I don't see why he *couldn't* have done all those things," I reply, my cheeks flushing. "He says he was in a special unit that did a whole lot of different things. We know he went into the first liberated concentration camp."

"Yes, and that's the only thing we know for sure," Bob scowls. This expression is the only manifestation, ever, of this mild, genteel man's displeasure. A somewhat subtle look in which his lips acquire a flat, narrow edge, The Scowl is considered cinematic by the press, who call him Mr. District Attorney, and downright scary by his children.

"But if he was just a regular Navy officer," I say, aware that my voice is rising, "he wouldn't have been tapped for that kind of unusual assignment."

I'm deflated by Bob's doubts, even though there is a whiff of suspicion about them. Although they are close, I sometimes detect a hint of rivalry between Dad and Bob. Perhaps I'm hearing it now. In spite of his modesty about his own heroism, I just wonder if Bob is a little jealous at the thought that my father actually fought the enemy with the Marines, on land.

"Mom, keep at it, keep trying to find out stuff," Josh says. "You're a great reporter. And I bet what you'll find out is what you want to find out." I could hug him.

Just then two heads peer in the window and I gasp. But it is only Harry and Martha, the children of my stepson Bobby Morgenthau and daughter-in-law Susan. They've all come up from New York for the holiday weekend and my children—about the same age as theirs—are excited.

We have dinner and then sprawl around the fire. We love to share moments from holidays past: "Remember the time when Josh dragged all those logs across the room, calling, 'Bobby, Bobby, let's put anathoh log on de fiah,'" I say. As a toddler, Josh mimicked the lilting Jamaican cadences he'd picked up from our housekeeper. Susan and I laugh as Josh, hiding behind a Piers Anthony book, blushes.

Bob and Bobby are talking about the deer that are overrunning the orchard, chewing up the newly planted trees. "They're so brazen they come right up to the steps," Bob says. "Maybe I'll get out that old Winchester of my father's. Josh, Bobby, do you want to do some deer hunting?"

"Are you sure that rifle still works? Haven't you had it since you were about five?" Bobby smiles.

"No, that was a Stevens .22. I got that one for my sixth birthday. I aimed at a grapefruit juice can but shot up the lawnmower by mistake."

"Dad, don't we need a Remington .220 to really do the job?" says Josh importantly. His grandfather has been teaching him about different types of firearms.

"When I was sixteen, I shot a grizzly bear at a hundred and fifty yards in Montana," Bob said. "He was feeding near the Grand Canyon."

"A grizzly bear?" Josh's eyes widen. "I'd like to do that. Grandpop, have you ever shot a grizzly bear?"

"No." My father is lying back, eyes half-lidded, on the couch, listening closely. They're talking about guns, after all.

"Dad, did you use a shotgun when you were doing your spy work in Europe?" I ask casually.

"Of course not," he grunted. "You wanted to get in and out of there fast. You didn't want to be hauling a big gun around."

"What did you use?" I say, heart accelerating. He's taking the bait.

"A pistol. A Colt .45. For starters."

"Daddy," I say, getting up, "let's go into the kitchen. We have some nice apple brown betty that I can warm up for you."

As I sprinkle more brown sugar over the apples and stick the dish in the oven, I think quickly. His response to having been virtually kidnapped and transported to Fishkill yesterday was telling. After a bit of snarling—mostly about whether I packed the right things for him—he was happy to be on his way here. Same with the missionary story: I asked, he told. Direct action. Perhaps I've been giving him too many outs.

I lean against the sink and fold my arms. "When you came back from the Pacific, that's when you were in this bureau of special assignments."

He eyes me. With new respect? "Both before and after I went to the Pacific."

"And why were you chosen for that special assignments unit?"

He eyes me again. "Who are you, Kojak?"

I smile. "Maybe. Everybody has to answer Kojak's questions."

"Uh-huh. Gee, I like that show. I liked the one about—"

"The question! Answer the question! Why were you chosen for that secret unit?" I say gruffly.

"Ha! Well, maybe it was because of my expertise with automatic weapons and demolition work. There were a lot of reasons—according to what mission I was on."

"Was one of the missions in Germany, the one where you wore the Nazi cap?" I ask, nonchalantly peering into the oven. Now I'm Columbo.

Silence. I try again. "Was it in Germany or were you behind the lines in another country?"

A long pause, then, "France," he says. "Occupied France." He takes out a pack of cigarillos from his shirt pocket. "Oh, I guess I can't smoke in here, can I?"

"No, no, go ahead," I say hastily. Never before have I broken my rule of no smoking in the house. "Here, let me get you an ashtray." I extract a crystal finger bowl from the china cabinet.

"I suppose the Iron Cross badge was on your uniform, the one you wore as a disguise?"

"That's right." He tilts his head and looks hard at me.

"Um . . . you were on a mission in France as a special American operative. Why did you wear a German uniform?"

"So I could carry out my mission."

"What was your mission?"

"I can't remember the details."

"Dad, you have a photographic memory."

"Not anymore. I'm serious. My memory of those times is very hazy. It was fifty or so years ago."

I think he's lying, but I try a different tack. "Okay, you were an expert in ordnance. Did you ever bring weapons, guns behind enemy lines?"

He pauses, lights up another cigarillo. All this smoke swirls around thickly above us. I lower myself down onto a chair to try to get to fresher air. "Maybe," he replies.

This is like dredging a river for dead bodies.

"I was told never to talk about any of my activities. I wrote one handwritten report, handed it in to the admiral in charge of the Bureau of Ordnance, and then I was supposed to forget all about it." This disclaimer, in all its different forms, has become my father's version of name, rank, and serial number.

"Dad, what was that admiral's name?"

"You know, I never thought I would forget it. But I just don't remember."

"And wasn't the Bureau of Ordnance just a supply unit?" I ask, all innocence.

"No," he says disdainfully, "it wasn't just a supply unit."

"It was a place for secret operations?"

"And there were undoubtedly a lot of other things that went on that you never found out about."

"If someone was trained in chemical engineering, they could have put together bombs. Which was it? Bridges, train tracks, what did you blow up?"

"Nothing." He flicks his ashes into the crystal bowl. "Or at least I myself didn't blow up any factories."

"Factories? You did industrial sabotage?" I think of the odd photos of machines I'd found.

"Not me. I told you that. There were people who put together the type of explosives that were needed and people who set the explosives. My team put the explosives together."

"What was your team, Dad?"

"I was in a special operations group in the Bureau of Ordnance. We would do a number of things, a variety of missions. But a great deal of the time we would just hang around the room, go to lunch, drink. Then the admiral would suddenly zap us off on an operation somewhere. We never knew where it would be—Chicago, England, Paris, the South Pole."

"And you were sent over behind the lines in Europe."

"A couple of times. From London. My contacts were there. One of them belonged to some organization with an acronym. Something with an 'S.'"

"SOE?" I ask excitedly. I've read about the British Special Operations Executive, the British wartime intelligence agency that had trained its American counterpart, the OSS, and worked closely with it.

"I'm not sure. But I was based in England for a while. Then I'd go in and out of Axis territory. Quickly."

"Were you attached to the OSS?" This is the $64,000 question. If he was with the OSS, he was definitely a spy.

"I was with the Bureau of Ordnance, U.S. Navy. They had a secret unit, I've forgotten what the real name was, but it wasn't anything that would alarm anyone or let them know what we really were."

"So when you wore the German uniform, you posed as SS, didn't you? That was an SS, a Gestapo cap—when you wore it, did the whole unit do the same thing, or did you work alone?"

"I worked alone or with one other person. His name was Jack Steele."

Jack Steele, the man with the damn pig in Guadalcanal! "He was with you in the Pacific too!"

"That's right. Huh. Jack Steele. A real live wire. When we were in Washington, he was going out with this beautiful girl and she dumped him. Let me tell you about it—"

"Okay, but wait a sec, Dad. You and Jack Steele, what were you doing posing as the Gestapo?"

"I can't talk about that. I was given strict orders not to write anything down or to reveal any information in my lifetime. I didn't know why at the time and I'm not real sure now."

"Did you have to photograph something with your Minox? Blueprints, plans, maybe some records in a Gestapo office?"

My father's cigarillo nearly falls out of his hand.

An easy enough guess. I'm getting it. Interviewing him is a bit like trying to find out what a young child did in school. Ask him, "What did you do today?" and he'll say, "Nothing," but if you ask, "What color crayons did you use today?" you'll find out what he drew.

Dad opens the refrigerator and gets out a bottle of water. "I was sure glad to get out of that one."

"Why?"

"Because I was discovered and almost lost my life."

"Oh, wow. Tell me about that, Dad."

"Cindy, I was sworn—"

Not again you don't. Time to play a trump card. "Dad, I found a receipt for a café in Gotenborg and some Swedish kronor and a list of Scandinavian names in the same box where I found the Nazi cap. Were your missions in other countries besides France?"

"A time or two I was in Sweden." I perk up at this; Pat told me to ask Dad about Sweden.

"Was that when you had to wear the Nazi soldier disguise? Did you work with Jack Steele?"

"Say, you know, Steele was a helluva nice chap, a handsome fellow. We went on several missions together. He had this lady friend he was madly in love with—"

"Were you both wearing Nazi uniforms when you carried out the mission?"

"What mission?"

"Dad, your grandchildren will want to know about their grandfather, the amazing things he did in the war, it's their heritage. I want you to do this for them." I feel a little twinge. Deep down, I know that I want him to do it for me.

He brushes a speck from his knee. "I've done some things I'm not proud of, and I wouldn't want either Joshua or Amy ever to know about them."

"What things?" What was so terrible about what he did? Was it a bomb he planted? Did it kill women and children by mistake? People left behind in a munitions factory when it was supposed to be empty? Or perhaps he committed sabotage and the Germans retaliated against the townspeople. I'd read that the Gestapo would kill ten innocent people for every Nazi killed by the partisans.

"Did you teach the French resistance how to use certain guns? Maybe how to repair them, take them apart and put them together?"

"Maybe I taught some people that at one time."

I swallow. "I've heard there were execution squads, teams that killed traitors. Did you train these people how to make a clean kill?"

The color drains from his face. "Who told you that? Did Lou Golden blab about that too?"

"I just know about it," I bluff, "so you may as well tell me."

"Do I smell something burning?" He sniffs and I think, oh no, another digression, until I remember the apple brown betty.

I sweep the smoking dish out of the oven, scrape the burned stuff off the crust, and dish him a bowl with a large scoop of ice cream. I know I can't bring the weapons training up again until after he's finished, so to entertain myself I time the minutes it takes him to eat each bite. One and a half minutes is his top speed.

After he's done, my father lights up again and shakes his head. "You'd never believe what Jack Steele did . . ."

"He shot someone?"

"No, no, after this beautiful lady dumped him—"

"Oh." I take a couple of breaths. Patience, patience. "What was he like on missions, Jack?"

"He followed the orders he was given. He was a real fine operative, short, stocky, built like a bear." He rubs his eyes. "Well, think I'll go to bed . . . Say, that was delicious," he says, looking longingly at the apple brown betty. "Say, I could use . . . ."

I narrow my eyes at him and whisk it into the refrigerator.

It is Thanksgiving morning, sunny and crisp. Burnt orange, lemon, and red, the autumn leaves tumble and fly like magic slippers across the lawn. A few apples still hang heavy on the trees, and chopped-off cornstalks lean drunkenly in the fields. At the bottom of the yard, flaming sumac rises up against the yellow crown of a tree.

Bobby and Susan have brought us a wooden, hand-operated cider mill and the kids have picked boxfuls of apples. Martha and Harry and Josh toss them in the hopper and Bobby turns the red wheel to grind them up. When the pulp reaches the top of the tub, we take turns cranking the handle of the big screw that pushes the press down into the bits of apple. A mighty stream of cider comes out the bottom and Susan holds the jug to catch it. We make three gallons. Bob pours out a mug and offers sips all around.

"Dee-li-cious," my father says. "Fresh and thick with a terrific aftertaste." He's standing on the deck in front of the house in his wool shirt and bathrobe—brand-new, cashmere, and free of holes—and my wool pom-pom hat on his head. I suppress a laugh at the sight of his spindly calves emerging from the bathrobe. He claps as Amy, wearing the pink hat and fleece jacket he gave her that reads "My Little Princess," does handstands on the lawn. I love seeing him standing there, even if he's chosen not to put on pants. If he wasn't sipping cider he would, of course, be sipping coffee. He's left his cup on the kitchen table covered with a napkin scrawled with the warning "Tom's Coffee. *Do Not Touch.*" He rues the years that he didn't cover his mug with this note because his daughter has thrown away hundreds of perfectly good stone-cold cups of coffee.

Bob comes over, gives me a kiss and begins talking quietly. "You know, I've been turning this over and I really don't think your father was the same after Ohrdruf. After all, he was just a simple boy from the Midwest. His best friend was Jewish. He could never comprehend that anything like that could happen." He puts a hand on my shoulder. "You're a great interviewer, sweetheart, but you didn't get everything out of him last night. I think he knows exactly what he did behind the lines, he's just not telling you."

"You mean you think he really was a spy?" Bob nods slowly. I give him a relieved smile. I need Bob to believe in me as much as I need to believe in my father. "What changed your mind?"

"Just the way he was talking last night, when you were interrogating him, the answers he gave. I can just tell. It makes a great deal of sense that they would pick him out of a mass of rookies. You just have to picture it; he had all these talents, he could have disguised himself as anybody, and he's so smart, there would have been nothing unexpected that he couldn't handle."

"But why do you think he didn't want Josh or Amy ever to know what he did in the war? He had to live with all this horrible stuff inside him his whole life. No recognition, no thanks from anybody. Why wouldn't he want people finally to know, especially his grandchildren?"

"That's just the way he is. Even if he hadn't taken an oath, I doubt whether he would ever have talked about it."

Bob rejoins the cider-makers, and I go up to the deck, where Amy is standing next to her grandpop. He's pointing out the Canada geese munching at the bottom of the hill.

"Grandpop, what do jellyfishes eat?" she asks.

"Those are wild geese!"

"But what do jellyfishes eat?"

He smiles at her wolfishly. "Little girls."

Amy shows him her *Ranger Rick* magazine. "Do you know anything about bumblebees?"

"I understand they can sting you bad," he says.

"When they're dead can they sting you?"

"No."

"My brother said they could."

"Well, I guess they could if you sat on their head with their stinger up."

"Oh, Grandpop," she laughs, "don't you know I'm really interested in science? More than Joshie is. I know more about it too."

I feel sad at this little touch of competition, Amy's desire to get from her grandfather what she saw Joshua get. Outside of his expertise on moths, the prodigious knowledge that he once imparted to Joshua has now thinned. Amy will never be dazzled by seeing the stars come together as fierce bulls or centaurs in the night sky. I bought a good telescope so they can peer at the stars, but I know that the only planet my father can still identify is Jupiter, and the only constellations Orion and the Big Dipper. Ten years ago he would have been out there relishing his turn at the cider wheel, but now he stands stationary, watching a universe whose curiosities he once rearranged.

Dad and Amy babble on when I have a sudden inspiration. I get the atlas and put it between them, opened to a map of the southwestern Pacific. I whisper in Amy's ear. Then I step back and wait to see what will happen.

Amy puts her finger on an island. "Were you there in the war, Grandpop?"

He squints at it and finally says, "Yes, but not there." He moves her finger to Bougainville. "I was here. That's where we fought the Japanese. And see that little island up there, you can hardly see it? It's called Emirau. We invaded it, but we had a special unit and the Japanese never knew we were there."

Amy frowns. "Why?"

"Because we were slick in the way we covered ourselves up and what we were doing and so forth. They would send planes to attack the big bases where our big battleships were, and we would radio the base and warn them that the Japanese were coming."

"Wow," Amy says. "Were there any animals on the island of Roo?"

"Emirau. Yes, and there were natives who didn't even know the war was going on. They didn't speak anything but their own little language and we couldn't communicate with them."

Amy leans forward conspiratorily. "Grandpop, did you know that sometimes I speak my own little language?"

Susan and I go in to take the turkey out of the oven, which sizzles golden brown, bursting with walnut stuffing. It is nearly twenty-four hours since I asked my father whether he'd taken ordinary French citizens and turned them into executioners, the question that had caused the color to drain from his face.

Our Thanksgiving dinner could be lifted from a Norman Rockwell painting. Family gathered round the turkey, butter pooling in the mashed potatoes, the kids' ringing their fingers round the rims of the crystal glasses, fingers here and there slipping stolen morsels into their mouths before everyone is served. Chatter and clatter and wine corks popping and everything is normal except that the quiet, unassuming gentleman pushing in the chairs of the women has taught people to kill in cold blood.

After dinner, Josh wants to go to a bowling alley in the neighboring town. So we pile into the car and drive ten miles only to find that all the lanes are full. There's a pool table in the next room, however, so we pick up cues in spite of the fact that none of us knows how to play. Josh gets one in the left corner pocket, but I can't get the cue ball to hit a thing, so I pass my cue to Bob. He sinks only two in twelve tries. Then he turns to my father, who's leaning against the wall, watching. "Want to shoot a few, Tom?" he asks. Dad shrugs but comes over to the table, chalks the tip of his cue, bends over, slides it between his thumb and forefinger, and sights his first ball. In minutes, only the cue ball is left on the table.

It's the first time I've ever seen Bob's jaw drop.

"Tom," he asks, "when did you become a pool shark?"

Dad smiles. "How do you think I paid my way through the University of Illinois?" he replies.

Chapter Eleven

It's Christmastime and we've persuaded Dad to spend it with us in New York. My mother used to make Christmas magical with dozens of presents and a tree laden with handmade sequin-covered felt ornaments. Dad played the role of Scrooge, growling about all the fuss. He's sitting in the living room now and I'm perusing my stash of World War II espionage books. The intelligence histories and memoirs I've collected recount a lot of espionage adventures but provide only spotty mentions of the more sordid side of the World War II spy game: premeditated elimination by the resistance of collaborators, Communists, Jews, members who were about to be caught by the Nazis. Who taught these men and women—even teenagers—how to do this—how to operate guns small and large, how to mix explosives? I'm coming up empty.

This isn't surprising, for I've learned that an abundance of World War II intelligence records—Navy, Army, FBI, even those of the OSS, which were purportedly opened to the public decades ago—haven't yet been entirely declassified. Many of the OSS files given to the National Archives in Washington have been pulled, even reportedly destroyed. It's the same for other wartime agencies: blank pages and obviously missing documents. The Freedom of Information Act has forced many official organizations to release personal files, but they often black out blocks of information.

My mind keeps coloring in the details I cannot find. I picture one of my father's trainees, a local baker, maybe, who's never fired a gun or used a knife or any other weapon. He slips inside the home of a Gestapo chief. The Nazi is cracking a boiled egg over toast, having executed a couple of Jews before breakfast. Crumbs are spilling down his tunic. The baker comes up from behind with a garrote, looping it around his neck and tightening it until the Nazi's head falls to the side and his tongue hangs out. Sometimes my father's student has been instructed in the use of the stiletto, like the one I found in Dad's cabinet, knowing how to sink it into a shoulder covered by a greatcoat at just the right angle.

Or maybe he faces the fellow and fires his gun before the Nazi can fire at him. Fighting fair and square. At least that's what I thought my father meant when, in one of his rare references to the war, he mentioned fighting "the fair and bare way." But I'm flipping through a history of the SOE and come across the name of William Ewart Fairbairn. A martial arts expert and a one-time commissioner of the Shanghai police, Fairbairn certainly didn't fight fair and square. He was apparently the dean of silent killing for spies.

Deep in the wilds of the Scottish Highlands, Fairbairn taught "dirty fighting" to novice operatives who were used to good English fair play and thus more than a little shocked at his uncivilized tactics. He authored a book called *Shooting to Live with the One-Hand Gun* and narrated training movies, some of which I have watched at the library. "There are no Marquis of Queensbury rules in guerrilla warfare," he announces to his students. "It's either kill or be killed. Capture or be captured. You will learn the technique of killing or crippling with your two hands at close quarters." Then Fairbairn demonstrates on some hapless recruit how to give a chop with the side of the hand to everything from the upper arm to the kidneys, how to overpower someone holding you at gunpoint, how to snap the wrist of an attacker, how to slam back his chin, press your fingers into his eyes, break his arm, slide your heel down his shin and stomp on his foot, and finish the job with a blow to the testicles. Also, how to press the thumb in exactly the right place on a man's neck to disable or kill him. Later Fairbairn taught the same methods to OSS recruits in American training camps. Had one of his student instructors been a certain Thomas E. Franks, who at seventy-five went on to jump a man half his age, pressing his thumb into the guy's carotid artery?

One book describes a shooting stance that Fairbairn invented and taught his students. The classic stance for shooting at a target was standing upright with the arm outstretched, as if in a duel. Fairbairn, however, advocated crouching, holding the pistol with two hands and rapidly firing two shots at waist level. A commonplace in cop shows today, it was an utter novelty in the forties and fifties. I thought about the time I'd spotted Dad in the basement, squatting and wheeling around, holding out his pistol. He was clearly shooting the Fairbairn way.

The number of guns issued in both Britain and America for use by the resistance fighters and the various Allied intelligence services were legion. I think about Dad's strange cache of guns in Milford. Many soldiers would linger to search the fallen for souvenirs, sometimes at the cost of their lives. But maybe Dad needed those foreign pistols to cover his tracks. If the Germans found one of their own with a bullet in him from an Italian Beretta or a Russian TT-33, they wouldn't know who'd pulled the trigger. The provenance of the gun wasn't all that mattered. A small gun was easier to hide. Agents were issued .32 caliber, hammerless automatics that were perfect for concealment. However, there was a gun that was even smaller.

I'm going to ask Dad about it once he's recovered from the exertions of Christmas in New York City. We've dragged Dad out to Fifth Avenue, ordering him to luxuriate in the snowy sights and sounds he always hated, but which he now seems to enjoy, looking at them through his grandkids' excited eyes. Rockefeller Plaza: skating to the wistful chimes of "O Come All Ye Faithful," looking up to see the giant tree twinkling with hundreds of lights, bumping and slipping into each other with frosty breath, walking among the band of wire angels Mother used to love, filling the pots of the skinny Santas, and lingering at the department store windows with their little scenes of past Noels beckoning you to come inside and for one small day, be merely content.

Defrosted and fortified with a hot chocolate, Dad is now sitting on the couch, leafing through the latest issue of *Black Powder Cartridge News*.

"Dad, does the word 'Stinger' mean anything to you?" I ask.

He looks up. "Yes, I downed a stinger once and I think my face turned as green as the drink. There's nothing worse than a mixed drink. I once—"

"No, I mean the gun! A tiny gun smaller than your hand."

My father puts down his magazine. "And why would you want a gun that small?"

"For use in wartime . . . by spies," I reply, sitting down.

He looks sharply at me. "How did you know about the Stinger?"

"I read about it."

"Huh," he says. "Yes, I remember the Stinger, which was a very good name for it because that was about all it could do unless you were nose to neck with somebody." He takes out his pen. "It was oh, smaller than the size of this and you fired it surreptitiously with one hand. You could use it and then drop it while you made your getaway. Only trouble was that if you were more than about ten feet from your adversary, all you'd do is give him a splinter."

"An OSS weapon?"

"You know, the Navy developed something similar. It was a glove that had a boxlike gun attached to the outside of it and you fired it by first making a fist. One tester nearly shot off his finger. It wasn't too popular."

"How do you know all this, Dad?"

"Oh, it was a long time ago."

"Which gun was best for taking someone by surprise, and not alerting anyone? Like taking out someone in a crowded area?"

"There's nothing like a silencer. There was something developed called the High Standard. It was a flashless silenced pistol. It worked real well." I think of the latest book on espionage I've been reading. When I turned to the page with photos of OSS weapons, there was a silencer that looked exactly like the one I'd seen in Dad's gun cabinet.

Dad chortles. "I understood that some big muckety-muck in the espionage world tested the gun by going into Roosevelt's office when Roosevelt was occupied with something else and shot several rounds into a pillow. The gun was so good, the president never even noticed it."

"That would be William Donovan, head of the OSS, who did that, right?"

He nods, then puts his chin down and looks at me over his glasses.

"Some of those weapons were pretty creative, right?" I ask.

"In fact, they were pretty hush-hush. The last thing you want is your enemy to know what you're up to. And it wasn't like today where every dirty trick the government pulls turns up in the headlines. People were innocent and easily shocked. Things weren't known. They weren't even imagined."

"I read that the British invented a cigarette that fired a cartridge, and then there was this pen that shot out tear gas."

"Oh, both countries came up with all sorts of harebrained things—exploding cigars and candles and suitcases, grenades that looked like baseballs that went off only when you threw them. There was a terrible tragedy over that one. I forget what the thing was called, had a name like that new pill for flatulence. Anyway, it killed a man—it was his own fault really, but he died from it all the same."

"Wasn't there something that looked like a pipe, except you didn't smoke it, you took off the handle and it turned into a firearm?" I ask.

"Something like that. But I think the Germans got onto that one right away." My father closes his eyes, thinking. "There was a very promising gadget, don't know its name either, but it was like an oversized plastic button filled with an explosive. You slipped it into the fuel chamber of a tank, and after a few hours it exploded and burst the chamber. Later on they found a chemical to add to it that would also ignite the gasoline. We needed things like that. You know, we were at somewhat of a disadvantage. We came late into the war and even then, our military wasn't what it should have been."

I'd forgotten how much my father loves talking about weapons. I have him in just the right mood.

"Say, you know, the British started it all," he said. "They had their own lab that made special ordnance ruses. Had some name like the Straw Barn. They went for the explosives disguised as everyday objects in a big way. They had bottles of milk that when you opened them would explode in your face. I think that in North Africa, they came up with bombs that looked like camel droppings."

"So, Dad, with your degree in chemistry, you must have worked on some of these spy toys. Like those limpet bombs that had magnets on them that you could stick on the metal underside of a ship. You know, the ones that were covered with a magnesium alloy and the salt water would corrode it and then the bomb would go off?"

"Now that wasn't just a toy. That was one effective device," he says. "They sunk a lot of ships, especially in Norway, where the Germans would send them up the fjords. And they weren't placed underneath a vessel; they were placed below the waterline amidships, so if the hole left by the explosion didn't sink the ship, then the boilers would be destroyed. They used them in the Pacific too, but the Jap ships were wooden, mostly, so you had to go down under and fire a spike into the hull to anchor the mine."

"Did you go down under? Were you a SEAL?"

"They didn't have SEALs then, they were called maritime saboteurs. But that wasn't a regular job. I guess I was kind of a troubleshooter. There didn't seem to be any damn thing they had qualms about sending me into. Especially if nobody else was around."

"You're a Renaissance man, Dad," I say, and he gives me one of his heart-melting, ear-to-ear grins.

He gets up to go to the bathroom and I try to connect what I know. I've read that all these trick devices were developed in the OSS's Research and Development laboratories, and, through combing archives and old Navy reports, I've pieced together a trail that may lead my father right to the OSS labs. The OSS's R&D section worked hand in hand with the government's Office of Scientific Research and Development (OSRD), which had ties to the Navy's Department of Ordnance. William Blandy, the head of Ordnance, was so close to the head of OSRD, Vannevar Bush, that he gave him one of his top people, G. L. Tyler, to head up a top priority section. Bush himself set up another special section of OSRD called Division 19, especially designed to produce special weapons for OSS. Bush even supplied OSS with the slightly mad genius Dr. Stanley Lovell, who started up the R&D's deceptive weapons section; Donovan nicknamed him "Professor Moriarty" after the scientific criminal in the Sherlock Holmes books. OSRD also worked with a naval research laboratory in Silver Spring, Maryland, whose mission was to develop new naval technology. This lab also had a number of people specially assigned to do secret work on unconventional weaponry and devices.

This is where my father, an expert in explosives as well as chemicals, comes in. I'd found a letter dated April 1943 from my father's father to his U.S. congressman from Champaign, Illinois, William H. Wheat, apologizing that his son hadn't been in touch; he implied he was doing confidential work, and it was only after an eleven-hour day that he returned to the place where he lived, College Park, Maryland. Why was Dad, who was attached to Ordnance at the Navy Yard in Washington, D.C., living in College Park, forty-five minutes away? On a map of Maryland, I found that College Park is just six miles from Silver Spring, where the naval research laboratory was located. Thus, I came to the conclusion that all the special weapons organizations and their labs were pretty much in it together.

My father comes back and sits down. I speak loudly, in the direction of his good ear. "Dad, in April 1943, you didn't live anywhere near the Department of Ordnance. You lived an hour away near a lab in

Maryland—a lab that developed some of these special explosives for OSS. So you were sort of connected with OSS from the beginning, right?"

He ignores my question. "Listen to this: there were these pieces of coal that were actually high-grade explosives painted to look like real coal. They had a sensor in the middle that detected heat. A couple of partisans could make a nighttime raid on a railroad depot and mix them with a flatcar full of real coal. Then it might get shoveled into the furnace of a locomotive or the furnace at some industrial plant, and BOOM, the boiler is destroyed, the locomotive is out of commission, the plant out of production."

"Wow. Did you work on the coal? On the limpets?"

"As I recall, there was a tiny incendiary you could put in your shirt pocket and time it to explode after you were far away. That became very popular in little towns where the Germans knew who everyone was and what they were doing."

"Did you hear of something called Project X-Ray?" I ask.

Dad considers. "Hmm. It rings a bell."

"They tested the notion of dropping bats with little fire bombs attached to burn up Japanese cities."

"Huh . . . Oh, yes. That one began with Eleanor Roosevelt. They had these scientists collect hundreds, thousands, of bats from a famous grotto. They were supposed to roost on the flammable paper houses of the Japs. They got shunted from one armed service to the other, including the Department of Ordnance and a special unit I worked with—"

Here's where I can connect the dots. "Was that special unit called Division 19?" I ask quickly. "Division 19 of the Office of Scientific Research and Development? Wasn't that its name?"

"Don't remember what it was called. But the project was crazy. You can't control animals as though they were inanimate bombs, especially when you drop them from airplanes. And do you know what they put in the bombs? Napalm." My father thinks for a minute, then begins to chuckle. "They put the bats upside down in parachuting egg cartons.

Then they were supposed to come out of hibernation and launch themselves onto the nearest roof. When they tested them out in some remote desert, the bats ended up flying wild. They had put too much jelly in the bombs and they burned down a whole airfield, hangars and all."

"Was that when Ordnance dropped out?" I'd learned from my research that the Bureau, which had been working on the time-delay mechanism of the bomb, finally threw up its hands at the impracticality of the project.

"I think so. I think just about everybody finally dropped out—the testing went on for years and cost millions of war dollars."

"Dad, talking about inventions, did you ever hear about something called Aunt Jemima?"

He nods. "A form of P.E., plastic explosives. It was a TNT mixture that you mixed with flour or milk, and it was like dough, you could shape it around any target. Easy to get through checkpoints because it was just a bag of flour."

"I've read all about it. It was an OSS invention, Dad."

He breezes right past that. "It could also be baked into biscuits and, in a pinch, for instance during a search, it could theoretically be eaten . . . how do you know so much about this, anyway?"

"You were in the OSS," I say. My heart is pounding. The moment has to be now. Admit it, Dad, admit it.

He looks at me pointedly. "I didn't say that."

"Well, you implied it."

"I made a commitment fifty years ago. I pledged myself to silence."

"But you must have belonged to *some* secret organization," I say.

"I was in the Bureau of Or—"

"Don't even bother, Dad!"

"Oh, I don't remember now who I worked for when. You know half the time they never told you what you were supposed to do or who was sending you. You just got detached from the unit at Ordnance to some damn operation or the other."

"OSS," I say, confidently. I have the evidence, circumstantial as it may be. "Let's stop pretending, Dad. You might have been with

Ordnance, or Naval Intelligence, but, aside from your duty in the Pacific, you were attached to the OSS."

"What is OSS anyway?" he says, looking at me innocently.

I glare at him, pick up his *Black Powder Cartridge News*, throw it in his lap, and walk out of the room. My father's operating the Fairbairn way. Definitely not fair and square.

I close the door to my study a little too loudly. Why on earth does my father think he still has to keep the secrets of a half-century ago? Unlike my husband, I've never known him to read about any war except the American Civil and Revolutionary Wars. I never saw a book about World War II in his home. Is he avoiding that war? Or is he toying with me? I've been steeped in books on the OSS, yet I've never read about some of the small ordnance inventions he described anywhere. He had to have been there.

I decide to get some fresh air, and when I get down to my building's little lobby, I find that I've finally received a book I'd ordered weeks ago from an out-of-print dealer. It's *Of Spies and Stratagems*, by Stanley Lovell—Donovan's very own crazy genius "Professor Moriarty"—a slim memoir about his work manufacturing the trick weapons for OSS. I already knew that Lovell had been ordered not to write anything until twenty years after the war and that even then he'd left out sensitive material from the manuscript, which was published in 1963. I rip open the envelope and begin skimming the old, yellowed paperback as I make my way to the local coffee bar.

Immediately, a tidbit pops out: According to Lovell, Bob's father, an ardent supporter of the OSS, had been as deliciously devious as Lovell and Donovan. It seems that Lovell needed permission from the Secretary of the Treasury to establish an illegal plant to forge enemy documents: passports, ration books, work papers, shop receipts—all the documents crucial to agents behind the lines. If Roosevelt gave a thumbs-up to the plan, Henry Morgenthau, surrounded by a phalanx of witnesses, would tell Lovell, "I was unable to see the president for approval because he has a cold." This code, Lovell later realized, let Morgenthau off the hook because if these "un-American activities" were later discovered, the secretary had witnesses who'd heard him deny taking up the plan with the president. "If anything went wrong, there was but one sacrificial goat . . . me," Lovell wrote.

I'm struck by the fact that Dad worked not far from his future in-law, Henry Morgenthau, the two of them laboring simultaneously and secretly, my father on clandestine weapons, Henry on saving the Jews, never knowing that fate would one day make them family. Although Henry would die before Bob and I were married, my father would know and be endlessly proud of the connection.

I'm vacuuming up the last of my frappuccino when I read about the secret weapons that the unit cooked up. I nearly choke on the foam. The weapons Dad mentioned are here—the limpets, the little time-delayed incendiary. A few, like the Aunt Jemima plastic explosive and the gas-tank booby trap, had actually been invented at the OSRD labs.

The gas-tank explosive Dad described was the Firefly, developed in Division 19 to destroy German gas tanks, dubbed "crematoriums" for their luckless drivers. "The success of the Marseille landings owed much to the little Firefly," wrote Lovell.

Another "harebrained" invention devised by Division 19 was the Hedy Lamarr, which simulated the screech of a falling bomb. It was designed to cause panic—like its namesake, the adored sex-bomb movie star of the time—and allow agents to escape in the chaos. During a demonstration before the Joint Chiefs of Staff, Lovell activated a Hedy, and suddenly there came a "shrieking and howling with an ear-piercing wail," which sent "two- and three-star Generals clawing and climbing to get out through the room's single door."

The grenade that Dad said was named after some "new pill for flatulence" was Beano, another OSRD invention. It was an effort to miniaturize the unwieldy, pineapple-size grenades used at that time. Apparently, an Army civilian engineer who knew exactly how it worked threw it up in the air to demonstrate how it could be handled like a baseball. "Of course the throw automatically armed the grenade," wrote Lovell. "When he stepped under the missile and caught it, he was killed instantly."

My father *had* to have worked for Division 19. Smiling, I propel my empty cup into the air and it lands right in the middle of the trash can.

Later that day, I take out some of the spy books I've collected, three histories of the OSS and another, by Roger Hall, entitled *You're Stepping on My Cloak and Dagger*, a humorous take on being in America's most flamboyant and heroic wartime intelligence agency.

I bring them into the living room. "Dad, espionage records from various branches of the service were declassified twenty years ago. Everything is known. Everything is out there," I say, only half truthfully. "Read these." I hand him the books. "They're spies who have told their stories and they've told them a long time ago."

By the next day he's returned the books. My father is a speed reader, but not that fast.

"Did you actually read all these books?" I ask.

"Oh, I got enough. The *Cloak and Dagger* one was funny."

"But what do you think? Are you surprised?" I ask.

My father's voice is emphatic. "I don't think these fellows revealed everything they knew. They've done some whitewashing and used some broad strokes."

"Dad, why don't you tell me how you were trained to be a spy?" I motion to a chair. "There's no harm in that."

He sits down gingerly; his hip is bothering him. "I had a lot of specialized training. All different kinds of training, on the East Coast, on the West Coast, in England. Some was to prepare me for special radar work and for other situations I might encounter in the South Pacific. The training for Europe . . ." he pauses. "Let's, well, let's say I skipped some basic training in these special schools because I'd already acquired some of the skills they taught: knowledge of weapons, explosives, chemicals, and some kinds of industrial machines that I'd gotten to know while working at General Alloys."

I smile proudly. "You must have gone right to the top level of expertise training then." He nods. "Did you spend a lot of time behind enemy lines? I mean, did you have a new identity and false papers?"

"I had doctored documents a time or two, but I usually only spent a short time in occupied Europe, quick in-and-out trips, and the rest of the time I would spend in London, sometimes undergoing even more instruction."

"What kinds of things did you learn?"

"Oh, let me see. . . . how to reveal invisible ink, about codes and ciphers, how to lose someone who was tailing you, how to follow a mark, how to pick a lock and crack a safe . . . . We learned from felons who'd been sprung from jail and later made agents in the field themselves. Also how to interrogate someone and trap them into revealing information." This is an art he's apparently forgotten, since he's consistently fallen into the traps I've laid for him. Does he want to be caught?

"We were taught to read and draw maps on rectangles of silk, which wouldn't disintegrate when exposed to water or rustle if you were patted down during a search." I think of the silk map I found in the cedar chest in Milford. "I already knew how to sew—you might not believe this, they put me into a homemaking class at school—but they showed us how to put pieces of linen with messages inside the lining of a pocket." I'd always thought it was odd that Dad sewed on his own buttons. "They showed us how to conceal important papers by hollowing out the leg of a table. I even ended up being a teacher in two of the classes. For weaponry and chemistry." He looks at me. "You didn't know this, but I had guns stashed all over the house in Wellesley." My face does not betray the fact that I knew this too bloody well. "Your mother hated it, but what she never knew is that there were damn good reasons for it—"

"What reasons?" I interrupt. "What reasons did you have for putting guns all over the house that could go off in somebody's face!"

"Now, look, you don't know what you're talking about!"

I just stare at him.

"Do you know that you can protect yourself by using a pen or a newspaper as a weapon?" he says sternly, then proceeds to take the sports section of the *New York Times* and in a second roll it into an impossibly tight, pointed rod. He gently slips it under my chin. "Ow!" I cry.

"Oh, I'm sorry," he says. "You know I hardly touched you. But I could have gone right through your flesh. It's something you should know, most especially in New York City, where you can get mugged just by walking down a dark street."

"How many times do you think I would be carrying a newspaper at night?"

"You can also use a simple house key, but as I've told you and your sister again and again, you should be carrying Mace."

"I should carry a knife," I say, trying to head off Lecture No. 47 on the Babylonian dangers of urban America.

"Say, that's not a bad idea," he jumps in. "There are several kinds—"

"Like a double-edged one," I say quickly. "I hear that special wartime agents would carry them, that was one of the things invented by this chap Fairbairn. Ever heard of a double-edged knife, Daddy?"

"Yes, I have," he warns, "and so have half the criminally insane. You know what you can do with such a knife? You can crouch in the darkness. Wait for your undefended prey to turn a corner. Then slash away at her—left, right, up, down—until she's in ribbons. And nothing will work against it—not a stick or an umbrella or a set of keys—"

"Nothing except a simple, purse-size can of Mace," I joke.

He squints at me.

"So what else did you do in that school?" I ask.

"They made us take a bunch of tests. One was for memory and I passed first in my class. I never forgot a face, or a name." This I knew. Dad could repeat a conversation to you that you'd had a month before. We'd be going to Colonial Williamsburg and he'd need only one glance at the map to get us there.

"There were tests to try to drive me crazy and to see if I would crack" he says. You didn't know it at the time, but the instructors were watching your every move. You never knew when you'd be deprived of a meal or have your toothbrush go mysteriously missing.

"They were particularly interested in how you drank and what you said when you did drink. Nobody revealed their rank or service, or whether they were civilians. They told you up front that you were never to break silence about who you really were.

"They tried to find out how quickly you could invent a scenario. I think there was this dummy in a room and spread out in front of her were train schedules, a stiletto, a couple of passports, other personal belongings, and you had something like three minutes to come up with a believable character."

Dad reluctantly tells me about another test: He was given some information about the exact location of a fictitious ammunition dump, and then put in a room under a spotlight and questioned for hours and hours.

"Did they do anything to you during the test, Dad?"

He goes silent. Then he laughs. "Yes, they did. I was subjected to hours of listening to the grating buzz saw that this short, sadistic little instructor called a voice."

He's holding back. I can tell. I casually mention every torture I've read about that didn't leave a mark—beating the bottoms of feet, hanging someone upside down, stretching them on a rack. "Water, some kind of water," I say absently. There's a sudden flare of acknowledgment in Dad's eyes. "Actually, Dad, I know all about what they subjected you to," I say. "They dunked your head in water and held it down, right?" He doesn't say anything. "How awful and scary that must have been, not being able to breathe, to be forced down in a barrel of water," I venture.

"It wasn't that much water," he replies.

"Just a big tub, huh?"

"No, it was probably less than a gallon."

I'm silent. Then it dawns on me. "They dripped it on your head!" Chinese water torture. "For how long?"

"A time," he answers.

"Did you break?"

"No," he replies, "of course I didn't."

I'd always known my father could stand up to any punishment. Once, when we were fishing off the *Pencilot*, he nearly cut off his finger while spearing a bluefish flapping around our boat. Nobody knew about it until they saw blood running from his hand.

Henry Morgenthau, a bit of an iconoclast himself, was the only cabinet member to support the OSS when it was a fledgling organization in 1941 called the COI (office of the Coordinator of Information). Most of Roosevelt's confidants, Harry Hopkins, Harold Ickes, and Henry Stimson, were against director Bill Donovan and his unconventional central spy organization, and it was widely derided by the armed services establishment.

One admiral at a Washington party told Donovan that his COI was a "Tinker Toy" society. Donovan bet him that his men could crack the admiral's safe and blow up his ammunition arsenal, all before the night was over. The admiral snorted. Donovan made one call, and within an hour several OSS Navy men gained access to the admiral's office, cracked his safe, and planted empty tubes of dynamite in the ammunition dump.

That night, I return to Lovell's book. It's easy to imagine my unflappable but devilish father in the company of Bill Donovan. I turn the pages excitedly, expecting Tom Franks to be on the next one. He never is, but his footprints are right there beside those of "Professor Moriarty" Lovell, another in the League of Extraordinary Gentlemen.

Chapter Twelve

It's the hottest summer in the island's memory. All the humidity in Martha's Vineyard seems to have collected in our home; it smells like my late great-aunt. Mold creeps up the 150-year-old baseboards, speckles the bathroom ceilings, and settles in the walls. The lace curtains turn up at the edges. The white wicker furniture has begun to peel.

My father is in agony, sitting nose to a table fan while I scrub the woodwork with bleach. Houses this old do not have air-conditioning. "I haven't been this hot since Guadalcanal," he grunts as I move around him, trying to rub the mildew off his rickety Hitchcock chair. "Sorry, I can't move."

I sit down beside him. He's wearing a yellowed undershirt, and his forehead is shiny with sweat. He's come for the month of August; he loves the sea, the fishing boats at Menemsha, the memories of the swordfish he once caught on his own thirty-six-footer.

It's been nine months since I tried to pin him down about the OSS and since then he's fought me off like a fish trying to break the line. I'm going to try a new direction: confirming the story Pat told me about the gun operation in Mexico. "Was it this hot down in Texas when you were on that special assignment?"

"Decidedly not."

"What were you doing down there, anyway?"

Dad sprinkles some water from a glass onto his head and aims the fan at his neck. "I can't think in this heat."

"Didn't they send you down to investigate a bunch of high-ranking officers?" I prompt. "Boy, you really got caught in the middle of that one."

"Huh. I was ordered to. These characters were selling ordnance parts to go-betweens. And those parts were ending up in the hands of the Germans."

"This was treason."

"Yes."

"How did you find out what they were really doing?"

"Came in as a buyer. I paid for a shipment."

"Disguised as . . . ?"

My father booms out a slew of sentences in fast guttural German, pounding his fist on the table so hard that the fan tips over.

"Oh, I see." I swallow. It is a chilling imitation—*if* it is an imitation. Could Dad have been a double agent, facilitating the delivery of weapons to the Germans and then pretending to break up the group?

"I got out of there quick because they found out that I wasn't a German national living in the U.S."

"What happened? I can't imagine you slipping and revealing your cover." And which cover was it?

"I didn't break my cover," he says defensively.

"Someone else ratted you out? Maybe somebody who pretended to work for you but worked for them at the same time?"

My father smiles faintly. "Someone who was doing the same thing I was but who'd been bought by the wrong side."

"What happened to him?" I ask.

"Cindy, can't you get a bigger fan? This one just about cools my nose."

"Sure, Dad." I stare at him for a minute, assessing. Then we go off to Shirley's Hardware.

* * *

The fresh of the evening has washed away the heat. We're all outside piled on the hammock, a gloriously oversized model that fits my father, Bob, and me, with the kids lying on top of us. Josh rocks us back and forth with his foot. Everyone is silent, waiting, for they've become used to Grandpop responding to my endless questions about the war. And they love to hear him talk in his languorous bass. Walter Cronkite reporting from the field.

I've finally received the "records" of Dad's military service that I'd requested from the National Personnel Records Center at St. Louis—all of one rather frustrating Summary of Service sheet. It leaves out half the places in the Pacific where he was stationed and has no mention at all of his European service. He's described as having six months in the continental U.S., six months of sea duty, and sixteen months overseas. But he only spent fourteen months in the Pacific, so where did he spend the two unaccounted "overseas" months?

I ask him but he ducks the question. "I was an inspector of ordnance," he tells us. "I went to several factories in different parts of the country where they made ammunition and weaponry." I should have known that he wouldn't talk about foreign missions in front of Amy and Josh.

"So you were supposed to check up on the way they made weaponry?"

"No, not always. The Bureau of Ordnance grew while I was there. We had just entered the war and we needed a lot more weapons than we could produce, so they gave a lot of contracts to private industry. Oh, let's see, they were companies like GE, Bethlehem Steel, Sylvania, all sorts of companies that made ammunition or products like miniature radio tubes, anything that the Navy could use. But you had to be real careful who knew what, because the country was full of Nazi moles."

"Moles!" Amy says. "Those cute little animals?"

Dad pats her on the head, and Josh says, "No, stupid, a mole is a spy."

"It's also an animal, Josh," Dad says.

"I know that," he replies.

"That's where you came in, Tom," Bob says. "Inspecting ordnance meant inspecting the people who made the ordnance?"

"Uh-huh. You had to look at the plants, you had to make sure their security was tight enough, whether they were doing thorough background checks on employees, even fingerprinting them."

"So you wandered around trying to sniff out spies!" Josh says.

"That's not a bad description at all," Dad replies.

"What was the biggest spy you ever found, Grandpop?" Josh asks.

"Huh. A vice-president of a company I won't name. He wasn't a spy exactly, but he let them operate and it could even have been inadvertently, though I don't think so." He shook his head. "He left top-secret material out in the open for anyone to photograph. And we then determined that there were a group of spies in the plant. Enemy aliens."

"Like the Jedi?" asks Amy.

"No," Dad chuckles. "They were real people. German people living here. Sometimes if we had a suspect alien, we'd call the FBI in to investigate."

"Did the manufacturers ever find out you were spying on them? I assume you were working for Naval Intelligence?" Bob asks.

Dad nods. "They didn't find out because most of the time we pretended to do completely ordinary things, like inspecting the rates of production, the way the weapons were shipped, the alarm systems and fences around the places."

"Weren't you afraid somebody was going to slip and give you away?" Josh asks.

"Well, you had code names."

"What was yours, Dad?" I ask.

"I think one time it was Gecko."

"Gecko!" I exclaim. The lizard you don't see, the one that blends into the background. Perfect.

The evening is darkening. A star has come out. "Is that the North Star, Grandpop?" Josh asks.

"That's right," my father says. "And see all those other bright spots that look like stars? Some of them aren't stars. You know what they are?"

"Planets!" shouts Amy.

For the first time I wonder, where had he gotten his expertise about astronomy? You can steer by the stars if you find yourself without map or compass in a foreign countryside.

"I don't think I could recognize many of the constellations now," my father says a bit dolefully. His voice has gone into Eeyore mode.

"You know, Daddy," I say quickly, "wherever I go, I can always see the Big Dipper." I inch closer to him now; our fingers are touching. "I don't even have to look for it, somehow it finds me."

He turns his head and smiles.

"I can see it too, wherever I go," Amy says, moving closer to me.

The next morning there are dozens of moths in the collecting tub. My father has invented the moth-catching contraption, using an old washtub hooked up to a big, fluorescent tube. Moths are inexorably drawn to the light, then fall stunned into the tub. The light that this homemade contrivance emits is so blinding that once our closest neighbors on the island, a half-mile away, called the police and claimed a UFO had landed.

When he was six, Josh would race out to the collecting tub at the first light to see if the night had yielded a giant fuzzy green luna moth fluttering its wings on the tin bottom. Now, a nonchalant fourteen, he walks, but still with a quick step. My father and Josh scoop up the moths and discard the commoners; the royal specimens they bring into the house like fragile treasure.

Once, my father loved collecting butterflies, but my sister and I, happy to bound through the fields swinging nets, recoiled when it came to spreading and mounting the catches. One New Year's Day, he lumbered, hung over, to the driveway for his paper, slipped on the ice, and injured his hip. This ended his butterfly-chasing. Without telling anyone, he gave his vast collection, which included some rare specimens, to the New York Museum of Natural History.

Then he discovered moths. You don't have to chase them, and their delicately patterned wings make them much more interesting than butterflies. Moths, most of which come out only at night, have become the passion of my father's life. And Joshua has become the son he never had, interested in boys' stuff like displaying insects by putting pins through their heads.

"Don't worry," I hear him tell Josh, "their life span is only two weeks. This way, they live on forever."

Jars containing cotton soaked in ethyl acetate line my kitchen counter, and the two of them put their prize moths inside and solemnly watch them expire with the fumes. Then they sit down at the kitchen table and stab pins through their thoraxes and attach them to a slab of corkboard. Spreading the wings is the next and most delicate step; my father guides his grandson's fingers as Josh carefully pulls each of the moth's four wings into position. Then Grandpop leans over miniature rectangles of paper and, in spite of the fact that his hands now shake slightly, labels each specimen in impossibly tiny writing. Polyphemus, the king of the psychedelic, with its wings of melting ginger. Cecropia, brandishing a bright red body and white collar. The ferocious-looking spotted tiger moth. The io moth, fixing us with the shiny black "eyes" and little white "irises" painted on its back. And this morning we're lucky; an enormous patterned sphinx has fallen into the trap.

My lepidopterists are enormously proud of their morning's work, showing off the mountings and propping them up on the window ledge. As I look at the little labels, I have a flash of memory. I am eight or nine. My father and I are playing a game. We sit at a table with a large piece of paper and two sharpened pencils in our hands. He writes a word in large letters and I copy it underneath, but write it smaller. Then he pens an even smaller version and I write smaller still. We continue on and on. At the end, I collapse in giggles, for his letters are so minuscule I can't read them without a magnifying glass.

I suddenly know why he'd been able to write so small. He'd been trained to write that way, render the alphabet in imperceptible scratches. Perfect for ferrying secrets. Pat had already implied that during one mission in Sweden, he'd been a courier. I've read that couriers were supposed to memorize their messages but that if the dispatches were too long, they wrote them in minute letters on rice paper. If they were caught, they could swallow the paper.

The next day we go up-island to the little port of Menemsha and stop in at Poole's fish market. Everett Poole is in yellow rubber pants held up by suspenders, hosing the fish blood off the cement floor. When he sees my father, he touches his cap. "Hello there, Tom," he says in his thick Yankee accent. He's known my father for decades. Here is where we used to dock the *Pencilot*, which was outfitted with a flying bridge for sighting swordfish, across from the commercial vessels that supplied Everett's father with his daily lobsters and fish. As Everett and Dad are chatting, I take off to watch the rough waters of the harbor, whitecaps rising up and foaming like horses. The Coast Guard has put up a warning flag.

That flag never mattered to Dad. We'd go out in the boat in any weather, bouncing and smacking through the sea, the red and green buoys swaying, until we were miles off shore. "Let's go back, Tom, you're crazy!" Mother would cry, and take to her bunk. "Lorraine, come back, going down under's the worst thing you can do for seasickness!" he'd bellow, but she never believed him. I did. I knew what you could do to stop the nausea: climb up the tower to sit with my father and keep watch for a telltale sword. Dad thought using a harpoon gun was bad sportsmanship so he had put out several strong lines. When I got too big to fit next to him in the tower, I picked my own lookout. I would lie down in front of the cabin windows, my head over the bow, my bikini strings untied, more to feel the salty spray on my face and to refine my tan than to look for fish.

Dad comes out of Poole's with a bulging bag: "A nice thick piece of swordfish—haven't seen it that pink and fresh for years. I got two dozen steamers, three crabcakes, and those lobster lollipops. For the kids." Around the corner, he points to a sprawling, shingled restaurant that's been there since before I was born. "Well, there's the Homeport, packed as ever," he says, indicating the long lines milling outside. "One day, you must have been three, not even four, they were having a two-for-one lobster special and we ordered one special because we were sure you'd eat, oh, maybe a nibble or two." I smile. I've heard him tell this story a hundred times. "And you sat there in your highchair while your mother and I looked on with our mouths watering, and damned if you didn't finish every bite of both those lobsters!" I laugh.

In one of the shacks along the harbor, an enterprising fisherman is offering up mortar shells he claims are from the battle of Normandy along with the usual bait. A little crowd surrounds him, enthralled by his stories.

I look out at the waves longingly. When Dad turned eighty, I lost my only surfing pal. He refused from then on to go into the water. Bob, for his part, has never gotten near a wave; five hours treading water in the chill and choppy Mediterranean Sea after his warship was sunk a half-century ago had cured him for life. So I'd ride in the waves by myself, watching my father on shore, a forlorn, rather comical figure clothed in sweater, trousers, sneakers, and an oversized panama, enduring the hot sun because he imagined that, if I got into trouble, he would dive to the rescue.

I persuade my father to take off his shoes and walk along the pebbly beach. "Oooh, eeeh, aaah," he says, tiptoeing along dramatically. "It's not funny, I have very tender feet!" I lead us down to the shoreline where there are fewer stones, though the sand, beneath the tide, is full of crushed conches.

Here I am, walking over broken shells with a man I never knew: a weapons instructor for the Resistance, a courier behind enemy lines, who knows what else.

My father, thrilling me with his tricks: riding down the hill with no hands—did he do this on the back roads of France, carrying boxes of important materiel? Surfing in the waters of Cape Cod, me on his back, catching the waves just at the crest so they would carry us like shells to the shore—was he such a good swimmer because he'd removed mines underwater? All those hobbies he'd thrown himself into—expert astronomer, marksman, lepidopterist—were those just different kinds of camouflage? If you have to play a part all the time, do you lose touch with who you really are?

"Cindy, I'm cold," he says plaintively. The tide rolls over his feet. "It's quite cold. I want to leave the beach."

We make our way back through the sand and walk along the crowded pier looking for the place where we once docked our boat. He puts his arm around me and we look up at the billowy sky. The sky is an aging courtesan, turning silver and gold in the dusk. At this moment, all eyes are upon her, waiting to behold the sun flush red and bow into the sea.

My father sits on a kitchen chair as Bob and I prepare dinner. "Isn't that a wonderful-looking piece of fish?" he says as Bob runs it under cool water and pats it dry. Josh is chopping garlic for his special mushroom sauté; the only television he watches is the Food Network. Amy is doing a backbend, trying unsuccessfully to get Grandpop's attention.

I bring a steaming bowl of clams wrapped in a red net bag to the table. My father takes out his jackknife and rips it open from end to end in one motion.

"Tom, how would you like to do the swordfish?" Bob is being a good son-in-law; he likes to grill it with lemon, but there's only one way my father has ever cooked swordfish: slathering it with mayonnaise and putting it under the broiler.

Dad looks at Bob blankly. "I don't know."

"Dad, of course you do."

"I don't know. I just don't know how to cook swordfish."

"Dad! What about the mayonnaise?"

"What mayonnaise?"

"The mayonnaise you like to spread it with!"

My father looks puzzled. "I've never put mayonnaise on sword-fish, at least I don't think I have."

We all stare at him. He's not kidding around. He really doesn't remember. Suddenly, I want to cry.

A week later, it's Labor Day weekend and it has not begun auspiciously. I've had a lovely massage in the privacy of the top floor of our barn, and as I groggily descend the steep set of steps, my foot slips and I bump down the stairs on my butt, bruising my tailbone. I limp into the house to find my father has hurriedly packed his bags and is asking to be taken off the island. Despite his devil-may-care exploits on the water as a younger man, he's developed an excess of respect for the weather (he watches the Weather Channel constantly) and has just heard that a hurricane might hit. So I ease myself painfully into the car, go down-island, wait for an hour in Vineyard Haven to get on a ferry, and drive him back to Milford. By the time I return from the four-hour trip, my back is killing me. The storm has gone out to sea. It's getting hot and everyone is eager to swim. My youngest stepdaughter, Barbara Morgenthau, is visiting, and all of us except Bob, who's on the phone following a case breaking in the DA's office, go off to Quansoo Beach.

This stretch of the island's oceanside coast is spectacular; the sand smooth and clean, the surf vigorous but gentle enough for even children to ride. Josh goes in with his boogie board. He's inherited his grandfather's talent for catching the wave at exactly the right time. Josh rides the first one all the way up to our towel, grinning. He does it again and again, but the tide is carrying him farther down the beach. I don't worry, for he's an expert swimmer. When Barbara goes cavorting into the water, a huge wave comes out of nowhere and swallows her up. I study the surface, worried, and finally, relieved, I see her head pop up, neck deep in roiling water. Meanwhile, Amy is punching my arm, yelling at me, saying something about Josh.

I look down the shore and see him theatrically careening up onto the sand, as though he's just survived the wave of his life. "He's just clowning around, Amy," but she's already halfway to him and then he falls flat to the sand and I'm running also. "Josh, Josh, are you okay?"

He can't tell me what's wrong. "I don't know, I feel funny, something hit me," he says in a whispery voice. I cover him up with a towel. I feel paralyzed, can't think of what else to do until an onlooker suggests calling 911. Miraculously, for once I've remembered to bring my cell phone and I numbly call an ambulance.

Also miraculously, the ambulance arrives within twenty minutes. Quansoo is on the southwestern shore of the island, at least thirty minutes from the hospital. As the ambulance roars out the dirt road, I miraculously spot my friend Wendy Gimbel driving in and yell to her to bring Bob to the hospital. And that, for now, is the end of the miracles.

The EMTs misdiagnose the problem as a broken rib, downgrading the urgency with which Josh will be treated. The X-ray technician makes the same diagnosis. "It'll heal," he smiles at me as he puts on his hunting jacket and leaves the hospital.

Meanwhile, Joshua lies in a room in the emergency area looking very pale. I hold his hand and try to soothe him. "It's just a rib," I say. "The doctor said so."

"Don't leave me," he rasps. I can barely hear him.

I watch his face; I see pain there, and now a new, grayish tint to his skin. "I'll be right back, I promise," I say, and as he reluctantly lets go of my hand, I rush out and ask for a doctor. The only doctor here, however—it's Labor Day—is currently doing hip surgery on an old woman. Nurses put Josh on a blood-pressure machine. "He's fine," they say. "His vitals are normal."

But I know they're not, and so does Josh. "Mom, I suddenly feel this incredible love for you, for Dad, and for Amy. I'm sorry I've never appreciated you before. It's so amazing, it's like real or something, it's hovering outside of me."

This is a boy of fourteen. And he's just gone deathly pale. I rush out of the room and smack into Bob and our best friends, the Kaufmans. "Bob, Josh is failing. We have to get a doctor! Nobody will listen to me!"

Marina Kaufman is a Moroccan-born beauty whose aristocratic parents, Sephardic Jews, treated her like the world was hers to command. She and her husband, Steve, Bob's former chief assistant, are Josh's godparents and would do anything for him. "Where is the doctor!" she shouts in her proud, accented English. When told that he's busy operating, she marches right into the operating room and tells the doctor, "You better get out here if you don't want a little boy to die on your watch!"

To our surprise, the doctor does leave his patient, putting the intern in charge of finishing the procedure. As he comes into the room, my son's blood pressure suddenly plummets. The doctor shouts at the nurses, "Get blood, get it now! And warm it." One wise nurse has intuited Josh's compromised state, and has the blood standing by. The nurses rub the bags between their hands. Then, in a flash, they have an IV needle in Josh's arm and are pumping the blood into his body. Watching the bags slowly empty, I concentrate on being the blood, racing against time to reach the vital organs. I watch Josh's face, see the color begin to return.

Blessed yet again, we discover that the doctor is a trauma expert who has worked with accident victims. His reading of the X rays is very different from the technician's. "There's no broken rib. This boy's spleen is ruptured. Badly. He's losing blood as quickly as we can replace it."

Stories have flown over the years about mishaps and misdiagnoses at Martha's Vineyard Hospital, a tiny facility that's underfunded and understaffed. Do we want this unknown doctor to attempt such a delicate operation? The spleen cleanses the blood, collects the germ-ridden flotsam and jetsam of the body. If he removes the spleen, will Josh's immune system be compromised? Could a big-city doctor save the

spleen? Bob and Steve whip out their cell phones and call every medical contact they have in New York and Boston. At least one doctor reassures them that people without spleens can live normal lives. Another
offers to send a medevac chopper to take Josh to a Boston hospital.

The doctor breaks in. "By the time you get him to Boston, he'll be
dead." We stare at him. "I have to go in there now or I can't save him."

Bob closes his phone. "Go in. Operate."

As Josh is being wheeled into the operating room, I stroke his
hair. "Everything is going to be all right," I say.

"I know," he replies, impatient, a man-child. "Just get me in there.
I want to get this over with."

The operation seems to take hours. Barbara has Amy at home.
Bob, Steve, and Marina are with us in the empty waiting room. I can't
sit. Marina, arm around me, walks me up and down the corridor trying, without success, to ease my terror. That's when I notice a door
that leads to a little chapel. "I'd like to go inside," I say.

I thought that as an adult, I'd lost my faith, or perhaps I'd just put
it aside. Now I go up to the front pew and bow my head and pray as
hard as I can. As a child, I'd bargained with God for my parents' marriage. Now my prayers transcend such calculation. I say only one sentence, over and over again: "Please, God, save him." And I feel I am
being heard.

I return to the waiting room, calm, in a dream. And just at that moment, in comes the doctor, his white hospital coat spattered with
blood. My son's blood. At first he says nothing, just looks at us. I freeze.
"He's okay," he declares. "But we almost lost him." I hear myself gulp-
ing back sobs of relief, but I'm really somewhere else quite peaceful.

"When I opened him up, blood spurted out, a geyser of it," the doctor says, using his hands to illustrate. "I stopped the flow with the palm
of my hand and I had to keep it there until we got things under control. The spleen was cut right in two. No way we could sew it back. We
just took the whole thing out . . . We used every bag of his type blood.
It's a miracle we had enough. I'd say we replaced his blood three or
maybe four times."

Before he leaves, the doctor raises a cautionary finger. "He's not out of the woods yet. His system has sustained an enormous shock. The next twenty-four hours will tell. What he needs now is rest."

Bob goes home to console a distraught Amy and Barbara while I sit by Josh's hospital bed through the night and into the next day. Having read somewhere that people in coma-like states can hear everything, I chatter away. I talk about his passion, art, I talk about my passion, writing, I talk about what I hate and he loves—cooking—and about what he hates and I love—baseball.

The doctor seems to be ubiquitous, constantly checking Josh, his IV, and the machine that records his vitals. The nurse, a crusty Irishwoman from South Boston, is also on my side. "He'll be okay, honey, he's young. If it was me or you, we'd be laid out in lavender."

They've filled Josh with so many fluids that his face is pink and swollen, as though he's just staggered out of the boxing ring. His body is still covered in sand so I pick it off, grain by grain, so as not to wake him. I'm getting pretty good at it—pick, throw, pick, throw—when, at 9:07 that night, he turns his head and whispers: "That feels good."

Teenagers are notoriously monosyllabic with their parents. But Josh wants to talk about the accident: "I remember the wave I was riding, it suddenly threw me up into the air, it really did just fly me over it and I landed on the sand with a smack."

"The boogie board. It must have hit you. This freak wave catapults you into the air, and the board slams into you."

He's silent and then he asks, "Why is this happening to me, Mom? I mean, one minute I'm me, swimming and surfing and being alive, and the next minute I'm me but I'm almost dead. Nobody else riding that wave almost died."

"Maybe there's another way to look at it," I say, trying to disguise the fact I've been asking the exact question myself. "Maybe the question is, why is this *not* happening to me? I mean, you had a really bad accident and you survived. The worst didn't happen to you. Yes, you're lying in a hospital bed, but all the things that could have happened to you, like breaking a leg, didn't happen."

"Okay, then, why *didn't* it happen to me? Why did one freak thing happen and the other not?"

"I think someone was watching over you when it happened. Someone who protected you, who wanted Josh to remain Josh."

"Minus one spleen. What does that mean anyway, Mom?"

"Apparently not much. You just have to take a shot every year or so to protect yourself against certain bacteria."

"Yeah, who needs a spleen, anyway."

"Right, it just gives you indigestion and bad temper." I smile and he dozes off.

The next thing I know, my father has gone missing. "I'll be right there," he said when we called to tell him about the accident. That was the last time anyone had heard from him. "How could he just disappear for twenty hours?" I ask Bob. "How can he do this to the grandson he adores! Call his house! Call the fucking Newport Creamery! Can't you handle this?" I snap into the receiver. The nurses raise their eyes at each other.

When I hang up, the Irish nurse pats my shoulder. "You got to get some sleep, honey. Come on." She leads me back into intensive care and opens a large closet near Josh's room that contains a cot. "This is my little hideaway. You lie down there for a while."

I put the hospital blanket over my head. I've just dozed off when I hear Josh calling me. I scramble up and run into his room.

"Where's Grandpop?" he asks, as if psychic.

"Um . . . he's on his way here," I say.

"Alone, with nobody driving him?"

A light dawns. I run out and call Bob again. "I think he's lost," I say. "Remember the last visit to Fishkill, he took Amy to the drugstore and they couldn't find it and drove around in circles for an hour . . . ."

"Well, I think we should notify the police," Bob says. "I'll do it. Don't worry."

"Thank you, sweetheart." I hang up.

In a little while, Bob's back on the phone. "We found him," he says. "You're right, he was lost, spent the night sleeping in his car. Apparently, he headed toward Fishkill, going west on the Mass Pike; then when he realized he was going the wrong way, he got off but couldn't find his way on again."

"Where the hell is he?" I ask.

"At a Mobil station in Waterbury, Connecticut. I'm leaving now and I'll lead him back home."

"Thank you, sweetheart . . . I wonder why he didn't call us before now? Guess he didn't want to be a bother."

"Probably was too embarrassed," Bob says. I know it's true and my chest tightens. He'd be mortified by the trouble he'd caused us. First he doesn't remember how to cook a swordfish. Now this.

A few hours later, I walk back to Josh's room after a coffee break and stop short at the sight of a broad back leaning over him. My father has his hand on Josh's shoulder and is talking quietly to him.

"Daddy?"

"Hi, Cindy," he says, not turning around.

"Where on earth did you come from?"

"I had a little trouble," he finally faces me. "These highways are very poorly marked now."

"But what did you do?"

"Oh, I went to Fishkill."

Maybe it's not his memory. Maybe in his hurry, maybe in his panic, he'd just forgotten we were in Martha's Vineyard. I put my arm around him. "Yes, these damned exits, you don't know where you are anymore."

"You got here, Grandpop," Josh sighs. "Awesome."

Chapter Thirteen

A few weeks' rest at home and Joshua is fully recovered. He stands in front of the mirror, fingering the raised scar that snakes down his stomach. "It's a war wound. Grandpop will love it. The girls will love it," I say. He gives me a withering look.

As for my father, pieces of memory keep falling away. He can't quite figure out his television remote control anymore, so he's asked his housekeeper to set it at one station: the news and later, the weather. He can no longer read maps and directions, although he can still find the Newport Creamery, two miles out of town.

Oddly, his long-term memory remains remarkable. He can tell the story of every fish he ever caught, the color and make of his first car, and the scene when Joshua finally convinced us to forsake his Christopher Robin bangs for a buzz cut.

And then, one day, out of this jumble of randomly receding remembrance, there comes for me a strange blessing: My father forgets that he is supposed to forget. He forgets that he's taken an oath never to tell what he's seen or done. The pressure that had built up for more than half a century leaks out like steam from a boiler.

All at once he begins to talk freely, even eagerly, about his missions. This is to my delight, but also my frustration. The names, dates, and sequence of specific operations or agents are as blurred and broken as his once-beloved moths now crumbling in our cellar.

"I couldn't tell your mother about the clandestine nature of my work, just that it was something confidential," he tells me. "I'd take off without notice and so she got suspicious. It drove quite a wedge between us, along with a few other things."

I'm in Milford now. I come every chance I get. This time I've left Amy behind, much to her disappointment, because I need to be alone with Dad: Pat the housekeeper has made an exciting discovery. "Cindy, I found something!" she told me on the phone. "Letters. Here's one of them: 'Thomas E. Franks is irreplaceable in the war effort.' And they're from the U.S. Navy!"

When I arrive, I find Dad fumbling with the tape player I'd bought for him. "This damn thing is broken," he says. "I want to put on some ragtime. The Knuckles O'Toole you gave me. Pat's the only one who can fix this." I put the tape in for him, then suggest we take it outside. Soon we're sitting listening to honky-tonk piano, my father jiggling his knee in time as we watch the birds enjoy a final frolic through the tumbling autumn leaves. Occasionally they come down for the seed he's scattered on the tattered lawn.

I gently turn the conversation to his military career. "I worked for Naval Intelligence for the first part of the war, in Washington and in the Pacific," he now readily admits.

"Can you tell me what kind of expertise you had when you were in the military?" I inquire, knowing as a journalist that asking the same question over and over, in different ways, will draw out more and more information.

"Ha. I'll tell you one. Dogs. I took care of the admiral's dogs, I really did. I'd told him about Bing, the most wonderful dog we ever had. Bing would follow me everywhere." I brace myself for yet another Bing story. "We lived not far from the railroad station, and one day I walked right out on the tracks in front of an oncoming locomotive. Bing snatched my diaper up in his jaws and dragged me off just in time. After I told him about Bing, the admiral entrusted me with his own dogs."

"Dad, what was this admiral like? Did he work for Navy intelligence or the Bureau of Ordnance?"

"The Bureau. As I remember, he was very cagey, very discreet . . . and very ingenious for a career Navy man. Did things his own way. He lent me out to this one setup, it was the pet project of some big shot in Naval Intelligence, I think, who set up these clandestine sections. I'd spent a year in Germany before the war because I was studying chemistry. I learned how to speak German, I learned about the customs. Of course, the best books on chemistry were written by the Germans."

I nod encouragingly. I'm scribbling notes and trying not to get distracted by the lit cigarillo that hovers above Dad's pant leg. "And this clandestine project?"

"It was a small, hush-hush group and most of them had permanent assignments there. I helped interpret statements taken from German prisoners of war incarcerated in American camps. And then there were documents that had been taken off them. I was tapped to analyze those that made reference to new kinds of weapons or explosive or chemical devices. We did the same thing with letters coming in from Germany that our censor had seized looking for the opportunities they might provide."

"Like what opportunities?"

"Classified stuff. Some of the documents were about chemical and bacterial weapons that the Reich was planning, or maybe they'd already been put into production and I was able to interpret the chemical side. I guess you might say I had become an expert in that field. We were looking for information that would help us with our own research on these weapons, maybe even allow us to duplicate them."

"You worked on chemical warfare!" I exclaim and then wish I hadn't. I'd marched in demonstrations against the development of chemical and biological weapons, but now I realize I've blown the moment.

"Oh, not really," he coughs, "I was just a lowly interpreter."

Right. Stupid me. "So this must have been one of those times that you were sprung from Ordnance school for special projects, in the first half of '43?" I ask, trying to break his embarrassed silence.

He nods. "I think so."

"You mentioned statements of German prisoners. How did you get them?"

"I wasn't so much involved in interrogation, not then anyway."

"What did you—I mean, what did they do to prisoners to get information out of them?"

"I don't think I want to talk about that."

I clear my throat. "Did they torture them?"

He shakes his head. "They came up with some interesting forms of eliciting information. First they'd be offered the chance to join the Allies, and that would work with some, but most of the officers were diehard Nazis. Then they'd threaten them about their families—we'd research the background of high-ranking officers, we knew about their wives and children, the names of their dogs."

"Was there physical as well as psychological torture?"

He shakes his head in disgust. "I think they invented some of the methods that have been employed in later wars. There were certain people who had a taste for applying it. Delivering blows that hit certain nerves that were so excruciating, the prisoner's knees would buckle under him. Keeping a prisoner in an uncomfortable position for hours, making him stay up all night and the next one and the next one after that until he didn't know who he was or who you were. That was almost as effective as a truth serum in getting the prisoners to give away order of battle and other vital intelligence."

I'm straining to ask more, but he quells my next question with a big, noisy yawn. "Cindy, I'd like a sandwich. I've had nothing in my stomach since breakfast."

And breakfast for him, the wandering ghost, was at 5 A.M. It's now six hours later. Session ended.

We go inside, and when I ask him what he'd like to eat, he says,

"Look in the icebox. There's some leftovers there from the Herschel Creamery."

I open the door and out tumble teetering stacks of takeout containers, their lids dated with pen in his handwriting. It's happening again. Some go back two or three weeks. Those I drop into the garbage can. He watches me, shocked. "Aw, Cindy, don't waste good food."

"Dad, some of this is so old it would kill you."

"When you do something like that, it makes me feel violated."

"Gee, when you talk like that, it makes me think you've seen a shrink," which he never had, at least I don't think so. Not since his stint in rehab, anyway.

I spread jam between two pieces of stale bread for myself and hand him a partially eaten container of baked ziti only three days old. "You warm this up and I'll go back out and set the table so we can watch the birds while we eat."

"Okay." His face clears and he reaches for a bird book on the windowsill.

When I come back into the kitchen, he's standing in front of the microwave, staring at it, the container of ziti still in his hands. He looks at me. "This damn microwave is impossible to work."

I swallow. He's been working the microwave for five years. Another piece gone.

"Oh, they're complicated, these contraptions. Let me do it . . . Dad, when Pat's not here, you eat these leftovers cold, don't you?"

"I like them that way."

We carry the food outside and he scrupulously sprinkles bird food a few yards from the table. "Say, here comes a sparrow," he says. "Now two blackbirds . . . they usually come in threes and squabble like old ladies. Sometimes, I have the uh . . . the goldfingers or whatever they're called with their little black caps. They drop in for a second, grab a seed, and fly away." A big red bird swoops down out of crimson leaves and majestically scatters the rest of the birds. "That's my friend," he points, "the cardinal."

"Dad, you remembered!" I smile, recalling the time almost a year ago when he couldn't name that bird.

"Of course I remember," he says, throwing more seed in the direction of his friend.

Cheered at this show of remembrance, I wave to his neighbors, the mother and her daughter who live upstairs, as they come out of the apartment house. I've bestowed upon them little gifts in thanks for regularly checking on Dad. The mother comes over to chat, but the daughter, Michelle, stands away and motions to me.

I see immediately the troubled look on her young face. "The other day we were sitting at a restaurant, eating our appetizer, and we saw your Dad finishing up his meal and leave," she tells me. "And when we came out of the place, we saw his car and so we went over to say hi, but when we got to the car, he was sitting there with his head slumped over the steering wheel." The hope that the cardinal has brought me drains away. "We thought he'd had a heart attack or something so we banged on the window and yelled, 'Tom, Tom!' because he'd locked the door and we couldn't get in. Finally he woke up and he rolled down the window and said, 'Oh hi!' as though everything was normal. Well, I don't mind saying that it worried me."

"Oh, Michelle, he likes to nap whenever he feels like it . . . wherever!" I chirp. "It's better anyway to take a little rest if you're tired and going to drive."

"I guess . . . well, I just thought I better tell you. I mean, I've never seen anyone take a nap with their head on the steering wheel."

When Dad holds up his three-day-old ziti and offers it to the women, I cringe. Then, on the inside of his upheld hand, I notice some pen marks. I take his hand and bring it toward me to look. He grabs it away but not before I see the words "red, cardinal" written there in tiny letters.

I feel a little dizzy. "I think I'll get myself a drink of water," I announce, and go inside. I try to put the handwriting and Michelle's story out of my mind. Anyway, I'm anxious to find what Pat has saved for me.

I open the cedar chest that is our secret drop point. There's the cigar box full of my earlier discoveries—the Minox camera, foreign coins and receipts, the silk map. There's also a button, strangely thick and heavy, that I found a few months ago. Tucked beneath them is Pat's find: an olive-green folder filled with old onionskin carbons. I flip through them, spotting a seal of the U.S. Navy on some. My heart skips a beat.

And then I see that some of the letters have General Alloys letterheads. The letter Pat quoted isn't from the Navy at all. It's from that fat old fart H.H. Harris, the man who screwed Dad out of inheriting the company. He's hounding the Naval Procurement Office to give Dad a military exemption so he can keep him under his thumb. Dad does an end run around Harris and applies for a commission to work in the Chemical Warfare Department or the Ordnance Bureau: "This war is going to last several years . . . and it will be won only by destroying the Axis armies in Europe and Asia," he writes to Harris in July 1942, saying that he therefore wants to serve his country.

Harris shoots off a letter to the Navy, arguing that "one-hundred percent of the business of the General Alloys Company is engaged in national defense and a great deal of it is of the most vital nature." He writes that Dad "was the first and only student to major in spectroscopic analyses of chrome nickel and nickel chrome alloys . . . he is in charge of making superchargers for aircraft engines and other work of a confidential nature, which will call for the utmost in metallurgical control and precision." Harris adds that my father also holds a key position in an unnamed special activity being carried out in connection with the "National War Program . . . we know of no way that we can replace the experience and technical training that Thomas E. Franks is contributing to the Defense program. Our Defense Plant will suffer seriously by reason of his going."

The Navy writes back that Mr. Franks has meanwhile "signed an immediate availability statement" and adds that Harris and his employee better work things out before they involve the Navy in the matter. In the end, Dad wins. In December 28, 1942, he enters the Navy as a commissioned officer.

The irony of Harris screaming at the Navy that Dad was worth more to him than to his country! But the letters provide me with confirmation. The U.S. Navy really was about to get a genius in chemistry and metallurgy, someone who was engaged in secret work with aircraft engines, who wanted to work with weapons and chemical warfare. Their eyes would be on him.

I hold the stack of carbons in my hand, so full of insight into a man as he once was. Proud, brilliant, patriotic, determined to go up against a bully, H.H. Harris, to enter a war that could end his life.

I look out the window. My father is nodding off, slouched in his chair. I think about the accumulated leftovers, the way he wouldn't get dressed in the morning sometimes, the way he mocked Amy and my attempts to get him to smoke safely. I assumed that his continual refusal to change these habits was a willful, even hostile act: You come into my home, rearrange my life, mess with my things, so I'll mess with you. Yet I see now: He wasn't proving the presence of will, but the absence of it. His short-term memory simply wasn't accessible.

I see him ten, fifteen years ago. We're sitting on the couch at the farm and he's leaning over, his forearms on his knees, looking down at his clasped hands: "Something's happening to me, I just can't remember things I should remember: the year I graduated from college, names of old friends, sometimes names of new ones. Cindy, write things down, I'm urging you, write them down before you forget them."

"No, Dad, no, no," I say, "of course you're not losing your memory, you just think you are. Everybody has trouble, Dad, and lots of times something will come back to you. For the longest time, I couldn't even remember the name of one of my boyfriends."

"This is different," he says. "Things aren't coming back to me. Some things that made a great impression on me, things in the war, in my marriage, are clear as day. But there are things that I knew positively, that I thought would always be here. They're gone."

Some years earlier, I'd visited my ninety-year-old grandmother at her cottage in Florida, in what turned out to be her last year of life. I was waiting for fried eggs, which she loved making for me. She cooked them by ladling bacon grease over the yolks, had done it that way for seventy-five years. I noticed how thin she'd gotten; her pinafore apron hung down flat over her chest. Suddenly she dropped the ladle and ran out of the room. When she came back, she settled onto her stool and shook her head. "I can't even make it to the bathroom anymore," she told me plaintively. "I can't go out to lunch with the ladies because I leak constantly, I can't hear what anybody says, and I'm afraid of falling if I go down the steps."

"Oh Grandma, it doesn't make any difference," I reassured her. "You can wear Depends, you can get a better hearing aid, you can get a stronger prescription. Everything will be all right."

But it wasn't all right. It's never all right. The people I loved had confided in me and I had denied the truth of their confidences. Fiercely young, I couldn't look old age in the eye, so I'd simply dismissed their miseries. With surging guilt, I look out the window. Dad is asleep now, his head hanging down onto his chest.

I carefully replace the Harris letters in their folder. I vow from this moment on to to protect him, to preserve his free will and to respect his personhood, whatever that turns out to be.

I take a walk and, when I return, am pleased to find that Dad is wearing trousers and one of the dozen shirts I've given him on Christmases past. He's peering at a War Bond poster on the wall. "That was sure some moment," he says, pointing at the cluster of victorious Marines planting the American flag on the hill in Iwo Jima. "An image that was in the home of everyone who had a television set."

I sense that this is the right moment to bring out the box of war memorabilia. I put the cigar box on the table. "I hope you don't mind my prowling around here, Dad, but I found these things that I wanted to ask you about." I pull out the Minox camera, the silk map, the foreign coins, and the odd button. I hold out the button to him "What's this, Dad?"

"You know, I gave all these things to your mother to keep and I never saw them again. I assumed she got rid of them. I'm a little sorry she didn't."

"I guess it's hard to see them again, huh?"

He stares at the box and then clears his throat. "The memories they bring up aren't pleasant."

I give him the button. He examines it for a minute and then tries to twist it apart. "I can't do it," he says finally. "It's stuck in place. You try."

I turn it like I'm opening a jar and it doesn't budge. "What's it supposed to do, come apart?" I say. He nods. I turn it the other way.

"You can't do it, because you've tightened it," he says, with a tinge of triumph. "Watch." He takes it from me, screws it away from him, and it finally comes apart.

"You could do it all the time!"

He grins impishly. Then he shows me the bottom half. Inside is a little compass. "You see, this button was made to open by turning clockwise. This was supposed to fool the Germans, but of course they got onto it."

"Wow, so it was sewn onto the clothes of agents so . . . ?"

". . . so if they had to get away fast, they could find their way to a safe house, say. Sometimes this was the kind of thing smuggled into POW camps in relief packages. The prisoners who could escape needed a compass more than anything else, otherwise they might find themselves escaping right back into the hands of the enemy."

"Ever use these? In your operations?" I gesture to the contents of the box.

He looks at them. "I was on two different missions in Sweden," he says finally, looking at the receipt from someplace in Gotenborg. He picks up the silk map. "I think the map was Jack Steele's . . . I think he had to make a drop somewhere on the outskirts of Stockholm."

"He was a courier too? For the OSS?"

"We both made deliveries there at one time or another. And I honestly never was sure which intelligence agency was sending me on any one errand."

"Where were they sending you from?"

He ignores me and picks up the silver coin, rubbing it between his fingers, "I believe this is a Half-Crown and I think they've stopped making them. I might have saved it from the time when I trained in a camp in the southern part of the country. You know, most of the time I was in Washington, at the Navy Yard, both before and after my tour in the Pacific, but then I got yanked out of the Bureau of Ordnance and sent to England and then on to various places in Europe. I remember I checked in with some British intelligence chaps. I've forgotten now what it was called . . . a bunch of initials, I believe . . . ."

"SOE," I nod. "You were liaised with SOE. You told me a while ago."

"I think that was it, or maybe the first time it was some chaps from the Admiralty, the Royal Navy. There was one time I think I went over there under the auspices of Naval Intelligence and then got hooked up with a different group.

"Sometimes I'd get no more than a few hours notice. I'd find myself en route somewhere, and the next thing, I'd be told to go sit at a bar in Stockholm, maybe, and wait, and then something would happen—a bar girl would put her arms around me and whisper something in my ear or I'd see a pencil rolling toward me and I'd slip it in my pocket. You see, I knew an ordinary pencil wouldn't just come my way out of the blue." He brought his thumb and finger close together. "Inside there'd be a little paper curled up—that's one of the ways they passed messages, by concealing them in a hollowed-out pencil. That's how I'd know what to do next."

"Why would you have to have all this secret communication in Sweden? I thought it was neutral right through the war."

"Huh, that's what everybody thinks. But they're dead wrong. Sweden appeased the Nazis for years. In fact, in the beginning, Sweden bent over backward to please the Wehrmacht because they had to; they sure didn't want to be overrun like the Danes and the Norwegians. They had secret police who trailed any foreigner—American, English, white, black, yellow, purple—because most of them, even the diplomats and businessmen, were undercover. This one hotel in Stockholm was lousy with spies. You sure didn't want to stay there and discover your room was bugged or your phone tapped. Any visitor who aroused their suspicions, they would pick you up on espionage charges in a minute. You might find yourself spending the rest of the war in an internment camp. Happened to many an agent."

"What did you do in Sweden, exactly."

"They sent me from England over to Stockholm and I stayed there a few days and then I went inland to a storehouse to inspect a shipment of roller bearings and ball bearings that were to go to the British . . . we wanted to be sure that the manufacture of these ball bearings was on the up and up and that they were made according to specifications—they were different sizes, small and large, the smaller ones were used for the engines and frames of aircraft. And you had to make damn sure that the stockpiles were free of the fingerprints of any Germans or their sympathizers."

I picture Dad with a crowbar opening the crates of ball bearings, making sure there was nothing about them that would cause a British bomber to fail in midair, or that Nazi spies hadn't stolen anything or filled the crates with dregs, or perhaps laid an explosive charge that would blow up in the face of inspectors like my father.

But who was my dad working for? The OSS didn't have a presence in Sweden in early 1943; it was much later.

I look at him hard. What if he was something worse than anything I could imagine? A disaffected Episcopalian altar boy from Middle America secretly turned fascist? My father, the one who was filling the crates with dregs. All this time, everything else a ruse?

I slap myself on the cheek. "Say, why did you do that?" asks my startled father. I don't want to tell him why; it's to get rid of these doubts, these absurd thoughts that keep recurring. I'll tell myself I'm being crazy, then I'll remember the cross and cap, consider how hard it is for him to tell me the simplest things, and I will wonder about his allegiance. It's torture to sit here with this impenetrable man and never, ever know one single thing for sure—is he lying or forgetting or trying to please me? In all my Gestapo-like extraction of this information, have I simply issued him an invitation to make up stories? Or, more importantly, is he the devil I don't know?

My father clears his throat. He's been talking, but I haven't even been listening. "You see, you had to have these kinds of inspections with Sweden because they were lousy with agents from both sides of the war and they were playing both sides down the middle. There were warehouses full of these bearings because the Germans wouldn't let the Swedes ship them to Britain."

"When was this, what year?"

"It was pleasant enough weather, the spring probably. I remember strolling along, looking into the store windows, thinking I might have time to buy your mother a dress. It must have been spring of '43. I was sent on a couple of European missions before I went to the Pacific and that had to be one of them . . . working on a project where a bunch of sailors were going to run the German blockade. They were some damn brave men, most of them seamen or fishermen, and they were going to be used in a big mission the British were planning. You see, the British were desperate for ball bearings, and for steel. They kept buying up every ball bearing Sweden could make and just stockpiling them in that country." He pauses and frowns. "I think . . . the plan, as I remember, was to load the stuff onto these fast boats and try like hell to get through the German patrols and out to England."

I point to the Minox. "Did you go to Gotenborg to photograph the shipments leaving for Britain?"

"No. I think the boats ended up going some months afterward. I'm not sure of the time frame because they broke the German blockade several times, I think, but I remember that at one point I went to the coast and used it to gather photographic intelligence for one of the operations."

He picks up the Minox and peers through the lens. "Haven't seen this for years. I loved this thing. Do you remember it?"

"I remember you kind of covering it in your hand and snapping pictures of Penny and me."

He nods. "It was a gadget classified for wartime use, and then finally it went on the open market. This original was a great little camera, though, reliable, took fairly good photographs considering it had such small components."

"When you took pictures in Gotenborg, did you pretend to be a tourist or something?"

"A tourist?" he grunts. "You can't be serious! There was a war going on! Nobody went anywhere unless they had to. There were no pleasure cruises—and the merchant ships that did try to cross the Atlantic got blown up by German U-boats. There was one plane, the Pan Am Clipper, which was a big, glorified blimp. Only military officers, VIPs, and special agents like myself were permitted to go on it."

"Okay, okay, Daddy," I say with mock meekness.

"I was disguised as a fisherman and a dockworker," he says, somewhat more kindly. "I think that stub you're holding was from a café where the dockworkers ate. And it wasn't just in Gotenborg either, I traveled up the coast, oh, about sixty miles, with a few other operatives; maybe this one was a British Navy operation, and we photographed other ports. They were along this ocean between Norway and Sweden—it was the outlet to the North Sea. If I had an atlas, I could show you. Do I have an atlas?"

"I've never seen one here. What were you photographing?"

"Certain people under suspicion and the exact geography of certain fjords, the towns, certain loading equipment. We were looking for signs of German ships, for destroyers, minelayers, any kind of indication that the Germans were aware of this operation and were preparing to sabotage it."

He frowns. "The last blockade operation, I was sent to a little coastal town to wait for these gunboats to come in from Britain. I know it was dark, and I know it was bitter cold, so it's got to have been the winter. January, I think. They needed someone who knew the gunboats and the docks and the people involved, and who knew how to check the cargo, fast and thoroughly."

"What were the boats carrying, more ball bearings?"

"No." He crosses his arms. "The cargo was top secret. And that's all I'll say."

"What was it, Dad? Come on."

"It was guns," he says too quickly. "They were crated to look like innocent freight, and they were dispatched quickly from the boats to barges, and then they were smuggled into disguised modes of transport to Denmark. I inspected them."

"What kind of guns were they?"

"All kinds. Mostly Sten guns, some pistols, .38 caliber Enfields, I think."

"Where did you inspect them? On the barges?"

"Not if I didn't want to get shot. Although by then, it had to be late 1944, or the beginning of 1945, and the Germans were pretty much leaving us alone. That sea, it was called the Skak-something—the sea that links up the Scandinavian countries. The Swedes by that time had switched their allegiance to the winning side. After all, we'd already liberated half of Europe. But Denmark was another story; the Nazis were there to the very end, and when they heard the Allied armies were coming, they shot up all their prisoners. There was nothing more brutal than a defeated Nazi."

"Where did you inspect the weapons, Dad? In Denmark?" I'm leaning so far forward, I'm nearly falling into him. "Did you go there? Maybe you met with the Danish resistance, taught them how to shoot?" Under the very noses of the Nazi hawks.

"They knew all about weapons by then," he says.

"Dad! Come on, were you in occupied Denmark or not?"

"That is something I just can't talk about. And the record of what really happened on that operation, I don't think you've ever read about it in any book."

"Why not?

"I can't remember, don't you understand?" He struggles up off the couch. "I just can't remember! All I know is that I knew then that no one would ever know about what we did. And I was right."

Chapter Fourteen

M y New York City apartment has become predictably smaller than it was when we bought it seven years ago, what with Josh's aquariums, rolls of Amy's watercolors, masses of Bob's farming material, and stack upon stack of his overstuffed legal folders from the DA's office. The file cabinets in my study can barely open because of years of research for magazine stories, and my teaching materials are stacked on the end of my couch, upon which I recline to have my greatest ideas.

Towers of books teeter on the study floor and migrate into the hall. In our bedroom, vases of pink lilies balance on a makeshift table made of more books. Many of my war titles come from private merchandisers with names like Oddlot or Dustbin Books and arrive from places as far away as Australia or the Isle of Man.

I lift up the lilies and extract two out-of-print memoirs and two war tomes that talk about the British blockade-busters in Sweden. They don't agree on exactly what happened, but I've just received a package from England that contains the correct story—or at least part of it.

The National Archives (known until recently as the PRO, or Public Records Office) in Kew Gardens is the British equivalent of our National Archives and Records Administration, and if anything, it contains even more classified, buried, or purposely obliterated historical documentation. The institution warns that many documents recording World War II European ventures remain classified and others were destroyed in a flood.

An experienced PRO researcher, Richard Robinson, scoured the files for me and finally came up with a sixty-three-page account copied on huge paper that I imagine is the size of the Declaration of Independence. The account tells of what was called Operation Moonshine, one of the missions I believe my father participated in.

Moonshine was the last of the Swedish blockade runs organized by a mustachioed buccaneer named George Binney, head of Britain's Iron and Steel Federation, whom British officials considered utterly mad.

The first operation, code-named Rubble, was simply to run the German blockade to deliver to Britain urgently needed steel and ball bearings. Binney secured four Norwegian ships that were trapped at Gotenborg and manned them with Norwegian refugee captains and British ore crews, some of whom turned out to be Nazi sympathizers—the kind of spies that Dad claimed he'd later tried to root out. Thus when the loaded ships tried to slip by unnoticed in January 1941, the Skagerrak—the sea whose name my father couldn't recall—was saturated with German destroyers and bombers. The convoy was shot up and battered by storms but finally arrived in the Orkney Islands with its consignment intact.

The second operation, Performance, was a disaster. When the loaded ships left Swedish waters, armed German trawlers fired on them, and when they tried to turn back into the Skagerrak, the Swedish Navy pushed them out into the arms of the Germans. Five of the seven ships were sunk, and 150 Norwegians were captured and sent to the Sonnenberg concentration camp. Almost a third of the men died there.

This didn't discourage Binney, however, who kept the blockades running. As I study the orders in my father's abbreviated military file,

I realize there's an unexplained gap in his whereabouts from mid-June to mid-July of 1943. That was when Dad could have been sent to Sweden just as Binney was plotting out his next run, Operation Bridford. Though it didn't take place until that October, Binney would have needed a sharp-eyed operative like my father to help scout out airfields to see whether hostile aircraft were lining up or to patrol the waters to check whether minelayers were planting mines—any indication that the Germans were wise to the newest rogue actions.

Dad could well have been part of the Naval Intelligence team that covertly patrolled the Skagerrak in 1943 in the service of Binney's operation; the British Admiralty and U.S. Naval Intelligence worked in close collaboration from 1942 onward. And I can imagine Dad taking snapshots of "suspicious" sailors, perhaps showing them to sympathetic dockworkers to determine if they had Nazi leanings.

Binney eventually switched to motor gunboats, or MGBs, the fast boats Dad had described. These famous little coasters, among the quickest ever built, could speed fully packed across the Skagerrak, sailing above the mines and dodging enemy fire. In all, the gunboats brought in 347 tons of bearings to Britain, enough to produce plenty of the Lancasters, Mosquitos, and other fighting planes that the British so needed.

Binney's final blockade run, Operation Moonshine, which ran weapons bound for Denmark, culminated in January 1945 in its only successful run. The joint Naval Intelligence–Admiralty operation, which ran intelligence for the blockade busters, had no doubt been the one in which Dad again participated. He was familiar with the operation, an expert, so they snatched him out of the Pacific Theater, put him on "extended" leave, and deposited him in the little Swedish port of Lysekil, chosen instead of Gotenborg for its quiet discretion and lack of spies.

I have trouble handling the oversized British Archives documents on Moonshine, so I spread them out on the floor. They tell how an SOE representative at a secret planning meeting affirmed Binney's planned operation, arguing that risky airdrops could deliver only four tons of arms per trip to the desperate Danes while the fast boats could carry some twenty-six tons. The Binney cabal dreamed up a creative feint for disguising the arms from both the Germans and Swedes: They told the Swedish officials that a big British steamer had been found that could smuggle large numbers of Jews from Denmark, which was occupied by Nazis, to neutral Sweden, where they could be hidden until they were ultimately transported to England. The steamer needed revamping, however. Luckily, British merchant ships would be able to transport the necessary parts to Sweden that winter, where they could be off-loaded and conveyed to Denmark. The Swedish officials, thus deceived, allowed the off-loading of cargo from three MGBs. On the top level of the crates, there could be seen winch runners, steering chains and other spare parts for the "mythical British Steamer"; on the second level, what could not be seen were 1,046 carbines, 936 Sten guns, four Bren guns, four bazookas, 120 bazooka rockets, and more than two million rounds of ammunition for the Danish resistance. They were "discharged direct onto a lighter, towed down the coast to some secluded fjord and there transshipped" to Denmark.

The account ended there. Just like my father, the Moonshine documentation had nothing to say about what happened to the arms in Denmark.

Operation Moonshine was the most treacherous of all the blockade runs. The Admiralty spies kept in touch with the boats via wireless radio and radar, in which my father was an expert, and reported that the Germans were mining the center of the Skagerrak, forcing the MGBs to hug the shallow coast or "get blown sky high." Howling winds and snow foiled attempts from September through January. And even during the successful mid-January operation, in the dark of a moonless night, one of the MGBs rammed into another, taking out half of their engine room. The captain pulled the pin for the explosives that would scuttle the ship in three minutes and raced to get overboard. His life jacket became entangled in the ladder, however, so he had to jump to the main deck to slip out of it. Then he swam in the freezing sea looking for a lifeboat. There was such chaos that sailors were forced to paddle one lifeboat with a big sausage and two frying pans.

This single successful run of Operation Moonshine was of crucial importance because the Allies were then driving through occupied Europe: the Allied Command, which had previously neglected the bold and brave Danish resistance groups, now wanted them to go all out to blow up the railroads, power stations, and communications lines to tie up German troops. For the first time, the Allies were pouring large supplies of arms and explosives into Denmark to aid them in these tasks.

There were other, later deliveries of guns to Denmark in 1945, OSS operations with code names like Twinkle, Camel, Creep, and Pink Lady, which parachuted everything from Suomi submachine guns to items like codeine, walkie-talkies, nitrated paper for making combustible cartridges, waterproof bags, and underwear. But I find no mention in books or archives of Binney's rather large January 1945 weapons delivery and the use to which it was put. Could the plans for the ordnance that was delivered on Operation Moonshine been so controversial, so secret, that those in charge saw to it that it "never happened"? Expunged it from the record? After all, the British had long tried to suppress details about the blockade runs: after the war, the government prohibited release of the relevant files for seventy years, although most—but not all—were actually opened in 1972. What information could be so unthinkable, as to be kept so long from the public? And why do these mysteries keep surrounding my father?

At least I have pieces of the puzzle finally in place. In June 1943, my father helped insure that Britain would get the crates of real ball bearings they so desperately needed for war materiel, and he was part of a longstanding intelligence operation to help ferry supplies safely. Then, almost two years later, they brought Dad back for Operation Moonshine and the Danish gunrunning, whose underlying details he would never divulge. I see him on the piers of Lysekil, pulling his cap down, pretending to light a cigarette while he snapped away with his Minox, his fingers frostbitten by the winds coming off the Skagerrak, ready to scrutinize the innards of the machine guns, wondering if some traitor on board had sabotaged them.

Suddenly the telephone seems to bounce off my desk. I never answer the phone. My father never does either. Answering the phone, we believe, is the job of the answering machine.

I hear Penny, her voice edgy, saying, "Pick up. Pick up." I try to prepare myself for the Predictable Crisis. Our childhood, after all, taught us that one a week was the minimum expected. I stare at the machine. It will, of course, be about Daddy, who happens to be at her house.

My father hates to fly almost as much as Penny does, but he hasn't seen his daughter and his other grandchildren for several years, so he'd steeled himself for the flight. Penny and I had been anxious. What was he going to do when he found out that he couldn't smoke for six hours? Light up in the bathroom, set off the alarms? Force the plane to land and eject him? But then he had walked up the ramp at the LA airport, smiling at the stewardess who was leading him by the arm. She reported that he'd sat rigid the whole flight, not leaving his seat once.

Penny and her family had been lavishing attention on him, but Penny had confided to me in an earlier phone call that she was shocked at his deterioration. She shaved him, helped him dress. Her husband, Bernie, convinced that he was subsisting on Cheez Whiz and spoiled leftovers, stuffed him like a Christmas goose.

Luke and Penny's second-born, Max, hadn't seen him for years. "But it's the weirdest thing, it's as though they've been channeling him!" Penny reported. "Luke uses all these 'Daddy' phrases, like 'Say, I'll sure make good use of this present you gave me.' They both have such subtle whimsy. One day Daddy and Luke were kind of rakishly sprawled on the bed and they started some kind of goofy staring contest. Daddy blinked and then he said, 'So, how are you Luke?' and Luke just laughed and said, 'Just fine, Grandpa.' You should see him with Max. Dad's amazed that Max is this little intellectual. They've been talking about everything from antique locomotives to World War II. Max talks to Dad like Max *is* Dad."

It had been a huge turning point for Tom and his youngest grandson. Max had been born ten years earlier with Fraser syndrome, a rare genetic condition. He'd been missing one eye and kidney, and had a cleft nose and a dangerously narrowed throat. The way Penny had handled Max's entry into the world awed both my father and me. "If anyone was born to be Max's mother," Daddy had declared, "it's Penny." She'd convinced doctors and nurses to pursue every medical avenue as aggressively as possible. She'd found an ophthalmologist who was willing to operate to save his one eye and hired specialists to manage other life-threatening conditions.

For the first year of his life, Max had a tracheotomy and an intermittent eye patch. Nevertheless, Penny and Bernie raised him to his strengths and taught him that his challenges didn't matter. Luke, eight years older, has been a soulmate to Max, caring for him, wrestling with him, and rarely letting him out of his sight. Once, Max's tracheotomy tube came out, cutting off his air. His panicked parents were fumbling with it unsuccessfully, while Luke, on his own, called 911 and calmly repeated instructions on how to replace the tube.

At first, Dad hadn't known how to react to Max. "When Dad came before, they just couldn't communicate," Penny had told me. "Dad's partially deaf and Max has only fifty percent hearing and they just couldn't understand each other. It was so poignant. Daddy was so frustrated he would just go out of the house and smoke." What she hadn't known then was that Dad thought about Max continually; he worried about his future, about how his unending operations would affect him. He grieved about all the battles he faced. Whenever he tried to talk about Max to me, he simply couldn't find the words.

Max is one of nature's miracles. He's an enormously appealing child, his hair deliciously silky and blond, his glasses masking his missing eye, his mind near genius level. He's been mainstreamed into a regular school and is pulling As. He's become an expert skiier, chess player, pianist, artist, and Boy Scout. His one eye sees well enough for two, and in spite of his hearing loss, he understands everything his grandfather says. And now Daddy is seeing how Max has endured and persevered through setbacks that could have destroyed most children. "I think it's brought back all Daddy had to endure in the war,"

Penny told me. "He really loves how tough-minded Max is, and that he's sensitive too. And that he just happens to possess Dad's own wry outlook on life."

But now something has gone wrong. I pick up the phone.

"Cindy," Penny says, trying to control herself, "this morning I came into Dad's room and he was sitting on the edge of the bed and he looked up at me completely bewildered and said, 'Who are you?' He really meant it. He really didn't know who I was. I said, 'Daddy, it's me!'" Her voice shook. "And then he did that little chuckle of his and he said, 'I was just kidding. I know it's you.' I asked, 'What's my name?' and he said 'You're Penny, my daughter.' But, Cindy, he really didn't recognize me, it was, I don't know, it was that his eyes were blank. He looked me right in the face and he said, 'Who are you?'"

I swallow. "Oh, you know how perverse he can be," I say lightly, though I too am shaken. "I'm sure he recognized you. In fact, I'm positive. If anything's gone downhill, it's his sense of humor. Or maybe he was just disoriented after the long flight, jet-lagged or something."

After Dad returns from California, I get a call from Bernie. I never get a call from Bernie. Now he's on the other end of the line urging me to find an assisted-living facility for Dad where he can be watched and cared for. I respect Bernie, a smart, no-nonsense man of Czech ancestry and a first-born like myself. But now I turn a deaf ear.

I have entered an unspoken conspiracy with my father. We both know that putting an end to his independence would put an end to him. Besides, what could Penny and Bernie tell about Dad from a visit lasting a few days?

Still, doubt nags at me. How well has Dad familiarized himself with the mounting unfamiliarity of his world? Is he furtively trying to repaint a fading landscape, trying to trick his family into thinking he's lost nothing at all? On the other hand, if he misses a step now and then, if for a second, say, he fails to recognize his own daughter, isn't that the exception that proves the rule?

And the rule is: Don't get caught. Keep your cover.

Hide what you did, hide what you saw.

Lie to your waiting wife that there's no mistress; lie to your mistress that your wife no longer waits.

Disappear for days and return with a perfectly credible story.

Write the names of birds on the inside of your hand.

Penny is a dog with a bone: "For heaven's sake, Cindy, at least take him to a doctor—a geriatric specialist maybe—and get a diagnosis once and for all."

I take him to a clinic in Wellesley. As we wait, Dad studies his watch intently. What's so urgent; does he have a train to catch? Then the nurse leads him into the examining room. I'm told to wait outside a swinging door, but I can see everything through the little windows. My father sits there in his underwear, looking a bit forlorn though steely-eyed as the starchy nurse probes his mouth and ears. Then she begins asking him questions. "What is today's date, Mr. Franks?"

"Friday, October 22," he declares.

"Very good," she says. "Now, can we count backward from ten?"

He looks straight ahead but his eyes travel downward to the Rolex Mother gave him thirty years ago. The nurse scans his medical forms. "Ten, nine, eight, seven, six, five, four, three, two, one!" He sounds like a drill sergeant.

The nurse peels off her gloves and leaves the room in such a hurry, she collides with me.

"Will a doctor see him now?" I ask.

"No, he's fine, not sick enough to see a doctor," she reassures me.

"Did you see any dementia?"

"Well, he passed the tests. Pay the receptionist outside and we'll see him in a year."

He cheated. His fancy watch, with the numerals and the date, answered the questions for him. Dad cheated and I didn't tell the nurse. In fact, I zip out of there feeling ridiculously relieved. No doctor. No blood tests. No chest X-rays. Unnecessary. He officially passed and that's all we need. For now. But somewhere I feel what's happening: Dad is in a tunnel, traveling on a runaway train that has no stops.

Chapter Fifteen

C indy, where's my car?" Dad asks for the third time, peering anxiously out the window of our Vineyard home.

"It isn't here. It's at your house in Milford. I picked you up there in my car," I reply, edgily. "I've told you three times. Don't you remember?"

"Uh-huh," he says, pouring his coffee into the sink. "That's right. I knew that."

A minute later he looks around, bewildered. "Now who took my coffee!"

The drain basket is full of murky liquid. "It's all right, Daddy," I say, defeated. "I'll pour you some more."

"Oh, thank you, thank you."

It's springtime, more than five months since I took him to the clinic. Now I can hardly bear to look at the blinding yellow forsythia. The sound of hummingbird wings, the air warming the windowsills, the pale leaves opening on the Russian olive: everything is new, dream-laden, and sad. My father goes deeper into his winter, hanging on so poignantly to those things that have not yet vanished into the whiteness.

When I arrived to collect him in Milford yesterday, he'd groaned and run to the bathroom. "I don't know what's wrong, I never felt like this," he said.

I vowed that short of trapping him in the car again, I would not plead or nag or try to manipulate him. I would dispatch this familiar routine with alacrity or drive right back to New York. I opened my mouth and, to my surprise, out slipped a sob. "But this was going to be a nice cozy weekend, just the two of us."

"Oh, that's right!" he said to my surprise. "Then let me go get packed."

On the ride to the Cape, he chatted away, his ills forgotten. When we finally arrived at the Vineyard, I felt tired and irritable as I hauled bag after bag out of the car while he sat there complaining about the draft on his legs.

"Well, then, get out of the car!" I snarled.

"I wish I could help you, but I just can't," he said, watching me drag his suitcase up the steps.

"You could at least bring in your sandwich bag," I muttered under my breath.

Inside the house, he began walking around with his head tipped to the right. "I can't straighten it out, it's too painful," he said.

"Then let's go see a doctor," I narrowed my eyes. "We can drive to the walk-in clinic in Vineyard Haven."

"No," he said, "they're liable to incarcerate me in the hospital and not let me out."

I stifled a sigh. "Let me massage your shoulders, Dad."

"No," he replied, "that might do more harm than good. It's a pain that comes and goes."

Today he's slept until early afternoon and his neck pain has vanished. He sits down with his fresh mug of coffee. "Gee, your kitchen looks nice," he says, smiling at the slightly slanted, freshly painted red floor. The kitchen is in the old part of the house, dating back to the middle

1800s. I love the old, cream-colored cupboards, the baby blue spatterware bowls and tin coffee pots hanging on hooks. Light spills onto the red-checked tablecloth.

"Remember when I bought the house, the crazy lady who owned it had painted it mustard and purple?" I say, and he nods. "I was eight months pregnant with Josh, down on my knees scrubbing the floors. And then the beautiful pine boards came up and you arrived in time to help me varnish them. Remember, Dad?"

"I sure do! I was worried about Josh, what all that Red Devil paint stripper might have done to him, but then when he did so well in school, I stopped worrying."

I get up and make lunch for him, frying some fresh bay scallops from Poole's fish market.

"Oh boy," he says, cutting the small delicacies into quarters. "What a treat! Fresh seafood. I haven't had these for I don't know how many years."

But it wasn't years; it was about eight months ago, in this very kitchen.

There are deep lines under his eyes, a shadow on his chin, but Dad's eyes are bright and alert. He has eaten his last scallop. With a sense of urgency, I grab my camcorder. "Is it okay, Dad, to talk about the war? Can I film you?"

"Oh, sure," he says pleasantly.

"Dad, why don't we go back to your being a weapons instructor. Did you ever see your trainees in action? I mean, were they good, did they use weapons the way you taught them, like in the way they dealt with the, ah, you know, traitors who had to be eliminated?"

"You're going to need some more sugar mix in that feeder, Cindy," he says, watching the flashes of red and green wings pass it by. "I can put it in for you." I see that there is already plenty of syrup in there.

The afternoon sun, beating down through the windows, has become stupefying. He unbuttons his shirt. It's beige . . . polyester with a ghastly pattern of intersecting circles. The kind you get at K-Mart. I unfasten the top buttons of mine, blue linen. The kind you get at Banana Republic.

"Dad, your trainees. Did you see them eliminate people?"

"I don't know about them. I only know about me."

"Hmm?"

"Why don't you turn that damn thing off," he says tersely. I flick the switch to standby and lay the camcorder in my lap. A second ago he seemed so placid and willing to talk. But now his voice is harsh. What did I say?

He shoves his chair back with an angry thump. He stares out the window for a long time, saying nothing, seeming to see nothing.

Then he looks directly at me. "I did the killing," he says.

"What!"

"It was I, me, I was an assassin."

Dread creeps through the room. "You don't mean, I mean, you didn't murder people, did you? It was self-defense, right?"

He assumes his gesture of defiance, balancing chin on thumb and cheek on forefinger. "No. It wasn't self-defense. I executed people. Twice."

I let out my breath. I feel heavy, as though I'm going to fall through my chair. Do I see remorse in his eyes? Not even a smidgen.

Then I notice his hands: taut, knuckles white as he grips the table. Behind his bluff demeanor, he's been holding himself rigid. He's waiting for my verdict. I manage a thin smile. "Oh well, that's war, I guess."

His hands relax. He looks at me and lets out a shuddering sigh. That's when I see the pain in his face.

I try to sound matter-of-fact. "Tell me about the first one. Is that when you wore the Nazi cap?"

He closes his eyes. Now he talks easily—not to the distressed daughter but to the dispassionate journalist. "That was, let's see . . . Waffen-SS. I was dressed as one of the Waffen-SS. Those were the elite SS troops. The uniform was an Obersturmführer's, the German equivalent of . . . I think it was lieutenant or maybe a rank above that. After the mission was done, I had to hand it back in, except I had a friend in the clothing division so I kept the cap. Do you know why I kept it? Because it had the death's head insignia on it. I kept it because I never wanted to forget who these German soldiers really were."

He takes a pack from his pocket and taps out a cigarillo. "That uniform, it was something. I don't think I've ever worn any material so fine. Our uniforms were cheap in comparison. It was a copy, of course, made by our people, but it was an exact replica down to the labels and the way the buttons were sewn on."

I'm clenching my fists; how can this man, who has just declared that he was an assassin, go on about haberdashery? But of course I know why; any diversion to delay the inevitable.

"The Germans had much better uniforms than the British or the Americans. They made them that way so that people in the countries they occupied would be impressed—and intimidated—by the Gestapo."

"So," I say in a controlled voice, "you wore that as a disguise to get into that Gestapo office? You went there to kill an SS?"

"No, I went there to pick locks, which I can do—one night, your mother and I locked ourselves out of the house on 2 Clark Road and I had the door open by the time she turned around. You should have seen the look on her face! She couldn't believe—"

"Dad, the Gestapo headquarters! You picked a lock there. Then what did you do?"

He shut his eyes. "It was late at night, not many people around. I was to go through file cabinets and get the files of certain names . . . people the Nazis wanted. And I was to take pictures of other things. But I was interrupted by a guard, a sergeant, and he wanted to know what I was doing. I could have talked my way through it, but instead I shot him and took my satchel and got the hell out of there."

I feel an incredible wave of relief. Killing a Nazi while engaged in an operation. If that was his idea of "assassination," then my father wasn't a killer, he was a hero. "Wow," I say. "You must have been terrified."

"Not really. I've always felt protected when I have a gun and at that time I had . . . let's see, it was a Walther, and a small revolver concealed on me."

"Where did this happen, Dad?"

He closes his eyes, resting his head between his fingers. "I just don't remember the name. I'd gone in by parachute before, but later on I went in on a small plane, a bomber that had been completely emptied out so that it was so light it could take off quickly. I met with members of the French resistance. We brought containers of weapons for them. I was supposed to show them how to use the stuff. They were new and green, some of them were women." He shook his head. "The life span of a saboteur in the resistance wasn't very long. The women, they learned quicker and better than the men." He paused. "You know, over the years, I've had the exact same experience out on the range in Framingham. There was this gal in Milford—"

"Dad, if you were a weapons instructor, why were you sent to the Gestapo office?"

"I suppose it was because I was good with a gun. And I was thorough. I'd guess they liked the way I used a small camera, what I came up with. But probably it was like most other things—there wasn't anybody else on the scene that could do it as well."

"Oh, Dad, do you know what you did?" I say proudly. "You saved lives, you stole the files of people who were probably about to be rounded up and shot."

"Yes, I guess so." He gives me what passes for a smile, but his brow is gullied.

"Dad, you said you had assassinated two people. What about the second?"

He gets up, goes to the big color map of Martha's Vineyard on the wall. "Say, I'd like to see where we are."

I motion for him to come and sit down again. "Dad, you were telling me about the second assassination."

He clears his throat. He opens his mouth, then closes it. Looks down, shakes his head. Three minutes elapse. "You've pushed me and pushed me," he says finally.

"Tell me," I say hoarsely, "who did you kill?"

He lifts his eyebrows and looks at me beseechingly. "My friend."

"Your friend?"

"He was a good man. A first-rate operative," he says softly. "Or so I thought. I didn't know what his real politics were." Then, oddly, he picks up his checkered napkin and absently knots it.

He shot his friend because his politics were different. Over the last months, I thought I had put away for good the old doubts about my father. But the question comes back now and once and for all I must ask it. "Dad, were you a Nazi sympathizer?"

He stares at me so long that I'm afraid of what the answer will be. Then he begins to laugh. "Are you crazy?"

"I don't think so," I say, uncertainly. "It was a long time ago, and you were young. I don't know that I care at this point."

"Well, you damn well should care!"

"Could you answer the question, Dad?"

He throws the knotted napkin down on the table. "No, I wasn't a Nazi! What on earth made you think that?"

"Well, you were talking about killing a friend, a 'first-rate operative' . . . ."

"He worked for the Allies! The Americans, to be precise. And he was feeding information that we obtained right back to what had become our enemies."

"Where did this happen?" I ask warily.

"I can't remember . . . I can kind of see the place . . . a dirt road off a main drag where tanks were rolling through, but I don't recall where it was . . . oh yes, I was attached to the Army, officially as an ordnance liaison." He moves his lips, silently. "I think it was a division of the Third Army, or no, maybe it was the Sixth. We were over-running what was left of the German troops. That little part in the east of France with the little German towns, if I had a map maybe I could find it."

"Alsace."

"Yes, I guess so . . . or was it Germany? We may have already crossed the Rhine, I can't remember. It was toward the end of the war there. I know I was slogging through mud and freezing my butt off."

"This was after you were in Sweden, gathering intelligence for the blockade busters?"

"Oh, I think so, quite a bit after Sweden. Several months." He runs his hand over his face.

"Why did you kill him?"

"Because I was ordered to."

"Why were you ordered to?"

"He had picked up vital information and was going to pass it on."

"So he was a double agent."

"Yes."

"Was he a double agent for the Nazis? For the collaborators?" I ask. My father shakes his head, looks uncomfortable. "The Russians," he says. "The damn Communists."

"The Communists?" I ask in disbelief. "But weren't the Russians our friends?"

"Huh! They were never our friends. The Communists had taken over half the resistance. Very organized and ruthless. They killed people who didn't agree with them, and they killed their own. The Russian armies, they were grabbing land right and left, and they were trying to take secrets about German technology. Cindy, I've told you and told you, the Soviets were almost as bad as the Nazis, Stalin killed millions more than the Nazis, they had a five-year plan to take over—"

"Dad, there are no Soviets left! The plan went kaput," I say, louder than I intend. My father killed someone just because he was Communist? "How could he be a 'double agent' if he got information for two allies who were on the same side? I mean, the Russians helped us win the war!"

"Hell's bells, Cindy. He was a traitor! He was going to let the Russians know where a store of German materiel—unassembled parts, blueprints, things like that—was hidden. This was a special type of weapon that the Germans had developed, we didn't yet know exactly how to duplicate it, and we didn't want the Russians getting hold of this stuff. Next thing you'd know they'd be using it on us."

I swallow. "So you were ordered to kill him?"

"Well, yes and no. I recommended that he be eliminated."

My stomach turns over. My father glares at me. Fierce, proud, poised on the edge of his seat like a boulder threatening to come loose.

He reaches into his pocket and takes out a tube of antacids. "You know, this conversation is burning a hole in my stomach," he says, putting two in his mouth. "It only makes things worse to talk about these things, not better."

I collapse back in my chair. "Yes."

We both sit quietly for a while. The only noise is the ticking of the clock above the stove. Finally I ask it: "How did you kill him?"

He peels the paper back from the roll, takes out two more tablets, and chews them. "I shot him with a Colt .45 automatic fitted out with a silencer." The same silencer I found in his cedar chest?

"Did it have only one bullet?" I ask.

"A handgun shoots a number of bullets."

"How many did you use?"

"One," he mumbles.

"You got him on the first try?"

"He didn't have much of a chance. We were walking along, talking, Jack and myself and this defector. Jack confronted him." Jack Steele, his fellow operative. "Jack told him we knew all about it. How he'd betrayed every one of us, not to speak of his country. I fell behind them and shot him in the back of the head, low down on the head, where death occurs instantly. We dragged him into the bushes at the side of the road."

Oh God. "What did he look like? I mean, after you killed him."

"There was blood."

"A lot of blood?"

"A good amount."

"Did it get on you?"

"Yes, it got on me," he says sarcastically. Of course the blood got on him.

"What happened then?"

He looks at me belligerently. "It was all very well planned. My superiors had planned it. They had okayed it, Cindy. That's why we went ahead. We got into an Army jeep waiting for us and went somewhere north, and eventually we were ordered to go to this camp they had discovered."

"You mean Ohrdruf? But wait, Dad, you told us that the admiral at the Bureau of Ordnance sent you to Ohrdruf. You told Bonnie at the museum that you flew there from the States."

"I was trying to throw her off the scent."

"You mean the scent that you killed your friend?" I ask bitterly. "So how do I know whether you're trying to throw *me* off the scent?"

He studies me. "I guess you don't. But I'm telling you the truth. The admiral was long gone. He was in the Pacific. My superior was an army intelligence man and I'd already been sent to join the liberating troops."

Though the house still holds the heat, the light outside is dusky now. Soon night will come. He looks at my face. "I *had* to do this, Cindy," he says. "If things like that weren't done, you might be living under a dictatorship, a damn police state, right now."

"Of course, Dad," I say, torn between the old rage and pity. How can he justify what he's done? How can he live with what he's done? "It must have been upsetting for you to kill him, if he was your friend," I manage to say, "if you had worked with him."

"Yes, it was," he says at last. "I knew his wife and two children. They must have been under twelve." He looks down. "I'd been to his home. His wife made me this delicious soup out of cherries."

A light dawns. "Was he going to tell the Russians about the V-2 rocket? The guided missiles they were assembling at Nordhausen?"

"Information that was something like that," he says, wiping his brow with his handkerchief.

I knew all about the V-2 rockets. The V-1, the German "flying bomb," had shocked the world when hundreds came searing across the sky out of nowhere in the summer of 1944 and demolished parts of London and Antwerp. The V-2 carried an even bigger payload and was so fast anti-aircraft artillery couldn't touch it. My father had told me he'd studied the V-1, the V-2, and other much smaller rockets developed by the Germans during the war. Indeed, after V-E Day, he'd received those orders dated July 1945 that named him a "liaison officer" on missile-bearing ships, and that stated he would "formulate operational policy as well as design changes" in the missiles.

"Dad, surely you know we got to Nordhausen first, before the Russians. Even if they had known what was there, they were too busy taking Berlin. We're the ones who grabbed every V-2 part we could and carted them off." The American forces had disassembled, packed, and moved enormous numbers of rocket components to the United States.

I know I'm crossing boundaries I'll regret, but after all our acrimony over Communism, his mockery of me, I can taste self-righteousness. "And surely you know that the Soviet Union figured out how to make the rocket anyway and that this rocket led to bigger rockets and that soon they sent Sputnik into the air and the Soviet Union won the damn space race anyway."

"Only at first," he says weakly. "We surpassed them eventually."

"But the point is, Dad, that even if you prevented this double agent from telling the Russians about the importance of Nordhausen or any of the other sites where they were developing missiles, even if it *was* him that tried to alert them to what the Germans were doing there, it still didn't make any difference. In the end, the Russians you hate so much got the plans they needed from other sources." I can't stop myself. "In the end, he died for nothing."

"Cindy, you damn well don't know what you're talking about!" My father takes off his eyeglasses. Then he begins to cough convulsively, putting his hand over his mouth, but I see his chin crumple. He pushes away from the kitchen table.

I follow him into the living room, where he stands looking into the black of the window. I watch his reflection and his skin glows silver in the glass; his large blue eyes seem to droop. Surely this has been the nexus of his nightmares, not only the horror of Ohrdruf, but this cold-blooded, cynical killing, this murder without meaning. I wonder what he really saw as his gun recoiled? *Quite a bit of blood.* Had the friend who'd welcomed him into his home turned around at the last moment? I think of the man's children face down on their beds, weeping, the widow screaming.

My father's reflection seems to tremble and his shoulders are heaving and I realize he's crying. I've never, ever seen him cry before. I suddenly feel ill. The OSS has nothing on me. I'm the master of water torture. I've finally extracted the gruesome past he'd buried so deeply. Finally discovered the Big Secret, but at what cost? What's he supposed to do now? Say, "Never mind, I won't think about it?"

I turn and go upstairs, leaving him to his grief—and me to mine.

I look at my bed, but cannot get in it. For so long, my father—an inventive, clever Daedalus, had tried to protect me. He'd made wings for me to fly. I'd invited myself into his labyrinth, determined to free us both, and when he'd warned me away, I hadn't listened. Like Icarus, I'd flown too close to the sun and plunged us both into the sea.

At least now I'm certain that he wasn't a Nazi. But, I'm too much like him. I use bare intellect to defeat my feelings. So I reach for the books I've brought with me; everything I can find about the Allies' final march, the conquest of the Third Reich.

He was right. The conquering Allied soldiers entered a ruthless world that seemed to have no exit. Rumors abounded about the Nazi scientists' research on the atomic bomb: Whichever power got to it first could destroy the others. The Communists slaughtered partisans in order to take control; they killed Jewish resistance members for no reason at all—and as Dad had said they even liquidated their own agents for "ideological impurity." Stalin's destruction of his own people was an enormity beyond imagining; scholars have estimated the number of murders to be between ten and thirty million. The Russians were moving from the east, raping Polish women, putting German heads on poles, seizing everything they could.

After the war, the Russian "grab" didn't end. The Communists confessed that they *had* infiltrated the young radical movements in America, including some that I was in. How my incessant pro-Communist diatribes must have alarmed my father. If he had continued as a spy after the war, if he had, for instance, penetrated the clandestine world of American Communists, he would have known even more about the Soviet plan to take over the world.

Tom Franks' decision to rid the world of one more Communist traitor had bought him a sentence of eternal suffering. In my ignorance and rush to judgment, I'd doubled his sentence.

Certain events seek shadow in our minds; they're sleeping silhouettes until something shocks them to life, and then a hundred little details come into the light.

The cries that came through my wall. Oh, that's just Daddy, I thought as a child. But come my adolescence, they grew weird, scary. And then the everlasting silence during his waking hours. At home, at mealtime, especially in the car, his wordlessness hung heavy. I'd thought it had been directed at me. I hadn't known about the emaciated boy wandering the camps, the skeletons in the pits, the spreading blood of a friend felled by his hand.

A ruined marriage, a lost job, hundreds of lost weekends, they'd flowed naturally from the rip in his universe fifty-five years ago. How could he answer a letter from his daughter in London asking him if man's existence was futile? How could he ask her how her life was going when his had stopped in Ohrdruf?

Maybe all those guns he hid around the house weren't evidence of his paranoia after all. He'd turned in corrupt base commanders and enemy plant workers, trained resistance fighters to kill, eliminated two men. And the OSS and the CIA had long ago admitted to "terminating" those who knew too much. At a factory in Dayton, Ohio, WAVES who were simply working the assembly line on a machine to break the German Enigma naval code were told if they ever talked about their work—even after the war—they would be shot. Perhaps, behind his in-different silence, my father wasn't indifferent at all. Perhaps, when he hid all those guns in the house, it hadn't been himself he wanted to protect. Of all the bedrooms concealing a weapon, his room wasn't one of them.

Did I ever know before that he was brave? I haven't lived inside a war, a revolution, a crumbling society, a state where I needed to show what I was made of every minute. But I knew now what *he* was made of.

Early the next morning, I bring him his coffee in the guest bedroom and sink down beside him on the saggy horsehair mattress. He props himself up, saying nothing.

"I'm sorry," I say. "I'm sorry, Daddy, I'm sorry."

He gives me a small smile and pats my hand. Last night's conver-sation is over. Nothing more needs to be said.

As we're packing up to catch the ferry, however, I take an inordi-nate interest in my shoes. I can't let him see my shame, the fear that what I've done to him will be mirrored in his eyes.

The great, hulking steamship picks us up in Vineyard Haven and casts off for the mainland. She's supposed to be cutting through the swells, but she isn't moving. She's just stuck in the sea like a ladle in a pot of old stew.

Even worse, we're stuck here in the belly of the ship, where the cars are packed in with no room to spare, because my father didn't want to bother going up to the deck. "Dad, there's something wrong with this old tub. If it's sailing, it's at half a mile an hour."

"That's an illusion," Dad says, and opens the car door. "Come, I'll show you."

We inch our way along the oil-stained cement floor between the cars, and he points to an open porthole near the bow. "Go and look."

The ship is rushing through the water. The waves like sheets of glass shattering.

"Well, you're right," I say grumpily. "But I was sure they were in some kind of slowdown."

"I don't think so," he says, poking his head through the open porthole. "See, you can see, ah, what's its name? The place we're going?"

"Woods Hole," I say, peering out behind him.

"That's right. Woods Hole, a direct line from Vineyard Haven. Gee, you can see why they use the color 'sea green.' I've always loved to look at the ocean. See how the waves roll over and over, like little kids. And sometimes you can see the sky in the sea if it's quiet, with clouds scudding along."

I move to his side so I can see his face. My father doesn't talk like this. His demeanor is oddly serene.

Just then, a wave of water surges through the porthole. "Oh no!" he yells, stepping back. He's soaked. His chin and nose are dripping, his shirtsleeves sopping wet. His glasses are fogged up. I grab my blue wool sweater from my tote bag and try to wipe his face, but fuzz just sticks to his damp skin.

"Stop, stop!" he says, "You're making it worse." Indeed, his face is now covered with what appears to be blue measles.

He shakes himself off like an unhappy puppy. "Every time I squeeze the water out of my shirt, more of the damn stuff comes in. Like a sponge." I try to stifle a giggle but out it comes. He frowns at me, but in a moment he too gives in to laughter, he's soon shaking with it, clearing away the heaviness of the morning.

I finally dab my eyes. Then I put my arms around his cold chest. "Daddy, dear Daddy."

I drape my sweater round his shoulders. This reversal of roles, this intimacy seems oddly right. I meet his eyes and what I see isn't sorrow, but light. Lightness.

We go up to the top deck so his clothes can dry in the sun. The sun blinds me. I can see nothing but spots, each spot a memory, running freely now, like a current through a safe harbor:

Penny and I are shopping at Filene's. We walk out the door and smack into the hands of a guard with the meaty face of an Army sergeant. My belongings are jumbled in my arms: purse, sweater, coat, and, unwittingly, an unpaid item dangling with tags belonging to Filene's Department Store.

With the guard's hand at my back and my sister in tears, I climb the three flights of stairs to the manager's office. Although I try to explain that I'd accidentally picked up the shirt, which hadn't fit anyway, the manager tries to browbeat me into a false confession. I ask if I can call my parents. He hands me the phone, but it's clear he intends to nail me. The police will come first, then the handcuffs.

"We have reason to believe that your daughter here is a thief," he says when my parents arrive. My father leans against the door, crossing his legs. He lights his pipe. He takes a long draw, then blows out a large puff of smoke that encases the smug face of the manager in a hellish miasma. "My daughter has never told a lie," he says in his deep, calm voice. "She has never deceived us. She has never ever been accused of doing wrong." I feel a little shiver watching him, standing tall with elbows folded, utterly unassailable. I have in fact distinguished myself at home as a fibber and a petty thief, but never, ever elsewhere, so he implicitly trusts my word. He will protect me at all costs. I know then I'm not going to jail. The manager might reign over the store, but my father's authority is greater.

Now it's Parents Night at Miss Ferguson's Dancing School and I'm stiffly moving around the room. Miss Ferguson, a tall, buxom woman, suddenly stops the music mid-measure. "Someone is leading the boy," she bellows, and I can hear her heels clicking round the wooden dance floor. I pity the poor girl, whoever she is. Then she stops and taps my shoulder. I'm mortified, but when the Father's Dance is announced, Dad holds me tight and follows my less than graceful steps. "You dance beautifully," he says loudly as we pass the old battle-axe.

My father, I had discovered, had been somebody in the world. And now, I realize, he'd been somebody at home.

I think of that night we had dinner at Mama Leone's when he'd told me about Pat. He wasn't simply being insensitive, as I had thought. He'd done it out of blundering love. He'd only wanted to bring together two people he cherished.

He'd stayed married even though he loved someone else, so that his children would be all right. He'd been loyal to H.H. Harris, forsaking far better opportunities to stay by his side, run his company. Behind his failures lay silent acts of heroism.

I look at my father, sitting there watching the passengers, his hair dry now, blowing back and forth in the breeze. Even with his double chin, skin slathered with sun block, arms sticky with salt, he is still so handsome.

He's taking out his handkerchief now, blowing his nose in that idiosyncratic way, a short burst from one nostril and a long one from the other. It will always make me think of him, that syncopated, owlish sound. He folds his handkerchief fastidiously, in one half, then another, and another, until it is a small square that he tucks in his pocket. Then, seeing me watch him, he looks down and bats his eyelashes. I wonder if he knows he's being adorable, and if he does, well, that makes him even more so.

In my travels through his subconscious, I'd hoped to find a dashing, romantic character, the one lost to my childhood. But what had started out as the point of my journey had turned out not to be the point at all. In the quiet of the morning, what he's done seems less than shocking. He'd killed a Nazi, good. He'd killed a double agent, a mistake . . . perhaps. But war abounds with mistakes.

The journey itself has been the revelation. For him as much as for me. In stripping away his dark mantles, I'd gotten back my real father— and given him air to breathe. The daughter who once didn't like him, who stopped the car only long enough to hand him a check, is now the one who lingers beside him, hour after hour, actually interested— no, fascinated—by him. He knows he has not just my respect, but my acceptance of him for who he is. Our time together has given him a reason to get dressed in the morning, a reason to talk, a reason to be.

I rest my head against his arm, which he puts around my shoulder. His shirt, almost dry now, is soft against my cheek. I breathe in the faint scent of English Leather.

I forgive you, Daddy, I say silently, I forgive you for all the things you did: for loving Pat, for forsaking your family. For using me, for depending on me to rescue you, for the drinking that blotted out your past.

I close my eyes and dream about a certain morning, a lovely sunlit morning when I rode upon your back, a little girl in love on the crest of a green, galloping wave.

Chapter Sixteen

M y father and I never speak of the assassinations again. But the gates are open and other recollections that he hadn't been able to retrieve stream out. I just sit back and listen as he easily describes his last months in the war. Though the memories are abbreviated, they explain why he stayed behind after so many other soldiers had gone home.

"I was attached to an Army division in Germany," he tells me. "They were clearing the towns of any opposition. We would go everywhere you could possibly go. Oh gosh, we busted right into Nazi headquarters. We went to all these industrial sites, sorted through all these documents. We photographed blueprints and plans and a lot of other vital information."

I think this means that he was part of the T-Forces, the special units attached to U.S. Armies that went after all the files on V-2 rockets and other ordnance before any of the other allies could get at them. The T-Force personnel—safecrackers and demolition experts, as well as shooters able to act quickly if interrupted—were from a polyglot of different services, including OSS.

This collecting was done in the shadow of one of the most horrifying human spectacles in Germany. Nordhausen, considered a subcamp of Dora-Mittelbau, was staffed by captive labor who worked nonstop; more than three thousand people died of exhaustion, disease, and starvation. They became so emaciated that three at a time could be put into the ovens. The Americans used some of the least wasted prisoners to help carry out V-2 machinery from the vast tunnels.

A week after he'd been an observer at Ohrdruf, my father saw the horrors all over again at a smaller testing site near Nordhausen. "These people were slave laborers and hardly better off than the people at Ohrdruf, most of them. They were emaciated and scarred from beatings," Dad tells me. "They were half-deaf from all the blasting; they walked hunched over. I've spent my life wondering how people could do that to people, what it is in human nature. You can't really comprehend it, no matter how hard you try."

My father eventually was returned to the States, but said he was sent back again to Germany to join an ordnance team that was interrogating hundreds of rocket scientists. This was apparently part of Operation Overcast, later evolving into Operation Paperclip, a controversial program that brought Nazi scientists, many of them war criminals, to the U.S. to work on American projects. One of the key men in the operation was Vannevar Bush, director of the Office of Scientific Research and Development during World War II, closely connected to the OSS and the Bureau of Ordnance.

Dad's role was to question some of the minor rocket scientists who'd been rounded up by American troops and to join the search for others. "The whole process kind of turned my stomach," he tells me. "I heard they wined and dined von Braun in order to get information and make bargains with him. He'd witnessed how they treated the slave labor in the testing sites. He'd seen people existing on one weak bowl of soup and a chunk of bread a day. He'd seen people hung for no good reason.

"Those Nazi scientists," he says in disgust. "There were hundreds of them who got off scot-free. They got a free pass into this country. They lived in the lap of luxury. Their whole families, cousins, aunts, uncles, were given housing and big salaries."

"But, Dad," I say, "Wernher von Braun was responsible for the successful American space program, and we got a man on the moon, so wasn't it worth it?"

"Not in my book," he replies. "To have rewarded someone who'd been in the SS or the Gestapo and taken part in the state-ordered mass murder of six million Jews? No, it wasn't worth it."

Soon the conversation begins to gutter. It's not long before Dad stops talking about the war, or about much of anything of substance. I pick him up and we drive to Fishkill in silence; not the kind of heavy silence I hated as a teen, but a comfortable, satisfying quietness.

Once, as I drive him home, I tell him how nice it's been to have him for the weekend.

"You don't think I'm boring?" he asks.

"Boring!" My eyes well up with tears. A question asked by the old, the useless. "Dad, you're the *opposite* of boring. And I am so proud of you."

"You are? I don't know why."

We like to snuggle up together and watch the Weather Channel; Amy, with a wise old smile, snaps pictures of us. My father wants to be with me all the time, especially when I'm about to leave. "Sit a minute, let's look for the birds," he'll say, or, "Would you like to join me for lunch?" and finally, "Why can't you stay?" I tell him I have a husband and kids, and he says, "Oh yes, I forgot."

When we're apart, I call him every few days. Each time he asks his favorite question: "How are your three children: Joshua, Amy . . . and Bob?" I don't disappoint him by failing to chuckle. The Newport Creamery has closed, so his new haunt is a restaurant right next door to the Creamery. "Did you go out to eat lately, Dad?" I ask. Each time he replies, "Yes, I've found a terrific place. It's called the 99 Club." I always ask him what he's had to eat, though I always know the answer: "I had a . . . a . . . oh, what is it called?" "A club sandwich?" I reply. "Oh, yes, that's it." We close with our standard good-bye: "Love you and miss you."

Then the spell begins to break. Too soon after the euphoria of the Martha's Vineyard ferry ride, the silences grow awkward again, the old discomfort returns.

There are no more stories. How much we had depended on them; they'd knitted us together. Now he's slipped his hand out of mine. On the ferry, I'd felt such love for my father. I was so sure of his love for me. Now, he is very far away. It's as though I've fed shilling after shilling into the heater in my chilly London apartment, the warmth enveloping me, only to have it fade after a few minutes.

Things are rolling back. He wants me to come every weekend, but he refuses to leave his nest. I'm twenty-five all over again: He needs, I give. On the telephone, he doesn't even inquire about my family anymore. I have to swallow the urge to ask, "Is that all you have to say?"

His adamantine self-reliance—that's what's driving me crazy. He runs out for milk and comes back empty-handed. He refuses help in the shower, but forgets what the soap is for. He pushes Penny and me away, insisting he can do everything himself. But he can't, and worrying about what will happen to him in an unguarded moment is draining.

I'm disheartened too by the poverty of his mind. He has only one book now. He picks it up and opens it randomly. I can't pay attention to my own book because I keep looking over to see if he's turned a page. He hasn't. He reads the same one over and over, or maybe he isn't reading at all.

Then, one evening, I put the Preservation Hall Jazz Band on the cassette player. During a trip to New Orleans, I'd loved seeing the venerable black musicians playing old-time songs. At the first chords of "When the Saints Go Marching In," Dad sits upright and declares, "Oh, my favorite!" and as the beat rises, the tuba drawling out a deep resonating solo, he begins to tap his palm on his knee—and then on mine, boom-baba, boom-baba, inventing a little tattoo. Then the band plays "Just a Closer Walk With Thee." It begins ponderously, the instruments in mourning. Then they quicken the tempo, released from their burden. It's a joyful clangor, but still you can hear each instrument individually, the banjo, the brasses, the oboe, doing their own intricate riffs. Suddenly the oboe takes off and slides up and down the scale, the notes jumping apart but melting together at the same time. My anger, frustration melt too. Dad looks down at me; we just sit there beaming at each other. How could I ever have doubted our love? My veins feel like they're being squeezed, the blood rushing through my body. I'm filled with a kind of primal wonder. I'm in church again.

How can this be? I long ago lost my connection with God. But now questions fill my mind. What caused my father and me to adore each other, lose that adoration, and then regain it in the end? Is it fate that works in a circle? Or something that lies beyond?

It's been a magical spring Saturday in Milford, for a sparrow has come up and eaten out of Dad's hand. Tomorrow we've planned an outing; he wants me to drive him two hours north to Gardner to see his old love Pat. In the middle of the night, however, I hear him moaning and hurry into his bedroom. He's bent over his bed, hugging himself, a sharp pain radiating through his back.

"No," he says, "no hospital," but he doesn't try to stop me from calling 911 and willingly gets into the ambulance. Once in the emergency room, he's completely composed. "Are you in pain, Mr. Franks?" the doctor asks. "No," he says unequivocally. He looks at me vacantly, as if I'm not there, but whenever I step out of the room, he asks where I am.

He is carted and trundled and shoved into scanning machines.

Only twice have I known my father to be offensive to a woman not his wife: the first time was when he told a stunned Pat Rosenfield that her bottom looked like two cannonballs. The second happens now, in the Milford General Hospital when he snaps, "Get your goddamn hands off me!" to a nurse in the X-ray department. I'm the only one who can get him to cooperate, and that only by persistent wheedling.

Dawn has broken and the test results are in. My father has inoperable lung cancer. I go back to his room and find they've filled him with Demerol and morphine and God knows what other drugs. He's asleep and doesn't know of his diagnosis, nor, as far as I'm concerned, will he ever. I walk leadenly around the hospital grounds, wishing my sister were here instead of thousands of miles away. And then I'm hit with an inconsolable hunger. I go back to the hospital coffee shop and eat a blue plate breakfast special, then a grilled cheese sandwich, a basket of onion rings, and a vanilla milkshake. This makes me feel sick, stupid, and even more hollow. When I take my tray to the kitchen, the server smiles at me and I immediately begin to cry.

We have no time left. What time there's been hasn't been time enough. Three, maybe four years—not long enough to make up for the four decades we missed together. Life unravels without you even knowing it, and soon all that's left is a spiral of images: a tattered blue bathrobe, a butterfly net, words slanting down a pink diary: "At least Daddy loves me."

I go back to his apartment and stare at his bed, the covers mussed, the sleeve of his bathrobe dangling from the back of a chair. I count five flyswatters scattered around the place and imagine him chasing the unfortunate fly from room to room. I look at the line of caps on his bedroom door, each one from a different gun meet, the wall calendar marking the days when Pat the housekeeper comes. His "stationery"— a pad of yellow lined paper upon which he has stamped his name, slightly crooked on the page: Thomas E. Franks, 5 Thayer Street, Milford, Mass. 01757.

I look at his table full of weekly pillboxes that he'll probably never need again. All those times he was too sick to visit us, I simply assumed he was faking it. But the pain in his back, his neck, it really did exist, didn't it?

At my fiftieth birthday party on Martha's Vineyard, he'd arrived without his teeth. I was beyond embarrassment. He did this just to provoke me, I thought. But the fact was, his false teeth hurt. They hurt him because they were cheaply made. They were cheaply made because he had no money. He had no money because I didn't give it to him. I, who had so much more than he.

Lou Golden had called me once. "You should really support your father," he told me. "I mean *really* support him. So he doesn't have to count every penny."

"We just can't do it, Lou," I told him. "We've got three households to maintain; we're already spread too thin."

"Well, that doesn't mean very much when you can't pay the light bill."

I consider how my son Josh, smooth-skinned and fit, strides quickly through the street, leaving me puffing behind. How many times had I resented my father for not answering his phone, not considering how slowly he'd have to shuffle to pick up the extension? By then, I'd hung up, angry and hurt. Josh can deconstruct Kant in a minute while I labor away, stuck on the same page. How does it make me feel? Jealous. Was my father any different from any other aging parent, robbed finally of sharing life side by equal side with his child? Broke and broken down, he had even less than most parents.

I wonder whether Dad will have any visitors in the hospital besides his family. How could he? He doesn't know anyone here. Not like in Hopkinton, where he'd taught the police how to shoot, where he belonged to a gun club. Who made him move? Me.

I recall the day when Doug Haward called me, alarmed at having seen Dad's old suits strewn every which way over his furniture. I wonder now if he was trying them on not to give up, but to hold on, each one bringing back a happy moment, a liquid mood, a time of innocence.

I think of that morning when he told me, "Pat thinks you don't like me because I loved her instead of your mother." I was so startled I hadn't heard the bigger question: "Why don't you love me?"

I would do anything to get that moment back. To get all these moments back. Every little guilty thing I did will be stuck forever in his obliterated brain. My failure to answer his unasked question will remain The Answer forever.

I come into Dad's hospital room the next morning and find him sitting up, asking every passing nurse whether she has a light. He fumbles in vain around his hospital Johnny for a pocket and a pack of cigarillos. "Say, they bugged me all night long," he grumbles. "Lights blazing and every minute someone comes in twittering, 'Hi, honey, time to take your vitals.'" And that's practically the last rational thing I hear him say for a long time.

A few minutes later, he cries, "Oh, look at the bird!" pointing at a recessed spotlight. Then, staring at the floral wallpaper border at the ceiling, he asks, "Is that a dog?" He plays with his towel, pulls at the sheet around his knees, keeps feeling for the nonexistent pocket in his nonexistent pants. "Dad, what are you looking for?" I ask.

"How should I know?" he snaps in reply.

I stay in Milford for a week and then, after I have a head-on collision with a car while coming out of the hospital driveway, I take a train to New York. I'm home at the most for thirty-six hours when he calls and says, "You'll never know how much I miss you." I'm back at Milford Hospital the next day.

I hug Dad hello. No response. "Dad, it's Cindy. Happy to see me?" I ask. He ignores me, gazing down at the bottom of a rolling tray. "What do I do about that wheel?" he asks. "I've brought you a donut and coffee, Dad," I tell him. He tries to drink from the bag.

I ponder my father's fractured state. Was the familiarity of his apartment the only thing keeping him together? Did he come apart once he was out of his element? I demand to see the doctors and they finally concede that the drugs they're giving him might be temporarily scrambling his brain. Also, he's refused to eat a thing for days. They talk as though my father isn't lying right next to us. Suddenly a hand shoots up from the bed. "Doctor, how do you do, I'm Tom Franks," he says, with a touch of irony and a great deal of dignity for someone whose Johnny is riding up over his bony knees. He clears his throat: "Can you save my life?"

I interject before the doctors invoke the prevailing principle of Full Disclosure. "Dad, that depends on you; you have to eat and try to get better." From then on, I get the nurses, who love him for his courtly manners, to spoon-feed him when I'm not there.

"I'm trying," he tells them woefully, managing to swallow one bite. Then he makes the "okay" sign and says "dee-li-cious" as though they've made the hideous chicken gruel themselves.

My fears that he's friendless are unfounded. Everyone wants to see him. I pinch some extra chairs and put them around his bed, which annoys him.

"They're absolutely useless!" he says, and then, as if on cue, his neighbors Michelle and her mother, Michelle's boyfriend, Benny Montenegro, and two pony-tailed waitresses from the 99 Club file in. He quickly adjusts his Johnny and smiles at everyone.

"Dad, here's Mary!" I say when another waitress, his favorite, comes in.

"Who's Mary?" he asks, but then quickly recoups: "Oh, you mean *our* Mary."

They talk and he listens and when they leave, he gives them each a little salute. We're alone and I cover his head with kisses, rub my cheek against his and tell him I love him very much. His face is pale and blotchy, and he looks straight ahead, oblivious.

I'm beginning to feel the strain, and Bob sends Joshua up to join me for the weekend. When my father looks at his grandson, now age seventeen, he cries, "Little Joshua!"

"Hi, Grandpop," Josh says. "How are you?"

"Just fine," he replies, his eyes lighting up. At least he's glad to see one of us.

Josh is an accomplished artist and he begins almost at once to sketch his grandfather. I, who have been dabbling in drawing, also take up my pad. "What am I, your model?" Dad asks. With Josh here, he begins to say more, but his responses are still disconnected from the questions he's asked. I wonder whether he's actually confused or just unable to get the appropriate words out.

Josh picks a button up off the floor. "Are you missing a button, Grandpop?" he asks. Dad, sitting with his long, rangy legs crossed, examines it and replies, "I've been asked my opinion about that and I'd say that it was about seventy-five years old." "Yes," says Josh, "it's a pretty old button." Then my father puts his head in his hands and just shakes it back and forth.

Josh and I go to the 99 Club for dinner. I look across the table at him; the mutinous boy I left at home has suddenly become a man, my moral support, my much-needed friend. I try to break it gently to him that his Grandpop doesn't have long to live.

"Mom, I probably shouldn't say this, but in my mind, Grandpop has been dead for some time."

I choke on a mouthful of food.

"See, I've been distancing myself from him because I wanted to shut out his decline, what he'd become, so I could remember him when he was important to me. You know, he would explain everything to me! And the moths, we would catch those moths!"

Grandfather and grandson filling glass boxes full of magnificent moths, sprinkling naphthalene flakes over them to keep tiny insects from nibbling the specimens. The grandfather teaches his grandson how to care for them, to preserve their bright color and perfect shape. But in time, the grandfather grows too old to tend them; the grandson becomes a teenager and loses interest. The moths lose their heads, their wings tear, mold deadens their colors; the creatures become ragged ghosts of their former glory.

My son, sitting across from me, his wavy hair tousled, handsome like my father. Josh's face has thinned out, lengthened; he has striking, pale blue eyes with strong, dark brows. And his upper lip forms a little V, just like Dad's. "I understand what you're saying," I reassure him. "But I have to remind you, he's been incredibly coherent about the war and his undercover work."

"Yes, but that'd be with you, Mom, not with me." Josh talks between big bites of his pastrami sandwich. "I think he knows more than he lets on," he says. "Listen, this is my theory. He's embarrassed. He doesn't want us to see him this way. You know how if you do something not well—like I played a lousy basketball game and I'd go to my friends and say, 'God, did I stink' so they couldn't think it first. So it's defensive. He puts his head down in his hands because it's almost a way of protecting his dignity. He knows we think he's diminished and pathetic. He's in a fallen state; he's defending himself. And I also think it's a little bit of a play for sympathy. If he's worthy of sympathy, then he can keep a little dignity."

After about three weeks, we move Dad to a halfway house near the hospital. He's more lucid but has declared he cannot walk and wants to stay in his wheelchair. The place is full of patients who complain and bark at the nurses, and they find Daddy such a pleasant relief that they regularly kiss him and sneak him pieces of chocolate. "Thank you, thank you, thank you," he invariably says, making them beam. At mealtime, he maneuvers to sit next to the nicest-looking female resident. He makes poignant little attempts to be social; his new greeting is to click his tongue make his finger and thumb into the shape of a gun and point it at someone he likes.

One day as I'm leaving, I wave and call, "I love you." "I love you too," he calls back. I stop. Tears fill my eyes. It's the first time he's told me that since he got sick. Just then, a man suffering from dementia turns to Dad and asks, "Do you love me too?" Dad pauses and then replies. "Of course I do."

* * *

Finally, Penny arrives. With her aversion to flying, she's taken a beastly long train ride from Los Angeles with Luke, who's now seventeen. He comes through the door first and Dad immediately recognizes him: "Tell me about Penny," he says. When he sees his younger daughter, he holds out his arms joyfully.

Penny and I visit regularly, fixing up his room together, bringing a nightstand and pictures of the family from his home. She gives him detective novels by Ed McBain and Robert B. Parker, not knowing that he can no longer read. He flips through them. "Those are two of your favorite authors, right, Daddy?"

He looks at her and haltingly says, "Ed McBain. I thought he was going to fall in the hole Parker had dug for him . . . but then he was turned loose." Penny stares at him, steps out of the room, and cries.

Chapter Seventeen

Penny is looking through a collection of revolvers in Dad's apartment in Milford; he'd always planned to give her one. I come into the spare room and watch her examining the weapons. A gun is one thing I certainly do not want. "They're all yours," I say to Penny.

"Why, thank you," she replies coldly.

Over the years, Penny's taken some valuable items from my father's house and even sold some heirlooms without my permission. I have to admit, however, that they're nothing compared to the U-Haul full of booty that Bob and I drove away with: the rare Chinese rug, Grandma Leavitt's oval Victorian dining table, some marble-topped tables, and various pieces of memorabilia. This was all at my father's invitation, mind you, since he claimed he could hardly move amid the stuff bulging from the small house we'd moved him into in Hopkinton. At the time, my sister was young, unmarried, and constantly moving, and—in my opinion—in no position to use these things. I never told her, since at that time we weren't speaking. When she found out about it, she was understandably livid. Every item I took must have felt like a nail extracted from her finger.

"Daddy said you made off with half of our heirlooms," she said in an icy voice over the phone. "Why am I not surprised? I've come to expect that of you."

Penny has a quirky personality and a wicked repartee that can reduce me to a delirium of laughter. She also has a hypersonic temper that can zap me right out of body and mind. Since the time she moved out west, we've managed to duplicate the mercurial relationship we had with our mother. We'll go for months, even years, not speaking, then get back together and become inseparably close, chattering on the phone for hours, giggling like kids, and then, inevitably, turning to our favorite topic—the outrageousness of our upbringing. Then, in one swift moment—just when we're sure that our frequent misunderstandings are a vestige of the past—we'll have some rip-roaring fight about a minuscule, but undoubtedly symbolic matter and begin the cycle again. We don't employ the fisticuffs of our youth anymore, but the fallout is equally painful.

One day we had a debate over a gold cross I was wearing. She claimed it was hers and I *knew* it was mine. Exhausted from caring for Amy, a newborn, I simply took it off my neck and gave it to her. We barely spoke for a year after that. I'd been so sure of my position at the time. Only later did it occur to me how often I'd been a teenage raider of Penny's belongings; small wonder she'd pressed her case.

Despite our differences, we have a bond that is sometimes eerie. Even though we're six years apart, we had our first child within months of one another. I'll think of her and suddenly the phone will ring.

During our good times, we'd rather be with each other than with anyone else. We'll calm each other through mammograms, job interviews, our kids' illnesses. Just as she'd supported me during Amy's birth, I flew out to Los Angeles in 1992 when she had Max. Realizing we're in the last half of our lives, Penny and I have lately developed methods of extricating ourselves from the turmoil and carrying on. The cold silences are shorter, the times of good feeling longer.

Now she and I are together again, but the right of possession is once more pulling us apart. It's clear that my father will never return to Milford; it's time to pack up his things and divide them up. The territory is treacherous; what one wants, the other one suddenly craves. Fortunately, Luke has come to the apartment with Penny, and he's a leavening influence.

While Penny examines Dad's gun cabinet, Luke peers inside at the impeccably polished, well-oiled collection and whistles: "Way to go, Grandpa!" A moment of male bonding with a man he's just begun to know. Penny and I look at each other and smile. "It's like he's just found out Dad is Wyatt Earp," Penny quips.

There are things that have gone missing, and slightly suspicious of each other, Penny and I are combining forces to search for them. What we both had coveted for years is a set of Victorian angels that once graced our Wellesley mantelpiece at Christmas. Trumpets and harps held high, the delicately painted porcelain figures sounded silent carols. Penny finally discovers them in a box behind the cellar woodpile. We whoop with delight.

"Oh wow, I can't believe you found them!" I say, running my fingers over their exquisitely detailed robes. "What do you want to do with them? Shall we split them up?" I assume an even division will please her.

Penny looks at me with a hatred I have never seen before. "I don't believe you," she says, shaking her head. Then, without another word, she stalks toward the front door. "Stop!" I shout after her.

"Okay guys, okay guys, chill!" Luke says, but Penny keeps going. She's heading down to the corner to hail a taxi.

At first, I'm mystified, but then I realize she must feel there's nothing I didn't want my fingerprints on, nothing that would be hers alone. I go after her.

"Please come back," I plead. "You can have all the angels. The whole set."

I listen while she confronts me with my removal of so much of our inheritance, as well as a host of other sins I never realized I'd committed. "I want an apology," she says. "And I mean a sincere one. For everything."

"I'm sorry, Penny, I'm really sorry," I tell her over and over. "I love you. I really need you here. Please come back." Finally she does.

While Penny is taking a call in the living room and Luke is sifting through some of Dad's old t-shirts, I open a closet in the spare room. Out tumbles much of my father's paraphernalia: cracked crockery, old jackets and shirts, caps from every sportsman's club in the state. Stacked up in the back of the closet are several cartons full of early Revolutionary War books. Out of idle curiosity, I begin looking through them. At the bottom of one carton is a disintegrating shoe-box containing three thick packs of old letters tied up with red, white, and blue ribbon. I look at the return address and swallow. I've never seen these letters before. They're letters my father wrote my mother during the war.

I hastily replace them, then tiptoe into the living room to find Penny gazing at a portrait of my mother, one of those milky Bachrach debutante photographs that makes the subject look dewy-eyed, moist of mouth, and impossibly young. During one of my Milford visits, Daddy had once found me looking at the same portrait. "That's one beautiful lady," he'd said, much to my surprise, and then, without further explanation, he'd sat down to read the *Boston Herald*.

I pick up the photo and look at it longingly.

"Do you mind if I take that picture of Mom?" asks Penny. I turn around to find her holding a Glock, which is pointed at my knees.

"Not at all," I say. I set the photo back down.

Next to the picture of my mother is one of me that I'd excavated from a junk drawer and put on the table. It's what they call a "Bachrach Junior." I am six and look like an angel, with light shiny hair, big eyes and dimples, the perfect child. Infuriatingly, the picture is speckled with little holes, as though someone had stabbed it with a sharp pencil. The only question is whether my sister did it as a child or an adult.

"By the way," Penny gives me a placid look, "that was a gun collector on the phone. I'm selling a bunch of those pistols. I've also called a book dealer to come and take away all these old books."

I'm about to protest when I remember the letters. They're a lode of archaeological treasure certain to be hotly contested. I quickly return to the spare room and stick the packs behind my shirt and under my belt. "I'm going to get some air," I call and make my way carefully to the door. One of the packs slips halfway down my pant leg and I slither out as though desperate for a bathroom break.

I think of locking the letters in the trunk of my car, so I can go through them at home, but how can I wait that long? I hide behind a tree at the back of the yard and surreptitiously slip the letters out of my pants. I untie a pack, then glance back at the house. I know I'm taking a risk. If my sister sees I've taken them without telling her, there will be a brawl the likes of which the neighborhood has never seen. If I don't tell her, I'll just be perpetuating our fractious history. But if I tell her, I might never see them again. These letters are the past come to life. What if they help solve the enigma of my father's life? I'm the one who's on the quest. I'm the one who can most use these artifacts. And after all, I can always make copies for her. Eventually.

The envelopes are thin and yellowed, edged with the blue and red border of the old airmails. My hands are black from handling the old books, so I wipe them on the grass. Then, very gingerly, I slide a letter out. It's dated November 4, 1943. The envelope bears a six-cent postage stamp and a silhouette of a fighter plane. At the bottom, there's a circle, initialed in pen: "passed by naval censor." It's addressed to "Mrs. Thomas Franks, 1250 Lakeshore Drive, Chicago, Illinois." By then, my parents had been married for about two years and lived in a small apartment on the west side of the city.

I hold the envelope in my hand with trepidation. Perhaps I need to ponder it first, get used to the idea that it exists. The address is inked perfectly, in fountain pen, although the "o" in "Illinois" has bled. I suppose ballpoints hadn't been invented back then. These letters were lifelines. What if the soldiers had run out of ink? What if a company's supply had been bombed and they went up in a shower of black spray?

The letter has been slit at the end, very neatly. How could my mother have stood it? To take the time to go find the opener, to slip it so exactingly into the edge of the envelope, to slice with such exquisite care. I would have torn the damn thing open. And now I take the letter out. A five-franc note from the island of New Caledonia falls out. It's crisp and elaborately decorated.

"Sweetie Pie," it begins. Sweetie Pie? Surely not my father's words. He'd never called his wife anything but Lorraine. Come to think of it, none of us had been called anything more tender than our given names.

Have neglected writing you for exactly ten days—I am very conscience stricken but have been awfully busy getting settled in our new camp. I also am teaching a class in plane identification now—I have to learn it as well as teach it which is not easy.

If the censor will let me, I am going to enclose a piece of the currency from the island we just left, where our mountain camp was. Two days after leaving, we arrived at our present destination. It was sure interesting to review what had happened here a little over a year ago as we sailed between the islands in the same path as our forces did when they first landed here. These are true tropical islands and certainly looked it from the ship. Coconut palm trees line the shore with the jungle and the mountains in the background making a rather menacing picture—I can imagine how our Marines felt when they invaded this island.

We disembarked and were taken to one end of the island to a camp. It is a real jungle camp set back from the shore about two hundred yards . . .

A lot of the palms are broken off about a third to half way up as a result of shell fire when the fighting was raging around here. There are still a lot of trees though and they all have coconuts. If you get real hungry you can go out and pick up a coconut, open it, drink the juice and eat the meat. I have never liked the coconut you buy in stores but this is different. The juice is cool and the meat is very good. I am making myself hungry—pardon me while I go out and pick up a coconut.

There are lots of insects including huge spiders but the most troublesome are the flies.—they appear to be the same kind they have in the states. And just as persistent.

I was cleaning my pistol the other night when something went clank, clank across the metal flooring. I looked down and right into the eyes of a monstrous land crab. It was about the size of a dinner plate with its legs spread out and the body was about the size of a large apple. It sure gave me a start.

Our tents have floors that are made of the metal strip they use for landing mats on airfields. At first, we had only cots with one blanket and mosquito netting. We have since been issued pillows and mattresses. You ought to see me do my washing. I have a little bucket, a washboard, and a bottle of bleach. I wash all my socks, underwear, coveralls, towels, handkerchiefs etc. I can wash a shirt and trousers in no time at all. I use a lot more Kleenex than I used to.

I got your letter about going west to Arizona or California, before leaving for this island. The only thing against it is that if I should get back suddenly I would want to head for the middle west and if you had a job in the west you couldn't pull up and leave on a moment's notice. So unless you have something really good in view, I wouldn't go.

I haven't gotten a letter from you for about three weeks— there must be an awful stack of them somewhere—it will be a lot of fun to get them all at once.

I miss you awfully, sweetheart and I can hardly wait until I can see you again. I love you so very much precious.

Bye now
Tom

p.s. There is a hint in this letter. See if you can spot it. Use a map.

I'm stunned. I have to read the letter again. I stare at the tiny, cheer-ful letters, the loopy "d"s, "p"s, and "t"s, the fine elegant slanting script, the "b"s and "h"s bending over happily. Wait—this isn't my father's writing. His hand was always straight, even tense, his letters intersect-ing perfectly, like a map of arrows leading nowhere.

Was my mother having an affair with some other Tom? No. I run my finger across the return address: "Lt (j.g.) T. Franks, U.S. Naval Argus #14, F.P.O. San Francisco." My mother was having a love affair with my father.

I quickly take letter after letter out and look at the endings: "I love love love you," "I think about you all the time," "The other guys go out to find women, but I stay and look at your picture all night," "I can't tell you how much you mean to me precious." I'd never heard my parents call each other a name more loving than "Icklebick." But here, after two years of marriage, my father appears to go weak just thinking about her. They did love each other. They had loved each other passionately. Once. Before I was born, before I could wish and pray for it, it had been.

On the back of the envelope, my mother has apparently written lat-itude and longitude numbers. That must have been my Dad's "hint," an indication of his whereabouts hidden somewhere in the text. A se-cret code; he was using a secret code! Among the letters is a tattered war map that shows the Pacific in detail, including the countries that owned or had captured certain islands. I'm directionally challenged, so it's with difficulty that I trace the coordinates on the map. Finally my fingers land right smack on Guadalcanal. My father must have been attached to a division that was sent to hold and mop up the island that the Marines captured a year back. "Guadal" was the base from which the Allies set out to hopscotch up the Solomon Islands. He implies that he's part of a small group that goes up to a camp at the end of the island.

I sit with letters piled up all over me, happy that there's no breeze to blow them away. But I have an odd prickling sensation. Is it guilt? Or fear? I look back at my father's back door. No sign, thank goodness, of my sister.

I pick out a few letters dated the summer of 1943, which bear the return address of Port Hueneme, California. These were apparently written before Dad was shipped out to the Pacific.

"Darling," one read,
I have been about as busy as I ever have before and I have walked so much on the hardpacked ground that my hip and groin are terrifically sore. I have been working until 8:30 or 9:30 every evening . . . the way to fix the Japanese would be to let some of their spies roam around Port Hueneme. They would get so confused by all the contradictory information that they wouldn't get untangled before the war is over. In the last week, my plans have been changed several times. First, I was going to leave Tuesday; then at the end of the week; then it was today. I have just been informed I am going to San Diego Sunday morning at 5:30.—what an awful hour. I have gotten to the point that if somebody came in right now and said I had to leave in fifteen minutes I wouldn't bat an eye.

What this San Diego deal will mean I don't know. I've had so many completely unexpected courses of training, that nothing would surprise me.

Please pass these letters on to my folks as I haven't written them. Writing letters is quite a problem—besides being busy and working late—the lights are turned out at 9:30 by an officer who outranks us. He also gets up an hour early in the morning, turns on the lights, and shaves with an electric razor. There is no place to go to write letters, there is no place to go period. There is no officers clubs, reading rooms, or anything. There is nothing here but Quonset huts. We live just like the enlisted men.

Will write you from San Diego. I miss you awfully and love you very much.

Tom

It makes me smile to hear him complaining about the lack of officers' quarters, the miseries of getting up early, his sore hip, his sore groin. This scribe is a tenderfoot. The Dad I know is a stoic. When did he become one? What happened in San Diego?

All of the return addresses put him in one Argus unit or another. The Argus units were mentioned in the orders I'd found earlier. One letter, from his base in Port Hueneme, seemed to imply he had a lot of clout for a lowly ensign and had some kind of special assignment: "I went to the Commander of the Argus units and had a showdown about why we have been here in Hueneme so long . . . this precipitated calls to Washington and conferences with the captain of the base." Another letter told of working under "adverse conditions at an anti-aircraft training center . . . there is continuous firing, black specks of powder everywhere . . . my face is like a beet and my nose a boiled frankfurter."

One letter dated September 11, 1943, also from Hueneme, is packed with colorful details:

Dearest Spousie,

Received a very pleasant surprise when I went to the Argus headquarters and found seven letters from you . . . They had been sent all over the base for some reason—I haven't read them yet—I am going to save them and read one every day I don't get a letter from you. You have no idea how I like to get your letters so please keep on writing them often.

My orders came through yesterday changing me from Argus 5 to Argus 13. So it is now definitely settled that I will go out with Argus 13. All of the equipment and some of the officers are leaving tomorrow.

It is rumored that we will go to San Francisco to take a ship out from there. I will try to call you from Frisco before I leave . . . it is almost impossible to get a call out of the base. There are only four telephones in one hut that the thousands of officers and men here can use. They are in constant use day and night. The boys

around here will set alarm clocks to get up at 3 and 4:00 A.M.
to try to get calls through. Even then there will be a line at each
phone. If I don't get to call you that will be the reason . . . .

The letter says that he had his heart set on doing some fishing in
the Pacific Ocean before he went overseas and he met a family who
took him in tow on the beach.

I went with them and had more damn fun riding a surf board
they had. I stayed for dinner and afterward played "Squeal" with
his wife and their three daughters. Two of the daughters were in
high school and the third was entering college this fall. The girls
were cute but giggly and played Squeal with all the sound effects.
Squeal is a game where each person has a deck and plays
solitaire but you can play on other people's aces and you yell
"squeal" when you are out. We played about twenty games—I
won once. About nine thirty they took me all the way back to
the base so I didn't have to hitch rides back in the dark. That
day was the first time I really enjoyed myself since I have been
out here.
In your letter #33, you mention that I haven't answered
some of your questions. I thought I had . . . let me know what
they are and I will answer them immediately.
I miss you so much, darling and wish I could see you if only
for a little while.

> *I love you, darling*
> *Tom*

P.S. Don't have time to read this over so if there are mistakes,
ignore them.

The letter has been turned to page eight and has a fresh, just-read
quality. I imagine my mother sitting on the stoop of their Chicago

apartment building, forgetting to put the pages back in order, holding the letter in the sun, stretching like a kitten beneath the warmth of his "darlings" and "I love you's." But then I see her face clouding. Her jealous nature asserting itself. Her husband is going out to sea, into danger, and she, unable to kiss and hug him good-bye, has to hear how much fun he's having with other women, sheer strangers.

I can hear those "cute" teenage girls squealing and my father laughing. He seldom laughed in our house. He never laughed in our house. How is it possible that throughout my teenage and college years, he never once cracked open a deck of cards and called to me, "Let's play a game of Squeal?" I would have loved to play Squeal.

How many times had my father been a part of another family? How many of his business trips were vacations with Pat and her two boys? The boys Mother always claimed my father really wanted? It was always the same: I never knew anything for sure.

I turn to see my sister at the back door, looking around. Quickly, I squeeze through a row of bushes that divide the property. She goes back in. This is absurd, but at least I'm safe for a few more letters. I riffle through them as though they were letters informing me whether I'll live or die. I find one dated August 20, 1943, from Port Hueneme.

Darling:

There is a USO show at the base this evening and an officers dance at Ventura 10 miles away. They are all away at one or the other. The officers' dance advertisement stated there would be 100 beautiful girls to dance with. I would rather stay home and write to my favorite girlfriend.

I am enclosing a very crude sketch of a Quonset hut such as we live in. They are about thirty feet long and about fifteen feet wide. The construction is of corrugated steel plate lined with Masonite inside and a wooden floor that is heavily oiled to keep the dust down. The result being that anything that is dropped

on the floor is black when you pick it up—from the combination
dust and oil. Jack Steele dropped his cap with a clean cover on
it. It was black when he picked it up—he was fit to be tied.

If I had only known how long I was going to be here, it
would have been wonderful to have you here. You would be
crazy about California. I sure miss you, darling, and wish you
were here.

The letter goes on to describe the bedside table he'd fashioned
out of an orange crate to put her picture on, explained how he didn't
need the money he was getting and would send it to her, advised her
on domestic matters. Then, on the last page, he wrote:

I was awfully sorry to hear about the miscarriage. I wish I could
tell you how I feel. Just think when I got back we would have
had a little baby in our family. That on top of your tooth must
have made you feel miserable—I wish I could have been with
you darling. When I get back we will try again to have a baby.

It is getting awfully cold so I am going to "hit the sack"—
that in English means "going to bed." A person who likes to
sleep is known as a "sackhound."

I sure do miss you, sweet, and I love you very much,

Tom

A miscarriage. I was always told I was a miracle baby, the first one
who didn't miscarry, and now here's a mention of the first one who
did. My father was tenderly calling up what could have been his child,
expressing his grief as well as his difficulty in doing so. But I wondered
whether my mother, who was overly sensitive to any slight, had been
put off by his not mentioning such a traumatic event at the beginning of his letter, instead of waiting for the end and then chasing it
with a joke about being a "sackhound." And would the very mention

of the hundred beautiful USO girls have made my insecure mother feel even more miserable, even if my father had written that he'd rather be with her? She was, after all, a woman living by herself, depending on her husband's affections. Was this where their troubles began, with artless impromptu letters bound to be misunderstood?

Now I find a letter that is exciting. Dated September 26, 1943, it begins,

> *I cannot say a single word about my present surroundings or what I am doing or where I am. I will be able to write you later explaining everything, or nearly everything.*
>
> *I asked the censor if I could tell you it's hot. It is HOT— stinking hot . . . The St. Elmo medal you gave me burns my bare chest, that's how hot it is.*
>
> *Your picture that adorned my orange crate that was a dresser at Port Hueneme, it is a real dresser now—not quite as steady as it was in PH, however (hint) . . . how about some snapshots or aren't you ready to send them?*

A letter five days later says, "I can't tell you anything except that I'm enjoying myself and living a life of luxury, comparatively speaking. I'm enclosing a menu for the dinner we had tonight. I had to cut the censorable name off the card."

I feel a stirring. I think of the OSS's training centers in elaborate estates in the countryside outside Washington, D.C. Dad had admitted undergoing a lot of training in the area. Some men and women worked hard during the day and luxuriated in comfort at night. Could this letter hint at what I've so long suspected but that Daddy never confirmed—that he'd attended one of those spy mills?

The next dated letter contains snapshots of sailors dressed as women, grinning, raising their glasses to toast Tom for "crossing the equator." The next one says, "Now arrived at an island in the South Pacific, arrived on a luxury liner that was made into a naval transport."

I feel foolish. He'd simply been on a ship that had transported him overseas, complete with a trembling seafaring dresser.

The letter goes on to relate his good fortune: "The island has a pleasant climate, like Southern California. My camp is in the beautiful mountains. It's a way station, not a combat zone . . . it's a grand outing—fishing, hiking, hunting, a stream for bathing." I find myself feeling ridiculously irritated with my father. I'm tired of reading accounts that sound more like summer camp than the pitched battles I know he took part in. When will he get to the "real war"?

I pull out a letter dated November 17, 1943:

Sweetheart,

Just a note on our anniversary to let you know I am thinking of you and that I miss you very much . . . our gear has finally arrived and there will be a lot more to do before our unit will be able to function as it should.

. . . a letter from you finally trickled through. There was no number on it, but it was dated October 24 so I am sure there are a lot of your letters piling up someplace . . . by the way, where is that photo you were going to send me—is it on the way or aren't you ready to send it?

. . . I am an O.O.D. today and sitting in the headquarters tent. It's rather warm except for a slight breeze. Rather warm means that your clothes are only damp with perspiration, when it is hot you are wringing wet. You noticed that I used Navy time—if you have a uniform and associate with Navy Officers I can't use anything but Navy time in my letters.

. . . I sure miss you, honey, and I want to see you so badly. Past Sunday morning I couldn't help thinking about how we used to have "Hunt" breakfasts with a couple of martinis first then go home and read the Sunday papers. Wouldn't that be fun now?

. . . I have to go now—there is a big boa constrictor looking over my shoulder and I will have to clean my gun after shooting him . . . I love you, darling, please keep on writing me long let-

ters because they mean an awful lot to me . . . All my love
which is lots and lots and lots, sweetheart. I miss you.

Tom

It's interesting that Dad kept asking whether my mother was ready to send a photograph. Perhaps she'd promised to go on a diet because she'd already started gaining weight. How sad that she couldn't send him the picture he wanted so badly.

But here, shoved in one of the packets of letters, is the promised photograph. It's Lorraine, bundled in a long coat with a Red Cross pin on the collar. She's already begun her volunteer work driving supplies and wounded soldiers around Chicago. Her fingers peep out from the bulky sleeves. She looks plump but not terribly heavy, and her round face and full lips are sensuous. On the back of the picture she has written, "Just ignore my 'fat' hands, please!"

What "gear" was Dad waiting for before his unit could function? He'd told me earlier that he watched for enemy aircraft in Guadalcanal. I knew there were Australian coast-watchers who settled on small islands and, with the help of the natives, obtained secret information about Japanese positions and kept alert for the sound and sight of Japanese planes speeding toward an Allied base. When a coast-watcher saw one, he radioed the information to the base so the plane could be taken out before it dropped its bombs. Coast-watchers were heroic, living in constant danger under subhuman conditions. In the beginning, most coast-watchers were Australians planted in isolated islands, but later in the war, Marine personnel were added and the coast-watchers were called the Allied Intelligence Bureau. I think about the name "Argus"— that giant with a hundred eyes who never sleeps. Who always watches. Was being a coast-watcher part of Dad's spy work?

Letter by letter, I go down deeper into history. It's strange, exhilarating to see my father as a young, complete man—his words resonate, I can touch the moments. My mother has been dead for decades, but in these letters she's the wife of a besotted new husband. My father now lies curled in the bed of a halfway house, dried-up, dying, but here I find him swimming fast through the rapids of life.

Discovering these letters changes everything. All along, before the horrors of war, before he had shut down and turned to Pat, it was Lorraine whom Tom had loved. I feel like shouting for my sister. Instead I simply rub my hands together so rapidly that twenty blurred fingers appear. If my life had run backward, my prayers would have been answered.

I put the letters back together and tie them up with the ribbon. They're not only full of brio, they're full of clues. They will give me the atlas I've longed for to chart my father's secret journeys as a spy.

At the very moment that I believed that I'd lost Dad, I've found him again: his real character, his words, his jokes, his worries—an unfastened man, a man brimming with feeling, one who dashes about, loves passionately, shows his vulnerability. I see him through eyes that have no memory.

Chapter Eighteen

Penny has to go back to California. We've packed up Daddy's apartment, turning it over to the landlord, and finished dividing his belongings. For once, no cartons full of our ancestral portion will go with him: only a bathrobe, some pictures, and a few plaid shirts. My sister has trouble extracting herself from his room at the halfway house, for she knows, even if he doesn't, that this is the last time she will ever see him.

"Bye, Dad," she says, leaning over to kiss him. No response. "Dad, good-bye!" she says more loudly, waving her hand in front of his face. He turns over, curls up into the fetal position, and appears to go to sleep. She walks to the door, goes out, and then comes back in.

"Bye, Dad!" she calls, her voice breaking. "I love you!"

The next day, he's sitting up in the common room, behaving every bit like the chivalrous gentleman. Pat the housekeeper comes to visit, and we're joking around about all the girls who love Dad.

I point to Pat. "Is that your number one, number two, or number three woman?" I ask.

"All three," he says, without missing a beat. He loves it when Pat visits; a smoker herself, she takes him outdoors for a roll around the block—and a couple of smokes. Once, when they come back, he silently puts his head on his arms, which are resting on his tray table. She sees his fingers wiggling and, thinking he's waving good-bye, says, "I'm not leaving, Tom," but he keeps wiggling them. Then it dawns on her; she reaches out and takes his fingers in her own, and he hangs on tight.

One evening, when I kiss him and smooth his hair, still soft, still the color of almonds, he takes both my hands. He looks hard at me, sad, resigned, and whispers, "Say, you *will* get me out of here, won't you?" But he has nowhere to go and somehow he must know it; somewhere he knows all his possessions, even his beloved guns, have vanished, along with his home. Yet he never mentions his illness, never asks about his apartment, never acknowledges where he is or how long he'll be there—and neither do I.

I've skimmed most of the letters and sorted them by date and year, from 1943 to 1946. With my father now hanging on to the edges of reality, I've been taking them out, savoring them. They're a forbidden pleasure. I haven't told anyone they exist, not even Bob. Who would understand how completely I enter into the intimacy of their universe?

I've been going back and forth from Milford to New York and right now I'm home. Everyone is asleep, so I put on my study lamp and take out the packets of letters I've hidden in my desk. I reread one from November 14, 1943.

Darling:

Just a note to let you know how I am. Your letters have been coming through fine. The three things that brighten life around here are mail from you, cold fruit juices at mealtime, and our shower . . . .

Sweetheart I am enclosing a money order for $60.00 for Christmas presents for our families. That will be enough to buy at least a $10 present for each one. If there is any left over you might spend it on other Xmas expenses.

Must stop suddenly. I miss you very much and can hardly wait until I see you again.

All my love,
Tom

"Must stop suddenly." Was there an odd rustling in the palm trees? Or had he caught sight of an enemy plane coming in from far away? I imagine him on that woebegone desert island, lining up, taking his pittance of a paycheck and somehow getting a money order home, just so there would be Christmas presents for his family. Christmas? He hated Christmas. He never bought presents for anyone, let alone as early as mid-November! To save my mother's feelings, I would buy presents labeled "From Tom to Lorraine" and put them under the tree. I don't think Mother was ever fooled, but she sat there, nose in the air, and never said a word.

There are several letters on Seabees letterhead in late October and November of 1943, which make me curious. I'd heard of the "Fighting Seabees." Bob's read up on them; they weren't just some auxiliary construction crew; they were some of the bravest soldiers on the front lines. They rebuilt airways moments after the Japanese bombed them, dug docks, built bridges and tunnels, and often put themselves more in harm's way than the average GI. The Japanese made them priority targets, aiming to stop them from rebuilding these vital hot spots. The Seabees also took part in the fighting, rebuilding broken machine guns and using the blades of their bulldozers to crush Japanese pillboxes during island invasions. Their symbol was, appropriately, a bee holding a tommy gun.

One of my father's Seabees letters is wistful: "Got your letter about going to New York. If your Father goes with you, as planned, be sure to take him to the Divan Parisien for some of their Chicken

Divan and to the Brown Derby for a look at their cha-cha floor show."
Who *was* this club-hopping bon vivant?

Here, on another envelope, are more coordinates: "Longitude: E
167 Latitude S 22." And inside there's a strange non sequitur: "I got
separated from a piece of baggage of mine." There's also so much
enigmatic talk about the weather, in this and other letters, that I think
it must be key to understanding the code Dad and Mother devised.
I want to see if I can crack it. I attempt to deconstruct the sentence,
trying various word substitutes, even anagrams, but get nowhere. At
least I can find the place on the old war map: Noumea, New Caledonia, in the "French Loyalty Islands." Ah yes, in Milford, I'd found
the currency notes from Noumea. And the dates and contents of the
letters indicate Dad was there for at least two weeks, undergoing even
more undisclosed training. As a Seabee, perhaps?

Another Seabee letter tells of my father suddenly being pulled out
of his camp in the mountains and put on a ship bound for an undisclosed place. He keeps writing the phrase "A little later," unnecessarily. Code, again? Do the three "l"s in a "little later" stand for latitude
and longitude?

Then I discover a letter written a month later to my mother's father, Henry Leavitt: "We will be moving up the line soon" and "will
see a great deal of action." He asks Henry not to needlessly worry Lorraine with the news. I wonder whether he'd sent the letter to her then
or after the war. Was this when Dad went to Bougainville, which had
been taken by the Marines in a long bloody battle in November
of '43? The Seabees built airstrips there that were crucial for the
Bougainville bombing of Rabaul, a strategic Japanese stronghold.

That's the last letter from 1943. I take out the 1944 pack. The first
eight, written in early January, are "V-mails," miniature, one-page
notes. It must have been the military's way of saving space and weight
in mailbags. The first one talks of Dad's Christmas in the South Pacific. My father thanks my mother profusely for the presents she sent,
and sends her a card showing a GI and a native with a spear looking
up at Santa Claus flying through the air on jet propulsion.

On February 3, he's clearly back in Guadalcanal. He tells of being a censor and reading the letters of enlisted men, which talk about "air raids that we don't have and battles we haven't had . . . This is one I heard today—it's a classic. They caught an army man in Noumea sending a jeep home. He had completely dismantled it and was slowly shipping the pieces as his own gear."

While on Guadalcanal, Dad shows the ingenuity that characterized the rest of his life. His men, existing on paltry, unappetizing K-rations, are hungry. One day he is snorkeling when he comes across a giant clam the size of a washtub wedged in some sharp, branching coral reef. He gets a rope, a block of wood, and a canoe with three men. The "razor sharp and I do mean razor sharp" scalloped edges of the clam are open and they shove the wood inside and the clam bites it in two. "If you ever put your arm or leg in one of them accidentally, it would be all over . . . by diving down twenty feet with the canoe paddles, we finally looped the rope around one end of it and pried it loose with the paddles. We worked for an hour and a half and the pressure on our ears was so painful that all you could work at one time was twenty seconds or so. And there was a shark swimming back and forth watching us." They finally haul the clam into the canoe; it weighs about two hundred pounds and Dad makes chowder that feeds thirty-five men. He draws an intricate picture in the letter to illustrate the event.

In fact, a number of letters have imaginative, whimsical drawings of tents, the barracks shower, the jungle, coconut trees. I'd never seen my father draw a thing.

A letter dated February 7 intrigues me because he seems to be worrying about everybody worrying about him:

*Darling, when I left Chicago, I didn't know anything about
what an Argus unit did. If I had known I would have told you.
You have the right idea in not mentioning it to my folks, they
would worry needlessly. Please don't worry about me, precious,
because it's going to be all right . . . our strength is growing out*

here daily. We blasted the Marshalls, we can pulverize an
island before invading it . . .

. . . Please don't forget to keep writing me long letters
because getting your letters are the brightest spots in my life.
I love you I love you I love you very much, precious, and I al-
ways will.

"I always will." How certain he seemed. I reach for a stack of black and white candids I'd salvaged in a Milford carton bound for the dumpster. My mother and father sitting on the couch smiling at each other, laughing, making goofy faces. My mother's ample bosom straining at her dress, which is patterned in big William Morris leaves. His hair, parted into two lustrous wings, looking in her direction, as though astonished at her perfection. And on her face: a smile of sheer happiness. He wears a smoking jacket with white piping down the wide lapels and a white lily in his pocket. In one picture, his lips form a silly pucker and out come perfect smoke rings bound to impress his wife. In another, there is a blur of hands as though they're wrestling, and in the last, my favorite, his arm is tight around her shoulders, cradling her, and he's looking down, exquisitely proud. She tilts back her head, with its dark satiny hair. A woman yielding.

I put the pictures down and take up a letter dated February 1944. My father says he's been detached from Argus for some kind of mission on a nearby island under the command of an admiral. A V-mail dated March 2 says he was offered a position aboard the flagship of a cruiser task force but his unit's commanding officer, who said he was the best officer under his command, wouldn't let him go. Mother must have been so proud.

In the next letter, postmarked March 9, though, I see signs of dissension between my parents. My mother is apparently jealous of the attention her friend Doris gets from her husband, Bill, who's in my father's unit. My father writes defensively about how Bill comes into the shack where he censors letters every morning, and "scrawls about 25 words on paper, drops it in the pile to be censored, and walks out—the whole process taking about three minutes . . . I said I had been hearing from you about how frequently he writes Doris. All of the guys spoke up in a chorus and said 'Well, if I was his wife I would rather get nothing than his letters.' Bill writes his wife v-mails exclusively . . . I stopped using v-mails after you told me you didn't like them as well as airmails. From now on, I will write only v-mails—maybe you will get them quicker." Then he writes "I love you, I love you, I love you, even if I don't write as often as I should" and tells her that he got her a cat's-eye bracelet like Bill got for Doris.

He mentions in this letter that he's been promoted from ensign to lieutenant, junior grade. He says it's "damn cold," so he must have left the heat of Guadalcanal for somewhere up north, probably to invade a Japanese island: "Have been awfully busy lately—everybody in the unit has. You can read between the lines . . . after our operation is over and we are relieved by the army there is a chance I may get back to the states, but don't count on it."

The next letter, dated March 19, gives me chills of apprehension. My father is on an LSD, a landing ship dock, which holds tanks and soldiers, on a long journey from the island where he's stationed, to invade island "X":

> . . . Tomorrow morning is D-Day (invasion or landing day) . . . an addition to our task force just showed up over the horizon, it consists of aircraft carrier, cruisers, etc., that makes our force a really powerful one. There are a lot of our planes circling overhead so we have plenty of protection. I love you terribly much and I miss you so very much. Write me lots of letters, sweet. I LOVE YOU. P.S. Get in touch with my folks as I will have time to write them a short note only. PPS. There will undoubtedly be a gap in my letters so don't worry if you don't get another one for awhile.

The writing is scratchy, hurried. D-Day. An island invasion. This is a story whose ending I know but don't know. On the back of the envelope is written "East—150 degrees, South—2 degrees." I take out three atlases and waste an hour trying to find where 2 degrees is. Finally, I figure out that he must be northwest of Bougainville, close to the equator, near the Admiralty Islands in the Bismarck Archipelago. Ah, this was Emirau, an invasion that was expected to be bloody, but when my father and the Marines arrived, the Japanese were nowhere to be found. The next letter reads:

> . . . *the landing was just like the movies, warships laying off shore, landing barges scuttling back and forth from the transports to the beachhead, amphibious tanks rolling up on shore, Marines plunging into the jungle . . . Anyway I have had the thrill of making a beachhead. My outpost crew came in here on D-Day with the Marine Raiders—which I got a big bang out of. After landing I took my team, which consists of eight Marines and four sailors and handles some specialized portable gear, up the beach to a point of land and set up camp. The main body of the unit went in a different direction and is some distance from us, for which I am happy because I am in complete charge here and can run my camp as I please . . .*
>
> *We are living in a rather primitive way . . . A year ago, if anybody had told me I could take a pail of water and have a complete bath out of it, I would have laughed at them. Believe it or not, from one canvas bucket of water I take a bath, wash my hair and shave and am quite happy about it because less than a week ago I was having to do the same thing on two hel-metfuls. By the way, we use our helmets for everything, as a wash basin, to cook in, to dig with, etc. etc.*

So I know that Argus is an independent group that has its own private camp, watches for enemy planes and clearly does other intelligence work, but beyond that I undoubtedly know less than my mother did.

The next two letters give me pause.

"Sweetheart," he writes on April 16, having just gotten two letters from her, "there is no need for hinting about things such as where I am. <u>Your letters to me are not censored and nobody sees them but me</u> so you can say whatever you want."

And then, on April 20, he writes a letter apparently in reaction to her questions about why other soldiers she knew were coming home.

You said in your last letter Did they ask for volunteers to return to the States? I nearly fell over backward when I read it. When I recovered from the shock I read your question to some other officers in the tent with me. They became actually hysterical. If there are two million men out here and they asked for volunteers to go back to the States, there would be two million volunteers as well as fights and mass murders to see who would go back . . . there isn't anyone out here who wouldn't lie, steal, or cut his best friend's throat to get back to the States and that includes your hubby. If there is any way I can finagle it I am sure going to do it.

What did my mother think of the fact that her husband read her love letter out loud so all the boys could have a good laugh? Poor Mother. Or did he do it out of shock: Did his wife actually believe he'd rather stay in that hellhole than come home to her? Perhaps all the men were laughing ruefully because they wanted so desperately to come home. It's hard not to imagine he's mocking her. But his letters to her have been so loving, so respectful. Was this the first of many painful attacks?

If I'd been Mother in this situation, I would have gone right to the censor's office and found out that, in fact, domestic letters *were* indeed censored; many enemy spies operating within the U.S. were uncovered solely because of coded letters they'd sent abroad. I would have found out exactly what the criteria were for soldiers to return home. I would have shot off a letter, listing all the backbreaking work I was doing for the war effort. It's a pity I have none of my Mother's letters to my father, but I imagine that in her youth she yielded to his authority, absent of her later bitterness. She would never have found the courage to take any such actions; she would have wound herself up in a cocoon of self-recrimination.

I imagine her after reading the letter, waiting in line for her ration books. She sees the other women dressed in "Patriotic Chic," the new fashion that conserves fabric by cutting the clothes narrowly. The three-piece suits, cuffs, flounces are gone. Of course, she can't fit into those straight skirts, nor the scandalous new two-piece bathing suits, not now anyway. So she just wears her big old clothes.

Tom's right. She cringes at the sight of a poster in the rationing office that shows a dead soldier with the caption "He died today. What did you do?" She should be thankful that she has a husband who's alive and uninjured. She should go home and take all her Bundt cake and brownie pans and drive to Brooklyn to the big pen they have for donations of aluminum and metal wares. It's amazing; they can make lipstick tubes into bullet casings, one shovel into four hand grenades, bacon grease into ammunition, and the aluminum foil from gum wrappers into aircraft.

She's going to keep her Red Cross job driving all those boys with suppurating wounds and shattered limbs to the rehabilitation unit. It's terribly depressing and she's dead tired at night, but she will not quit, as Tom suggested she do. The war effort needs her.

Tom's letters have her coming and going. How can he make her feel so small and naive, and then shower her with so many declarations of love? Why is it so farfetched to suppose the FBI would censor letters going overseas? The government is constantly warning you not to talk about your loved ones overseas. The enemy could be as near as your next-door neighbor, that's why they say, "Loose lips sink ships."

And why *shouldn't* she ask if they took volunteers to return home? Tom *wanted* to go to the Pacific. He *wanted* an advance base. He told her so. Was it really so dumb of her to think that some people wanted to be there? Seeing those other men coming home made her think perhaps he didn't love her enough to come home. Oh, she's a boob, he's right. But it's just that she misses him so much, the smell and feel and sight of him. She's so lonely. He's been away some nine months now. The time it takes to have a baby. It's worn them both down, made them irritable. And he must be exhausted too, deprived of normal comforts, maybe traumatized by the shooting, killing, patrols of Japanese making surprise attacks. As soon as she gets her ration book, she'll go home and write him. She'll say she was just being ridiculously facetious. She'll begin the letter "My dearest dearest love."

The light from a nearly full moon streams through my window. I have to get up early to get the kids off, but I can't stop reading. Here's a letter from May 3, in which Dad tells the tale of Oscar, the lizard, complete with a humorous sketch. The lizards there, he says, are rather shy and run away if you approach them.

"Oscar, however, made friends with me all by himself. He climbs up on my sack around ten o'clock every day . . . and crawls all over me very unconcerned. If I have my knees in the air he will often perch on top of one of them and snag flies as they go by. He usually leaves around three in the afternoon and goes back to the jungle." Later, he writes "Oscar didn't show up today—maybe he had a date with his girlfriend and was too busy. I'll bet he wasn't half as busy as I will be the next time I have a date with you."

A date, eh? I'm surprised by this rather frank reference to love-making, given my mother's distaste for it.

The paper in the next letter is stiff, disintegrating. My father goes on for six pages describing in great detail the island of New Caledonia, its appalling slovenliness, the different races, and their costumes and customs: "The Javanese women wear a skirt that almost reaches the ground and looks like it is just the cloth wound around them. They walk several steps behind their men, who are liable to appear in anything from an ice cream suit to a pair of overalls." Reading his wide-eyed descriptions of this Third World town, I realize how young and untraveled he is. He hasn't been to Ohrdruf yet, hasn't seen what men are really capable of.

Whenever he mentions alcohol, he seems to go out of his way to assure her that he isn't drinking too much. I can't tell whether he actually is. He writes that he went to the officers' club and got a "mild buzz on, but was home in the sack by ten . . . Tomorrow night our C.O.

is giving a dinner for the officers and I will probably have a little as there will be quite a lot of liquor flowing. It's something I have to go to and can't decline like the usual excursions into the officers' club to throw back drinks with both hands." Had their addictions taken hold by then—his on alcohol, hers on food? I doubt they ever talked about it.

Then he writes, "One thing I have been very appreciative of though, darling, and that is the fact that all your letters are cheerful, you never gripe, carp, or needle." Being a censor, he says he reads the most awful letters men get from their wives and cites the example of one recipient.

I have been expecting him to write a letter any day telling her to go straight to hell . . . she should be shaken until her teeth rattle. No matter what anybody says life out here isn't fun and you get on edge and short tempered easily and frequently for no reason at all. Something in a letter that you don't like or understand you brood about it for weeks. You don't know how glad I am that you write nice letters, darling, they make me awfully happy . . . .

I got your letter the other day that ended with your saying how much you miss Junior. You have absolutely no idea how much Junior misses you. All I have to do is think about you and Junior begins to react—I could write a whole book about how much Junior misses you. He certainly has a lot of lost time to make up for when I get home.

I do a double take. *Junior?* This makes the "date" mentioned a few letters ago seem positively Victorian. So my prudish mother hadn't merely lain back and "dreamed of Venice." Instead, she'd named his penis! And declared she missed it! You didn't have such pet names unless you had sex, and a lot of it. My father had even promised a virtual orgy when he returned home. For the first time, I step out of my intense identification with my parents. I can hardly imagine them falling hungrily into each other's arms. Not once did I see even a spontaneous hug between them, although I once overheard Mother tell Dad, "It's important that you kiss me good-bye in the morning in front of Cindy."

Even at my young age, I recognized the resulting perfunctory pecks as phony, and the ritual was quickly abandoned. *Junior.* What next?

I reluctantly put the letter down and go on to the next one: August 1944. Daddy has landed in what, according to my calculations, is probably Guadalcanal to join the Argus 14 group,

> *. . . the same type of organization as Argus 13 . . . Sometime in the future 14 will go in on an operation just as 13 did . . . I have seen all the plans and know all about it and I am not trying just to make you feel better; it actually will be much much easier than the 'push' 13 went on and that was easy enough . . . .*

In a later letter, he says,

> *Some time in the future there will be a break in my letters . . . Don't Worry, it's an easy operation but the circumstances are different from Emirau so there will be a longer time before you hear from me. In fact, this could be my last letter for some time. Seems like I've been separated from you for years, instead of 14 months. Junior thinks we have been separated ten times that long.*

Junior again! Did this make my mother blush as much as it made me? No, of course not, Junior was her creation.

After September 9, there's a gap in his letters and then my father's at sea, "on board an invasion transport." My calculations tell me he's on the way to the brutal battle of Peleliu, which took place on September 15, 1944. He offers up a quaint treatise on the men's pervasive "foul language":

> *Along that line a funny incident happened at an officers wardroom on Bougainville . . . a USO girl asked an officer if he was able to get much liquor out here and he answered "No, not much, just this fucking beer." When he realized what he had said he turned a dull shade of gray and was completely paralyzed—unable to say anything at all or even move . . . the*

naughty word is the most commonly used profanity for some reason. Its use as an adjective is almost universal . . . Everybody wonders just how many of that kind of stunt he is going to pull when he goes back.

By the way, he writes,

When you see newsreels of the Marines charging up on the beach with fixed bayonets they aren't running to get at the Japs they are running as fast as they can to get away from the troop transports that brought them.

    Dearest, you mentioned some time ago about going out to the west coast to live with Barb. There is nothing wrong with that except that it is possible that we might not make connections there.

I feel my mother's irritation: He's trying to control her. He's not forbidding her to do anything outright, but he's subtly undermining her wishes, encouraging her to stop working at the Red Cross, discouraging her from moving out of Chicago to Arizona to seek adventure elsewhere. Now he's discouraging her from moving to the West Coast to be nearby in case there's a chance of seeing him, just as he'd done when she wanted to move near Port Hueneme. And, in a letter from 1945, I found out that she wanted to go overseas with the WAVES but that he wouldn't hear of it. She wants to be closer, but he seems to be pushing her away. Does he even realize he's doing it?

    Yet their love is still palpable. On November 12 he writes a letter timed to get to her by November 17,

. . . which you may remember as a very significant date. It's awfully hard to celebrate our anniversary alone—I would give anything if I could just be home for that day only, sweetheart . . . think how much fun we could have if we were together. Just think, we would go to the Empire Room and then make a round of places like the Camellia room, etc., getting slightly plastered

on the way, or it would be just as much fun sitting quietly at
home. Just anyplace would do as long as we were together.

By the way, darling, I will bet that you do not know what
anniversary this is. Don't go look it up—it is our Silk Anniver-
sary. I wish there was something made of silk I could send you,
precious, but the only thing on this dammed island is palm trees
and insects.

This would be their third anniversary not their "silk" or twelfth anniversary. My careful father had been uncharacteristically careless. I'm sure that now he's on the island of Ulithi, an atoll farther north in the Western Caroline Islands that served as a key fleet anchorage. It was so tiny, however, that I'm sure my father couldn't find a snippet of silk to send her.

I didn't know my mother had ever written a poem until I read Daddy's November 24 letter.

I enjoyed the poem you wrote in your letter, sweet,—did you
really feel that way about me leaving. I sure hated to leave you
too, darling . . . the poem about the Red Cross was sure
funny—I read it to my tentmates . . . your little v-mail poem
was cute, honey. Did you make it up all yourself? If so, we have
a budding young poetess in our family. The lights have gone out
and I am finishing this by the aid of a flashlight.

Is he being sincere or condescending here? Pat had described his careful critiques of her poetry. Did he look down his nose at his wife's cute doggerel and later praise his mistress's more momentous meditations?

A letter dated December 2 ends with a lyrical vision. I swallow. It's so much like my father's surprisingly poetic description of the sea on the ferry during our last visit to Martha's Vineyard. He'd pulled something long buried out of himself then. Here he goes out and sits on the beach and watches.

The reef extends about two hundred yards out from shore and
then drops suddenly off into very deep water so that when the

waves come in, they hit and break on the edge of the reef into a white foam that comes tumbling into the shore. The natural phosphorescence makes the foam intensely white against the black background of the water. This combined with the full moon, the palm trees and the silvery beach makes a beautiful picture. I would gladly trade all such beautiful pictures for a drizzly, cold night in Chicago with you.

On December 11, an unabashed lover's quarrel:

I was sure glad to get your letter, sweetheart, as it has been ten days or more . . . like you, I haven't written for about a week—I just was not able to get a minute to myself. I was awfully sorry to hear that you were so down in the dumps you couldn't write. I hope you feel better by now. The sixteen months I have been gone palls on me also, darling. The conditions under which I have been living are also beginning to pall on me to beat all hell . . . we haven't been paid in three months so I can't even buy you a money order. I am just as sick and tired of being out here as you are of having me out here. There is not one dammed thing I can do about it however except hope I get sent home when I can be spared and hope that is soon, damn soon.

You may have gathered I feel as bad today as you did when you wrote the letter I just got. I feel that way quite occasionally too, whether I show it in my letters or not.

He certainly wants her to know who has the right to feel most miserable. It's a foreshadowing of things to come—my mother ticking him off, my father getting more and more riled as he thinks about the insult. And does my mother realize how selfish she seems by not writing him because she's "down in the dumps"?

Just two days later, my father is penitent:

The letter I wrote you day before yesterday was sort of sour and I am sorry about it, darling. When I wrote it I was in a particu-

larly bad frame of mind as everything had been piling up for quite a while . . . You asked about washing in my helmet—I have washed in my helmet ever since I've been out here, I have also used mine to cook in . . . they also come in handy as a "chamber" when you are in a foxhole at night and don't dare stir out. They are really handy gadgets.

You will get a kick out of this one—we were sitting around talking before hitting the sack when one of the boys brought out some cookies he had gotten in a package. I said "I got a package of tea today, let's have a cup of tea with the cookies." So Jack Steele put some water on to boil, someone else got some sugar and condensed cream. The very last thing I got out was the tin box of 'tea,' took the adhesive off you had sealed it with, lifted the lid, and out came the figs you had sent me. The boys became practically hysterical with laughter at the look on my face. For the next couple of days somebody would say 'let's have a cup of tea' at which everyone would laugh.

Two days later, he talks about listening to Tokyo Rose, who broadcast from a Japanese propaganda radio station.

She has a very breezy way of coming on—it usually goes something like this 'Hello my little orphans of the South Pacific. How are you tonight—thinking of home? We will have some music right away to cheer you up . . . You poor dears, you must be lonely tonight, thinking of your loved ones so far away.' Occasionally she will get off rare ones like this 'I am getting mine, your wives and sweethearts are getting <u>theirs</u>. (slight pause) Are you getting <u>yours</u>?'

I got the little folder with your pictures in it and it sits beside your big picture on my 'dresser.' . . . The Coleman lantern is beginning to wheeze. I hope it holds out until I get this in the envelope. I miss you so, darling, and words can't express how badly I want to see you and that goes for Junior too. I love you, Tom.

The pet penis pops up again. I feel like a voyeur. I *am* a voyeur. A kid peeking into my parents bedroom. I still cannot imagine "It" sizzling between them. It's time to say goodnight. I gather up the letters and tie them back up with the red, white, and blue ribbon.

I go into the living room and put the Ink Spots on the stereo. Strange how I've always felt drawn to the culture of the forties. Women pinning shoulder pads underneath their dresses, the long rows of satin-covered buttons, men's jaunty Borsalino hats. I've haunted thrift shops looking for sweater sets and white beaded purses, original LPs of Bing Crosby crooning "I'll Be Home for Christmas" or Kate Smith singing "The White Cliffs of Dover." I've never tired of watching movies like *Mrs. Miniver*, *It's a Wonderful Life*, *Casablanca*. These things always fill me with a deep and inexplicable nostalgia for times I never lived through.

I belong inside these letters; in them lies the map of my other life. I was my mother, yearning for my soldier husband, I waited until I had just the right picture to send overseas. I bathed in my "handy" helmet, Oscar the Lizard perched on my shoulder. I was there; not even born yet, but there.

During my next trip to the halfway house in Milford, Dad and I are sitting together when suddenly he cocks his head, as if hearing something. "Lorraine?" he says, "Lorraine?" Then he turns and looks at me and says, "Lorraine?"

"Right here, Dad," I reply. "I'm right here."

Chapter Nineteen

"Oh no," Dad says as we pass over the Triborough Bridge. "I'm going to have to live in New York, aren't I?" He's been released from the halfway house and I've made plans for him to be near me. I've explained to him many times that to accomplish this, I have to bring him to the city he's always hated.

Not that he'll ever really live in it. He'll never get stuck in traffic, visit movie houses or restaurants, see waves of heat rising from the sidewalks. He'll live in a wheelchair and a hospital bed at Mary Manning Walsh Nursing Home, not far from our apartment.

I decorate his small but airy room with pictures of Bing and his grandchildren, his shooting trophies, and a raft of little stick-on butterflies, which I attach to lamps, drawers, and walls. When he sees the room, he exclaims, "But this is some of my stuff! What's it doing here?" Then he settles in without complaint. At the end of the day, when I get up and say good-bye, he tries to hoist himself up also. "Say, are we taking two cars?" he asks.

"No, Daddy, you're staying here," I tell him, "You're living here now."

"Righto," he says cheerfully.

Memory can be so pure, so fresh and immediate. When my children were little, I had to leave them to slow down time, to savor their incandescent moments. Watching them in the bath as they squealed and bounced, pounding the water with the palms of their hands, or feeling their velvety skin and inhaling the scent of their caramel breath. I would replay those instants over and over in my mind, each time a new exhilaration. What does Dad's memory bring to him now? The slice of a feeling, a fickle flash of remembrance? Or is everything cockeyed, clocks in a Dali landscape?

Loss of memory is often a blessing, for it extinguishes all other losses. My father doesn't understand time now; he doesn't remember what I've told him in the past and barely understands the present. At least I think he doesn't, although . . . there was that two-week vacation I took. When I returned, I told him I'd been away. "Yes," he replied, "I noticed that."

And he's still crafty. He's lost twenty pounds and his clothes droop off his body, so I keep him company at dinnertime. It's like trying to get a toddler to eat; each bite of eggs, which I've heavily seasoned to mask the cafeteria flavor, is a victory. When I look away, he spoons some of his dinner into his glass of milk. One night, we sit across from a resident with severe dementia. "Is it Wednesday?" she asks nonstop. He gives me a surprisingly knowing look. I circle my ear with my finger. He turns so she cannot see him and smiles at me.

I talk about Penny and her family, about Bob and my two kids and five stepchildren. He nods at each story; "Oh yes . . . huh . . . I'll be darned." If he understands these stories, what else does he understand about his present circumstances? The thought is unbearable.

Mary Manning Walsh, arguably the best nursing home in the city, offers many activities, but he won't participate in any of them. One night I wheel him down to the weekly bingo game anyway. I'm dismayed to see that he cannot even match the numbered squares with the numbers on his board. "They called 12, Dad, where is 12?" He throws up his hands in bewilderment. "I don't know!" But when the game ends, he smiles at me: "That sure was a lot of fun."

Then I understand. He will remember to remember one thing until the end: He must protect me. He knows me too well. And I, him. I call the wheelchair His Chair and we never mention the words "nursing home." We nestle up inside each other's illusions.

My father lingers through the summer. Joshua gets a volunteer job at Mary Manning Walsh so he can be closer to his grandfather. My housekeeper Nerissa and her beloved predecessor Renia feed him dinner when I cannot come. He bats his eyes at the resident who eats beside him, but she loses interest when he never says anything but "How nice you look."

We often bring him home for dinner, piling his wheelchair into the trunk. One time, he surprises us by actually eating. He finishes his little piece of turkey, and then he starts on his paper napkin. I hop up to take it from him. His face, for a split second, collapses, and it fills me with panic.

"Let him alone," Bob says.

"Let him eat his napkin?"

"Yes, if that's what he wants to do."

Dad comes home one last time. My stepchildren and their families are there—impeccably turned out, impeccably dignified. And there is my Dad, sitting on a chair, pale, expressionless, the waistband of his pants rolled down. "Is your father all right?" asks Jenny, Bob's oldest, alarmed at seeing his chin fall to his chest. "Oh yes, he's just napping. He does that," I say tensely. When Bobby, Susan, Harry, and Martha arrive, he suddenly wakes up. He gives Martha a big smile, and she comes and sits on his knee. He flaps his hands weakly, like a bird. She laughs. I want to cry. He is lordly, rolled pants and all.

Two weeks later, he lies semi-comatose. We've taken him to New York Presbyterian Hospital because he cannot remember how to eat; he simply chokes on his food. They put him on an IV for nourishment. They've taken away his hearing aid, false teeth, eyeglasses.

I sit by his side. I want to be noble, but I feel tired, I feel hungry, I feel bored. I slip out at the slightest excuse.

One day, out of nowhere, I say, "Jesus is with us, Daddy." I flinch.

Where did that come from? Opening his eyes, my father emerges briefly from the darkness to say, in a deep voice, "Ha, ha, ha."

I fret about the fact that he is thumbing his nose at the Almighty just when he needs him most. But then I remember a story Pat Rosenfield Cosentino told me long ago. Dad had been driving along a road in Ohio when his car stopped cold, right before a curve. He opened the hood. A wire had torn loose from the battery, so he took the foil wrapping out of his pack of cigarettes and looped it around the anode to restore the current. Just then, he heard a car roaring around the corner. He prayed to God that the car wouldn't hit him. It swerved just in time.

I figure that if there is a God, he is magnanimous. If my father called him once, then he'd called him forever. If there is a heaven, whether he believed in it or not, he, the unsung hero, is just the person to get in.

Of course, it's not just his salvation I'm interested in. If I'm honest with myself, behind my unrelenting push to get to the root of my father has been the hope that I'd find goodness in him—and therefore in myself. And I have. Everything he accomplished, I now own. I'd been the child left behind on the empty playground, the offspring of two damaged parents. A bad egg, or so I thought. Seeing myself anew in his image has given me confidence to claim my place.

One day, as I'm coming home from the hospital, a neighbor stops me. "Hey, is it true you won the Pulitzer Prize?" My usual response to these familiar words is to shrug and say, "Oh, that was a long time ago." But now, to my surprise, I look her in the eye and say, "Yes, I did."

Penny and I don't want to let him die. The doctors are after us, the nurses shake their heads, the social workers try to corner me and I manage to give them the slip. "If he was my father, I wouldn't have let him get to this juncture," says the director of the Geriatrics Department. Daddy is essentially starving himself to death. They want to let him do it. He is bedridden but conscious enough to answer simple questions and to repeat his mantra every time I come to the hospital: "Oh, so nice to see you, Cindy." He says the same thing to Penny on the telephone.

In a conference call with the Geriatrics Director and a collection of social workers, the staff tries once again to persuade us to let him go. Penny, on the speakerphone, is adamantly opposed. The director then appeals to me: "Think, Mrs. Morgenthau, what would your father say about being in this state. Would he want to live?" I speak loudly so Penny can hear: "I asked him that question. Or kind of that question. I said, 'Daddy, are you all right this way, or would you rather be somewhere else?' He said he was just fine where he was."

The director looks at me pitilessly. "Picture the quality of life he'll have if we keep him alive on tubes."

"Well, he was concerned the other day about the global situation. He wanted to know what we should do about it." The director looks at me incredulously. In fact, Daddy had babbled on incoherently, asking, "What's happening to the world, what are we going to do about it?" I was so upset by this that I told him I had to go. "Oh, don't go," he said, "stay, please." But I didn't. I went home and went to bed and had nightmares about how I'd failed him.

The nurses put a feeding tube into his stomach. He keeps pulling it out and they keep putting it in. Finally, the opening becomes infected and the infection spreads. Before we know it, my father has sepsis throughout his body. "It's a matter of days now," the director tells me. But she's wrong; it's a matter of weeks. She argues for a morphine drip, because she insists that he must be in great pain. I ask my father if he is and he replies, "No, not a bit." Finally, however, when I see him gritting his teeth, I race for the nurse and ask her to put in the drip.

One morning Penny calls me at home. She knows how much I want to be with him when he goes. "He's dying, Cindy. I just talked to the hospital. They're going to keep him alive for you. You only have a half hour at most."

When I get there, Dad is bloated from injections of saline solution.

Something tells me he won't die like this. Penny calls again. I put my cell phone next to his ear so she can talk to him. When he hears her voice, he starts and opens his eyes. I can hear it too, small and tinny through the earpiece: "Bye, Dad, love you, love you and miss you."

They say the comatose can hear you, so I shout out as much as I can muster: what a wonderful father he's been, how I'm so glad he taught me how to read the constellations, recognize butterflies, shoot a gun. The director comes in. "Could you please lower your voice?" she asks kindly.

"But he's deaf. I want him to hear me," I explain.

"Let's give him some quiet," she says. "That's what he wants right now. Peace and quiet."

I watch over him long into the night and chat with Penny on the phone. We try to joke: "It's just like Daddy to keep us waiting," I say.

"And instead of feeling the pain, he's sleeping through it," she answers. "When the going got tough, Dad always took to his bed."

I sleep in a cot next to him, and when I awake, I hear a catch in his breathing, as though he has something in his throat. It is October 15, 2002. I call Penny and place the phone on his pillow so she can be with him too.

My father's face is no longer swollen. His eyes are wide open, clear and shimmering, and he seems to be looking at something, seeing something far away. It's amazing to watch. His beautiful blue eyes trained on something with an intensity I've never seen. I want to put my hand in his, but I'm afraid to touch him. I don't know why. It's as if he doesn't belong to me right now. I can't bring myself to say the things you're supposed to say, like, "It's all right, you can go." So I just keep telling him over and over that I love him. His breath comes slower, shallower. Finally there is no more breath and his mouth falls slack. Then I see a smile come over his face, or at least it seems to be a smile. It's there but not there. Above the left-hand corner of his bed, there is some kind of movement, some vibration, like the air whirling. It's very strong, but not scary. It just vibrates there, making me happy. I hear Penny's voice coming through my cell phone but I can't move. My father has just died. How could I possibly be smiling? How could *he* be smiling?

I finally pick up the phone and tell Penny he's gone and what happened when he went. She wants to hear it over and over, she wants to know what he looks like now; she wants to be there. I stay beside him until two very nice men from the funeral parlor put him in a body bag.

Then I get into my car to go home. But I'm not alone. There's someone else in the car. I feel it. I look over; my father appears to be in the passenger seat. I don't consciously choose Bob Dylan's "Nashville Sky-line," but I find myself inserting it into the CD player.

For the next several days, I play Dylan over and over whenever I'm driving. I do it because when I do, my father gets into the car with me. I feel his smile, feel him instructing me to suffer no remorse, no sorrow that he's dead, but happiness that he'd been alive.

My father loved to drive and so do I and so does my sister, who braves the freeways of Los Angeles two hours a day. When I call her and tell her about Daddy's mystical appearance in my car, she gets very quiet. Then she tells me that Daddy has been riding in her car too.

The disturbance in the air I'd seen above my father's hospital bed comes back. Long after Dad has left the car for good, this little molecular tremble appears at whim. It likes Bob Dylan too, especially "Girl of the North Country" and "Lay, Lady, Lay." But it doesn't shrink from other musicians: Bryan Ferry, Fats Waller, Madonna. It happens like this: The music will soar from major to minor and back again and I will hold my breath and it won't come. Then, when I least expect it, the little whirlwind settles at the top of my windshield. And gladness fills me.

Either I need to see a psychiatrist, or it's really God. I decide that it's God. And that my father, the devout agnostic, is the one to blame. Forgiving my father allowed me to let go of a lifetime of rancor. He'd taught me to believe in miracles. And he'd delivered me to a father far greater than he.

I am ecumenical but I want to refamiliarize myself with Christianity. I begin to dip into the Bible, to read the theological writings of G. K Chesterton, C. S. Lewis, and others. But for all the evidence that many of these writers give for the historical reality of Jesus Christ, this doesn't make me believe. Nor do the Scriptures, with their multitude of contradictions and their portrayal of an angry and vengeful Old Testament God. The New Testament God, who made himself flesh in order to die on a cross and take away our sins, is a total muddle. Instant and eternal salvation in exchange for the simple utterance of belief? Hitler in heaven?

Yet I can only explain my sense of renewal by using the paradigm of the Resurrection. I become an intuitive Christian rather than a biblical believer. I acquire a sense of faith and trust that God is embracing my family and me. I'm astonished to find how many of my prayers are answered—sometimes not as quickly as I would wish, but in God's own time. I learn he has a sense of humor, and that it's okay to pray for the tiniest of things: "Oh Lord, may I kick ass in this tennis game." I join a Bible study group at the ungodly hour of 7:30 A.M., but its ten intelligent, loving women keep me coming. I learn to read between the lines of the Bible and my fear of running up against a vindictive God fades. My God is Jewish, he is Christian, he welcomes everyone. He is generous and forgiving; I am his child whom he made in his image. He yearns for my love as much as I yearn for his. The only time he gets irritated is when I race around, caught up with worldly things, and pay absolutely no attention to him or what he is saying to me. Then I stop and listen to Psalm 46: "Be still, and know that I am God."

I phone Penny and lo and behold, she has had a spiritual renaissance too. We had both cooled on religion in our teens, perhaps in rebellion against our Mother's extreme devoutness. But now, Penny tells me she has not only experienced a conversion, she's become a practicing member of the Catholic Church. I nearly drop the phone. "I figured if I was going to be religious, I might as go all the way," she explains. She goes to mass every day, says the rosary regularly, and has taken Teresa, for St. Teresa of Lisieux, as her middle name.

It all began years ago when Max was born, she tells me. "I prayed intensely. I said 'God, I can't handle a dead baby, but let him live and I will accept anything, I will do everything I can to make him whole.'

And my prayer was answered." As I had done when Josh was near death, Penny made a bargain with God, but not a lasting connection. Now it was different. "Something has been pulling at me since Daddy died, perhaps it was the smile you saw on his face. I went to our local church a few times. It smelled like the church we went to as kids, that stone and wood smell. And then one day, I was looking up at the cross of St. Luke's—he was the first physician in the Bible and each edge of the cross is bowed wood, symbolizing crutches—and this gentle wind blew over me and inside me and I sat down with a thud. Oh my Gosh, I thought, this is it, this is what the Holy Spirit feels like. It was as if God was saying, 'Yes, I really am.' And I knew that I was finally on the Journey."

Eventually, my happy whirlwind goes away and so does Penny's gentle breeze, returning only rarely. This puzzles and frustrates us both. Then, an African priest sits down with her: "He told me that those moments of holy exhilaration were a way to bring me to God. The carrot, to be blunt," Penny tells me. "Now, I am attached. My love of God is deepening in a different way. After all, he said, look where you are every day: in his house."

I find the little two-hundred-year-old Trinity Episcopal church in Fishkill and take Amy with me every Sunday. Josh sniffs at these proceedings. Bob, like many Jews, refuses to step into a church. He gives my Venetian glass cross his legendary Scowl, but he makes no comment on my spiritual search. He comes from a long line of cultural rather than religious Jews. His family traditions didn't include bar mitzvahs and minor holidays, but we've always gone to temple on Rosh Hashanah and Yom Kippur, feasted on Passover, and lit candles through the days of Hanukkah. We also celebrate Christmas not only in deference to me, but because Bob's assimilated parents and grandparents, whose ancestry was German, celebrated it too.

At night, Amy and I pray and sing hymns together. Then one day, she turns fourteen and becomes a pagan: "I think God is only in nature; the rocks and the trees, and maybe in animals." Some time afterward, she announces, "I don't believe in any god, I believe in myself." I drag her to church anyway in hopes that she will come back to him.

At the age of nineteen, Josh suddenly becomes alarmed by my religious leanings. "Don't ever mention Jesus Christ," he advises. "People will think you're some anti-Semitic fundamentalist." I explain to him that Grandpop's restaurant attack on an anti-Semite is what had started me on this spiritual journey. For once, he doesn't answer me back.

The death of a friend may affect my husband deeply, but you won't see it in his face. That is, until my father dies. Aside from the mortuary men, Bob was the only one to touch my father. He'd rushed up from his office, but by the time he came into the room, Dad had passed away. When Bob saw him, his eyes filled. Then he patted his foot. "It's okay, Tom," he said, "it's okay now."

My sister and I don't want a funeral. We don't think my father would have wanted it. Instead, as he's cremated, we recite prayers with the mortician. We think that's the end of it. But Bob doesn't. His face takes on The Scowl.

"We have to give him a proper send-off," he says. Then he picks up the phone and arranges for a memorial service to take place on the USS *Intrepid*, the historic World War II aircraft carrier-turned-museum that's permanently docked on Manhattan's West Side, on the Hudson River.

Penny's whole family makes the trip from Los Angeles and arrives a few days before the service. I've tried to make her feel part of the ceremony, making copies of old pictures of Dad for her, thanking the *Intrepid* in the funeral program "on behalf of the Morgenthau and Franks-Hribar families." But I can imagine it is hard for her, stepping inside her big sister's world at such a vulnerable time. She hangs back for a while when we set up for the service in the designated room at the ship's stern. But then she steps up and introduces herself to the participants and the staff and puts up a picture of Luke and Max next to my children on a long display table. We place other photographs on the table near the ship's rectangular windows: Dad, age nine, hugging Bing, Dad at Guadalcanal, looking thin as a walking stick.

This is to be a military funeral complete with the pageantry appropriate to a war hero. Bob sees to that. Inside the blue cover of the program is a beguiling Navy portrait of Dad, looking pensive in his dress whites; I'd fallen in love with it and had it framed on my desk. Inside the booklet is the order of service, then a full-length photo of him in fatigues, beside his barracks, a gun on his hip, a helmet on his head. His hand is poised in midair, a cigarette between thumb and forefinger, as though he's stopped to investigate something beyond the picture. Above it are the words "Always Remembered," and below it today's date, November 7, 2002.

There are no friends of my dad's at the service, just our friends, many of whom knew him. Pat the housekeeper couldn't come and neither could Lou Golden, who lived across the country.

Pat Rosenfield Cosentino had just had a hip replacement and it was too far for her to travel. When I called to tell her Dad had died, she cried and said, "I knew it, I knew it was going to happen soon." And she also cried when we told her that the memorial would take place on the *Intrepid*. "Your dad would have loved it, Cindy." That's the kind of thing people say automatically. I rather suspect he would have been embarrassed—"Why all this fuss?"

Like my father, the *Intrepid* is a veteran of the Pacific Campaign during World War II, a battle-scarred survivor of seven bomb attacks, five kamikaze suicide strikes, and even a torpedo hit. I'm pleased to discover that the Japanese nicknamed her "The Ghost Ship" for her ability to slip back into action after repeated hits—how fitting for Dad.

About fifty people board a ramp, closed to the public and specially installed for the service, and walk the length of the ship with her galleries of vintage planes and helicopters to a long, low-ceilinged, rather plush room at the fantail. Next to the podium is a table holding the urn containing our father's ashes. It's draped with an American flag. Both Penny and I just stare at it. Daddy, tall, dignified Daddy, now a twelve-inch container of bone and ashes.

An honor guard of ramrod Marines marches in holding flags so tall they brush the ceiling; this is the Presentation of the Colors. Then

a diverse group of children from Bob's charitable organization, the
Police Athletic League, fills the room with the sweet melody of "God
Bless America."

The rabbi, William Kloner, who also happens to be a rear admiral, gives a passionate eulogy. He's never known my father, but we've
told him Dad's story. "Just look at that picture," he booms, pointing
to the barracks snapshot that we had blown up into an 18" by 24"
portrait. "There he is, ready to go, dead set to serve his country,
and he served it silently, performed feats that would never even be
noticed . . . ."

I've picked Psalm 23, "The Lord is My Shepherd," and Penny has
selected Psalm 25, "To you, Oh Lord, I lift up my soul." After these
are recited, Rabbi Ronald Sobel of Temple Emanu-El says the Kad-
dish. The indoor part of the service ends with the Navy Hymn, "Eternal Father, Strong to Save," and at this point I smile at Penny: Yes, we
are both thinking, Daddy would have enjoyed this.

Penny and her family step up to the podium. She pays homage to
her father as a "gentle agnostic. He never made any excuses for it or criticized others for their faith. He knew his internal drummer had a different beat and he accepted it." Bernie reads a passage by Albert
Einstein: ". . . I cannot conceive of an individual that survives his physical death. I'm satisfied with the eternity of the mystery of life." Max,
ten, completes the circle by reciting "I Didn't Go To Church Today"
by Ogden Nash. Max has also written an essay: "If our Grandpa saved
our country," he reads, ". . . then every single one of us is a hero inside
and out." Luke, speaking with flair and drama, proceeds to read Carl
Sandburg's "Chicago," which brings to life the haunts Dad and Mother
had known in their youth.

The Morgenthaus speak next. Amy, twelve, in a voice like a bell,
says that when told of her grandfather's death, "I was both happy and
sad. He was caught in a net like a butterfly and now he was released.
I was happy that he would never feel confused or tired or lost again."
Josh, hand in pocket, says: "When I was ten years old, he sat me down
and said, 'It's about time you learned about the theory of relativity.'
I think it was kind of a rite of passage for him. Later on, no physics

teacher could ever make me understand it like he could." I speak un-emotionally, but in the end, my voice betrays me: "So Dad . . . for your support, your understanding, and your abiding love . . . I want to say, thank you . . . thank you . . . thank you."

Bob speaks last. Tom Franks, he says, was a man in whom "still wa-ters run deep." He alludes to the concentration camps and says, "Tom never could deal with what he had seen." Then he breathes deeply. "If I'm in a ship on stormy seas, or on a desert island, or walking down a dark street . . . or behind enemy lines," he concludes, descending the podium with chin trembling. "I'd like to have Tom with me."

Afterward, we walk out onto the ship's fantail and stand behind Leviathan anti-aircraft guns. A howling October wind sweeps across the deck, sending everyone's hair flying about. Sailors in dress blues point their rifles in the air and give my father a resounding ten-gun salute. A Marine Corps sergeant with white gloves carefully folds the flag that covered Dad's urn of ashes and presents it to me. Then they play "Taps." I am dry-eyed. I've said my good-byes, but Penny is fight-ing back tears. I turn and give the flag to her.

In military fashion, Tom Franks' two daughters and their families place hand upon hand and toss a wreath of flowers into the Hudson River. We watch as it spins round and round, getting smaller and smaller as it moves like a life buoy out to sea. Penny and I turn and em-brace each other. At last, our father has gotten the recognition he de-served. There will never be any pins or medals in velvet-lined cases for him, but his story has been heard; he's been honored by all.

People mill about and have refreshments while Dad's favorite Dix-ieland and Knuckles O'Toole albums are piped into the room. Then a Coast Guard boat takes us to the Statue of Liberty. Penny has brought a bottle of Champagne and little glasses. She uncorks the bottle and pours a glass for everyone, including the crew. Then Luke and Josh to-gether scatter Dad's ashes upon the waves.

The project Bob lovingly shepherded—the Museum of Jewish Heritage: A Living Memorial to the Holocaust—officially opened its doors in

September 1997. Now, months after Dad's memorial service, the museum is putting on a special exhibition, "Ours to Fight For: American Jews in the Second World War," about Jewish GIs in World War II. At the opening, my husband walks me through the dimly lit rooms full of memorabilia that tell these soldiers' stories: letters, photographs, torpedoes, bombs, helmets marked with bullet holes. There's a movie depicting the first Shabbat service held in the newly liberated camps. The final presentation is a panorama of three large screens showing film of the concentration camps. I sit on a bench, sickened but spellbound. I've never seen some of these clips before. Narration of the film comes from speakers located high above the screens.

Then, suddenly, a cold draft passes over me. I hear my father's voice. Loud and clear, as if coming from the sky: "There were pieces of bone, hair, skull, corpses where you didn't know whether they were male or female . . . ." My father's Ohrdruf testimony. I'm hearing someone's voice that I never expected to hear again.

A person you love dies, and you can look at his photograph, you can read his letters, but you can never get back the sound of his voice. Yet here it is: that voice speaking to me down the years, strong and soothing, a voice that taught, that comforted, that fathered. His voice is just the way I remember it, yet also different. It's more deeply colored than when he gave his testimony. Behind his matter-of-fact, almost belligerent tone, I hear something I hadn't heard at the time: the sound, faintly, of sorrow.

Then Bob takes my hand and leads me to the wall. There hangs a shining silver plaque. It thanks the people who have narrated the movie. And there, standing out among the rest, is the name: Thomas Edward Franks.

Chapter Twenty

I've found Jack Steele. Dad's jilted, pig-bereft bear of an intelligence partner. His best friend during the war. The one who, in some ways, knew him better than I.

I'd tried to track Steele down a long time ago, when Dad first began opening up about the war. After all, the two had spent nearly the whole time together. They'd been assigned to Ordnance in Washington, sent behind enemy lines in Europe, and served in the South Pacific in the same mysterious Argus unit. Even when Dad was in severe dementia, Jack's was the one name outside the family that he couldn't seem to forget.

But I'd stopped the hunt for Jack too soon. I think the truth was that I was afraid to find him. At the time, I was scared I'd find out that my father had done something unbearable. I was equally scared to find out that he'd done nothing at all.

Dad has been gone for two months. But not for me. An old boyfriend once called me "a person obsessed without an obsession." Well, now I have one. My father's death has left so many gaps, so many question marks. I want more of him, want to ferret out as much as I can about what he really did from 1943 to 1945, perhaps the two most crucial years of his life.

So I take out my slim Steele folder again and resume searching. I've discovered that it's almost impossible not to be found by the Internet in seconds. If you're a peeping Tom, all you need is a few dollars, a name, and a search company, and you'll have the address, telephone number, neighbors, banks, credit histories, criminal records, and marital status of your victim at your electronic fingertips. There's just one catch: a common name like Robert Smith will yield hundreds of listings. So will a Jack or a John Steele.

I first phone all the Steeles listed in Massachusetts; Dad had once mentioned Jack living in Worcester. Then I call some thirty more John Steeles in retirement states like Florida and California. All dead ends, although one John Steele describes the lingering chilblains he'd gotten in the Ardennes; another tells of being rescued from a torpedoed destroyer.

Then, to my glee, I come across Jack Steele's serial number on one of Dad's military documents. I immediately call the Veteran's Administration.

A southern female voice asks me if I'm next of kin.

"Well, kind of," I lie, "I need to find him to tell him Dad died."

"Oh!" she replies. "My Daddy just died too."

"Oh, I'm so sorry," I say. "Then you can understand . . . why I'd want everyone who loved him to know."

"Yes, I suppose so, but we would have no way of locating a veteran who was in any specific war."

"I have a serial number," I say, and slowly read off the numbers.

"Oh drat, my computer just went down. Again. Hold on."

"Isn't modern technology just the worst," I say. "It slows you down more than speeds you up half the time."

"Oh yes. The stories I could tell you!" and she does, for the next twenty minutes, as I purr out my sympathy. By the time the computer is up and running, so am I.

She's found him. I'm elated. Her voice lowers conspiratorily. "I shouldn't really do this, but . . . let's see. Steele, John Henry. Is that him?"

"Yes! That's him."

"Arlington, Texas," she nearly whispers.

"My God, thank you," I cry. "I can't thank you enough."

"You're welcome," she says. "I kind of broke the rules here, but it's okay."

I tell her again how grateful I am. But there is silence.

I start to hang up when she says softly, "Oh no . . . oh dear."

"What?"

"He died. He died about six months ago."

I collapse back in my chair. After I recover from the shock—and finish kicking myself for not searching him out earlier—I realize that I can still track down his children. I've located their names and Jack's old address, but they are at large somewhere in Arlington. Intelius.com, Virtualchase.com, Switchboard.com, PeopleFinders .com, and Militaryofficers.com are black holes that suck me in with the empty promise of actually finding them. The neighbors are no help. Then, one bleary-eyed evening, I find the redoubtable Mrs. Perkins. Her peppy Texas twang chimes through the phone lines. She talks about the weather report in each region of the state, the pepper pot she's cooking, the advantages of poodles over any other dog. Finally, she says, "They live up in Plano. They're real private. Their numbers ain't listed. But I'll give 'em to you."

I reach Jack's son, Lee Steele, first. "My father never talked about the war. He just told the same funny stories over and over about being in the Solomon Islands." Did these kids hear endless iterations of the damn pig story too?

Lee's sister, Christine Steele, isn't the least surprised to hear that her father might have been a secret agent. She'd lived with her father the last years of his life and had just moved out of his house. "Dad absolutely had the persona of someone who had been a spy," she says over the telephone. "He was secretive, he was sly, he seemed haunted, like he'd seen some atrocity or done something that he just wanted to get out of his mind.

"I associate the name Tom Franks with something kind of murky and mysterious, one of those things Dad would bring up and then drop," she tells me. "In the last couple of years before he died, he began to do that, drop little bits and pieces about the war. He told me he was in 'Advanced Reconnaissance Group US' and that he set up secret radar stations. I'm pretty sure Dad was in Europe—he hinted at it, but he wouldn't go anywhere with that one. Something wasn't right there. He never wanted to go to Europe on vacation.

"He came out of the war smoking heavily," she tells me. "He had such bad ulcers he had to be hospitalized . . . Something happened to him that he never wanted to remember anything about. He didn't show physical affection, but actually he was emotional, and very sentimental. He just kept it all back. He was this big guy, an engineer for Brown and Root, an executive at Bell Aircraft, former captain of the football team, president of all his clubs, and one night I caught him crying when Hoss's fiancée died on *Bonanza*.

"He was very sensitive to anti-Semitic things. He would get all sullen whenever the concentration camps came up. He would talk about man's inhumanity to man.

"Finally, his drinking got out of control; he had blackouts and had to be put in a detox center. At the end of his life, he had some form of dementia but he was good at putting on an act. He was clear as a bell on the phone, but when I came over, the bed was bare and I pulled three or four sets of sheets out of the dryer. Stuff everywhere. The toilet was stopped up, dried food on tables. In the hospital, he was so stubborn and ornery, he would pull the tubes and wires out. They wrote 'noncompliant' on his chart."

I hang up, shaken. What was Jack Steele, Daddy's doppelganger? Secretive, emotionally frozen, phobic about revealing what he did in the war, tormented about the Holocaust, at the end tricking people into thinking he was fine when he was not. Death by drowning in tobacco and alcohol.

I might not have been able to ask Jack Steele if he'd been my father's spy partner, but he seemed to be telling me anyway.

Where in God's universe my father is I don't know, but I can hear him, now released completely from his vow of silence, his bottomless voice urging me on, his hand at my back: "Go ahead, find out."

I've repeatedly written the FBI and the CIA under the Freedom of Information Act, requesting Dad's military records, but they remain as stonily silent as Dad once was. I talk to an array of experts in intelligence, including specialists at the Office of Naval Intelligence, the Naval Records Depository in Norfolk, the rocket program in China Lake, California, and the University of Michigan, where certain war records are stored, looking for duty rosters, company lists, anything that would contain my father's name.

I attend World War II history conferences. I talk to historians. I contact Charles Pinck, head of the OSS Society and his father Daniel Pinck, an OSS veteran. I join the society and post notices on its website, hoping to come across someone who worked with Dad. This brings me in touch with lots of fellow explorers, including Thomas Ensminger, a retired civil servant whose father flew supplies and agents into wartime enemy territory. He has written two books on his father's "Carpetbagger" unit; he becomes a regular pen pal and helps me with connections. I get more assistance from Sam Roberts, author of *The Brother*, the well-known book on the Rosenbergs and an expert at obtaining official records. Joseph McNamara, a retired Marine officer familiar with military intelligence, chases down leads, as does the eminent historian Richard Breitman, who tries to follow a report he heard that American agents, perhaps one of them my father, posed as Nazis and infiltrated certain POW camps in Germany. Still, no one can find mention of Dad, his Washington spy group, or the puzzling Argus unit in the Pacific Theater.

One day Bob comes into my study with a sly look on his face. He puts down a thick book of entries by fellow Amherst alumni, from the class of '42, reminiscing about World War II. His finger is on a certain entry by one Roger P. Baldwin.

"Oh my God," I cry. "He was a lieutenant in an Argus unit! And they were using radar to spot planes!" I look up at Bob. "A far cry from watching for them through binoculars." But Argus was no ordinary radar operation.

Baldwin describes Argus as "an amphibious radar early warning outfit, specifically intended for first wave island-hopping," but goes into little detail, only that it was a secret American weapon in the Pacific, to spot enemy planes. No naval historian I consulted had ever heard of Argus, and here my husband had cracked the enigma by diligently reading his alumni mailings.

"Historians," I roll my eyes.

"They're not perfect," Bob agrees. "What people still don't know about the war is unbelievable, records not kept, major disasters swept under the rug." In 1993 journalist Charles Osgood broadcast a radio report on a major scandal: On November 26, 1943, a British troop transport ship called the HMT *Rohna* was sunk off the coast of North Africa by a German glider bomb, and 1,015 American and more than 100 British and Allied soldiers were drowned. Their families were lied to and told they were missing in action in Europe. This was the biggest naval disaster since the sinking of the *Arizona* in Pearl Harbor, and for almost fifty years the Army and the Navy had suppressed it. Bob shared Osgood's sense of outrage. "If the *Lansdale* had known about the German activity, we might have been better prepared for their glider bomb attacks and the aerial torpedo that finally sank us in the Mediterranean."

Was Argus also a target of the Navy's complicity? I'm spurred by Bob's discovery to visit the National Archives and Records Administration (NARA) in Maryland, outside Washington. I enter the high-tech, round, glass building. The lobby is vast and gives off a sterile, sanitized air. I must leave my coat, purse, laptop, pens, paper, and anything else I have on me in a locker. This is what it must be like to be searched and booked for a petty crime. Then I have to fill out endless forms, get my picture taken, and wait for a laminated ID card, which I must show at every turn. Only after I apply for and dangle a second card from my neck am I authorized to enter a small, overheated room where VIPs can go for research help. John Taylor, an ancient, stooped character of archival eminence, and Barry Zerby, the chief naval historian, offer to help me. When I explain that I'm here to learn more about Argus as well as my father's duty in a Bureau of Ordnance (BuOrd) secret operations group, their faces take on a dour cast.

Predictably, they've never heard of Argus, and as for the special BuOrd unit, Zerby warns, "I've been here twenty years and I've never seen correspondence relating to such highly sensitive material."

Nevertheless, Taylor and Zerby both begin flipping through big black books until they come up with what they hope might be relevant material. I write out multiple copies of retrieval slips, wash my hands, am given plain white paper and a pencil, and am ushered to one of the tables in the main room, where I sit idly for two hours.

At last, a waiter's cart is rolled over to me, teetering with dozens of fat, brown folders. Inside the BuOrd files, I find original letters, reports, orders, and memos from the forties. The intimacy of reading someone else's mail, especially when I stumble across letters from such World War II icons as Secretary of the Navy Frank Knox and Fleet Admiral William D. Leahy, is exhilarating. As I turn over each onionskin carbon, I feel like I'm sliding down into an urgent and uprooted world where boys loved passionately one night and killed passionately the next, where German U-boats blew merchant ships to smithereens, and perfectly aimed bombs arced through the air over London.

The correspondence is arid but heady. Here is a memo citing a group of enemy aliens living near a weapons plant in Nevada; they were being investigated with an eye to deportation. I wonder if they were the same German immigrants turned saboteurs that Dad had mentioned.

Everything I find in the old, brown folders confirms that the Bureau of Ordnance was a culture steeped in secrecy. Albert Einstein did confidential consulting work for them, and Morton Sobell, a member of the Rosenberg spy ring, took a job there. Nazis were infiltrating the country, and the bureau was dealing in wartime armaments and secret weapons. It was just the kind of place where clandestine units could flourish.

By the end of my second day at NARA, I've finally found a few marginally interesting BuOrd memoranda—but no smoking gun, nothing about any spy unit. With less than an hour before closing time, I run to the machines and begin copying all I've got so fast that I lift the top up while the blue light still glares from the machine. Suddenly I am blinded. When I open my eyes, a wiggly black line with a tiny head and legs comes out of nowhere. In truth, all I have for my two days of research is a sore neck, writer's cramp, and a little man in the corner of my right eye.

Next I head for the Washington Navy Yard, where my father once lived in one of the little brick houses. In the Navy Library, there is a multivolume history of the Bureau of Ordnance. Straight off, I find some intriguing news. My father's military designation SO had meant Special Ordnance duties.

I call Kathy Lloyd, head of the Navy Museum's Operational Archives branch. "Could 'special ordnance' have meant my dad was a spy?" I ask her.

"No," she tells me. "That was just a designation change. It didn't mean anything."

I call Bob at the office. "I'm not so sure about that," he says. "Every book I've ever read about World War II says that SO means clandestine Special Operations."

In Volume 5—*Naval Administration*—I find that William H. P. Blandy, during his tenure as Chief of the Bureau of Ordnance from February 1941 to November 1943, mined America's technical schools and corporations for chemical and metallurgical engineers, particularly older recruits like my thirty-year-old father. An engineer himself, Blandy prized these experts, for he planned to expand the bureau threefold. He also established a system whereby "special staff assistants" in different divisions were directly responsible to no one but him. He liked to have his own special coterie.

Last, I visit Washington's new International Spy Museum, an historical cornucopia of spy stories and secret agent devices. Encased behind glass, I find the trick glove made by Naval Intelligence that Dad had told me about—its leather palm holding a gun the shape of a large cigarette pack—as well as a replica of his old Minox camera. I buy a totebag full of new spy books. As I lean back in my seat on the train home, the little man is still dancing in the corner of my eye.

Chapter Twenty-one

"Blandy? Blandy . . . I've heard of him." Bob puts down his bite of stuffed pepper and pushes away from the dinner table. This is an act so uncharacteristic—you don't get between Bob and his food— that I know he must be excited. He goes straight to his bookshelf and takes out one of his favorite books, *Victory in the Pacific, 1945*, volume 14 of Samuel Eliot Morison's *History of United States Naval Operations in World War II.*

I've just discovered that it was William H. P. Blandy who personally signed some of my dad's orders sending him out for "temporary duty . . . in addition to his regular duties." Not simply the Bureau of Naval Personnel, which signed his other orders, but the head of the Bureau of Ordnance himself.

This exciting discovery is all because of Charlie Rangel. After the St. Louis Records Center had finally told me my father's "complete files" were lost, Bob asked Rangel, member of the House of Representatives for New York, to look into it. And now, within a week, I'd received them. The center gave an explanation for the long delay: I'd failed to request in writing a "DD214" and a "201" file. And, after all that, the "complete files," like the one-page service summary, turned out to be contradictory and incomplete. But at least I got the Blandy orders.

In the absence of hard evidence of my father's spy activities, Bob and I are leaning toward the circumstantial. We have become like hounds on the scent.

"William Henry Purnell Blandy, Admiral, United States Navy," Bob reads from Morison. "He was an engineer . . . sanguine Celtic type, with a humorous Irish mouth overhung by a large red nose . . . quick mind, grasp of essentials . . . driving energy . . . Chief of Bureau of Ordnance until late 1943 . . ."

"Oh, wait! Is Blandy the admiral Dad was always talking about? The one his unit reported to?" I ask.

Bob nods. "Now I remember. Your father said several times that he reported to the chief of the Bureau of Ordnance. That would have been Blandy. He might have been a career Navy man, but it looks like he was a very unusual one. People like that, they often had elite groups of their best men. When they wanted something done on the QT, they'd be set in place, ready to go."

"And I know that Blandy had connections to OSS, through his friend Vannevar Bush, for one—Blandy even lent him one of his people," I say.

Bob tucks a pillow that had been needlepointed by my mother behind his head. "If I was this brash Irishman, I would have spotted your father in a minute and lent him to my cronies whenever they needed an expert to go behind enemy lines."

I punch Blandy's name into a search engine. It turns out that Blandy, after service at BuOrd, had training in the Amphibious Force— just like Dad. They also left for the South Pacific around the same time, at the end of 1943. Just a coincidence?

I reach Blandy's granddaughter in Montana. She talks in a soft, rather dreamy voice. She has been going through her grandfather's papers. "They are scattered all over his house," she says. "I just found his ID card from Operation Crossroads behind some bookshelves." That was the code name for the nuclear weapons testing in the summer of 1946. "He was head of it, you know, when they tested the A-bomb on the Bikini Atoll."

She allows that her grandfather "believed strongly that there were Communist infiltrators in the country." Perhaps he had taught Dad to believe that, too.

"Would he have had a special spy group?" I ask.

"I assume he would have," Catherine tells me. "Grandpa was a very independent spirit."

I ask Catherine whether her grandfather had dogs. "Yes," she tells me, "They weren't allowed on the furniture. I can't imagine Grandpa walking them himself. Yes, I think they were probably walked by others." Dad had, of course, been the walker.

Blandy was clearly an iconoclast who had a sense of humor, according to Catherine. "He died when I was six but I have a clear memory of being on a beach in a Cadillac convertible. He put a stick through the steering column and drove with his knees. He yelled out, 'No one is driving this car!'"

I wonder whether a trove of Blandy's papers are still hiding under cushions, on pantry shelves, in bureau drawers. "Most of them ended up in the Library of Congress," Catherine tells me.

So off I go to Washington, once again. Unlike the antiseptic NARA building, the Library is in a high-ceilinged old marble relic full of mahogany and red velvet. I begin to pore over documents about Admiral Blandy and the first thing I see is a letter from the Library informing the donor of the Blandy dossier that anything "inappropriate for the library to retain" would be returned or disposed of. Aha. Another case of document sanitation.

Wartime newspaper articles about the Ordnance chief paint the picture of a man who not only made quick decisions but who was part of the Navy gun culture in Washington, an assemblage of officers who believed in the warrior ethic and relied on weapons as the "fist of the fleet." On his desk he had miniature torpedoes and shell casings. One newspaper article says Blandy wouldn't tolerate strikes at defense plants. In a speech he made in Georgia, he declared that the leaders of strikes should be run "out on a rail as if they were wearing swastikas on their sleeves."

I return to the National Archives, this time with a professional archivist. Marc Masurovsky, a stern, determined chap, was instrumental in exposing the Swiss Banks that had hoarded gold stolen from Holocaust victims during the war. At NARA, he zips from floor to floor, his eyeglasses slipping down his nose, unearthing clue after clue about my father.

And, eureka. One of the first things we find is a cryptic message indicating that certain unidentified Ordnance officers were sent to reconnoiter the Swedish coast with Royal Navy intelligence. This occurred at the same time my father recalled that he was dispatched to Sweden as part of the British operation to break the German blockade.

"I bet you that Blandy detached your dad to Naval Intelligence, which linked up to the British Admiralty in summer of 1943 for the Swedish missions," Marc tells me. "And that's where he was picked up by the SOE, the British version of the OSS." We find evidence that British wartime intelligence dominated Scandinavia until late 1943, when the OSS was allowed to come in and work with the SOE.

"Then, in 1945, he was brought back from the Pacific in order to join OSS," Marc says. "By then Donovan had become tight with Navy Ordnance."

OSS and Navy Ordnance were probably cooperating even earlier than that. We discover two 1943 letters from OSS's Donovan to Blandy, indicating that the two are in cahoots. We also find out that one Lieutenant Commander Draper Kauffman, closely associated with OSS, ran a demolitions school at the Navy Yard, where my father would very likely have studied—and maybe even taught recruits to use a variety of fuses and explosive devices. Kauffman was also linked to the Seabees, as was Dad.

Marc and I pore through pink carbons of action reports and travel vouchers in the OSS files, hoping to find my father's name. The OSS reports make us thirsty: "To Gin/Bitters (copy to Port)/ From: Toddy." Two other code names are Whiskey and Sherry. "The OSS agents in the ETO were famous lushes," explains Marc.

Marc leans back in his chair and posits my father's trajectory in the world of espionage. "In a state of emergency, like World War II, government agencies become more autonomous . . . The FBI, State, the War Department, the Air Force, the Navy's ONI, the Army's G2 and G5—each of them had its own secret units. And the subagencies, like Ordnance, were not to be outdone. Lots of intrigue. You can see War or OSS soliciting Blandy for weapons instructors and demolitions experts. Once your Dad had done his somersaults and was famous for infiltrating and breaking up those corrupt naval base commanders, he would have been a natural.

"There are plenty of indications that your father was up to something. All those 'temporary assignments,' so he could have been sent in and out of places. You look at his orders and they give him a lot of autonomy. He has enough pull to decide on 'varying his itinerary' and flying by priority air. Usually the Navy decided that, and it was rare that they allowed underlings to use planes instead of trains or sea transport."

After two days of grueling work in the archives, we of course still haven't found Dad. Marc isn't surprised: "These big guys never left traces of these special units."

I talk to various experts, and they agree with Marc: It's unlikely I'll ever find mention of Dad or his spy unit. Some think such orders were only given orally. "It was too dangerous to do it any other way," says Ed Marolda, head of the Naval Historical Center. "Special operations do not like paperwork. Even today, from the Gulf War, you won't hear about secret things they did or used. They may want to use the techniques again." Joseph McNamara voices a different opinion about my father's vanished paper trail: "Any government agency has buried documents in files all over the place and what can't be found passes out of memory and then it's as good as useless, like it never existed at all."

Or, say others, any written accounts were simply destroyed or kept under wraps. Nearly the entire history of the OSS counterintelligence organization X-2 has been stricken from the files of NARA. Recently the

CIA refused to declassify data on Nazi war criminals brought to the U.S. to work on weapons projects.

I return to New York to report my failed mission. "I'm never going to find anything," I say woefully to Bob.

"I think you are, love," he says."There's got to be something out there." He reminds me that an important speech written in longhand notes by his father, then Secretary of the Treasury, had recently turned up in some stranger's attic. "I suspect that Blandy's personal records were filed in his head, and that's why your father saw him tear up the hand-written reports he gave him after every mission. That's one reason the OSS had code names, so that the principals could never be identified."

One day I receive an urgent e-mail from Thomas Ensminger, who tells me that an historian friend has found what could be my father's name on a list of twenty thousand OSS members: S. T. Franks had entered the service the same time as my father. In his youth, my father was called Sonny Thomas Franks. I could imagine him—impressed with the secrecy and danger of his assignments, or even in a streak of mis-chievousness—giving those somewhat misleading initials. I try through all my OSS sources to track down S. T. Franks but, as usual, with no luck.

One evening, I learn that the husband of my friend, writer Wendy Gimbel, had a father who was a spy in Nazi Germany. "He admitted to us that he'd been a spy with a certain cover," Doug Liebhafsky tells me, "though he never told us any details. After he died, I was going through his dresser when I found this odd wartime ID card. It iden-tified him as working for the Navy Bureau of Ordnance."

The Bureau of Ordnance as cover—it would have been the per-fect shield for my father. I need to put this all together.

I lay out the military records from St. Louis on my living room floor and begin roughing out a time line. Dad was in Navy officer training in January 1943 in the Bronx, then moved to Ordnance School in the Washington Navy Yard. Unlike ordinary students, though, he was dispatched to the Naval Operating Base in Norfolk, given permission "to carry all and any photographic equipment," and told to perform unspecified duties there with the Amphibious Force of the Atlantic Fleet. No orders to Europe, but then, as Marc has said, my father seemed to be a troubleshooter sent here and there; any covert action was most likely passed on orally or expunged from his record.

Dad indicated that his first European assignment, to Sweden, was in late spring of 1943. Sure enough, there are no orders for June, just a yawning gap in time between his orders on May 20 to inspect ordnance in Pontiac, Michigan, and apparently attend anti-aircraft artillery school there, until July 14, when he was sent to Port Hueneme, California, where he was frequently detached "temporarily" for other duties. During that time period, his separation papers list that he went to Pontiac Ordnance School for eight weeks, but Daddy told me he'd stayed there hardly more than two. Moreover, an individual order I'd found said his duty there was "inspecting ordnance," not attending school, and I think that was a cover-up for his real assignments.

My theory that his orders were a cover and his leaves of absence were often taken up with secret assignments is bolstered when I figure out that on February 23, 1943, in the middle of a two-week leave, he is sent on "temporary additional duties to inspect ordnance" in Norfolk and Charleston "and other places you deem necessary." That could have been the mission to uncover the incompetent behavior of commanders at the naval base down there.

Just before that assignment, on February 19, he'd filled out a beneficiary slip, naming my mother as next of kin—even though he'd already made out such a report less than three months before. Moreover, on May 1, during a period when there was a conspicuous absence of orders, he took out additional life insurance of $10,000, which was a great deal of money back then. His file is actually full of beneficiary slips, which Bob characterizes as unusual, recalling that he himself had made out only one. Another beneficiary slip was submitted a month before he was shipped out to the Pacific in October 1944 and several more during his tour there, including one before the bloody invasion of Peleliu. I'm guessing that he filled out many of these slips right before a secret spying mission, one that carried the very real possibility that he might not return home.

The records have him periodically taking long leaves, totaling more than three months, yet his separation papers state that he'd taken only twenty days. Indeed, upon his discharge in late 1945, the service owed him more than two months' leave. Mother had complained in a letter that her friends' husbands were getting orders home; couldn't he ask for one? Oblivious to his secret operations, she must have been crestfallen when even during his leaves he didn't come home.

A letter to my mother on Christmas Eve 1944 says that both he and Jack Steele had been pulled out of the Pacific "very very unexpectedly" with only a few days' notice. At that time, he made out a beneficiary slip. Records document that he completed an urgent return to Washington on January 2, only to be given four weeks' leave. On January 6, his father had written him that "someone called for you but I didn't tell them where you were, in fact I told them I hadn't heard from you at all."

My father had told me that after he returned from the Pacific in late December, he'd been whisked away to Scandinavia. So I surmise that he, along with Steele, returned to Sweden at once for the Danish gun-running Operation Moonshine, which tried to run the blockade from September 1944 to February 1945, although their only successful operation was on January 15, 1945. Dad already knew the ins and outs of the blockade-busting operations from spring of 1943. He might have come home after January 15 and then later returned to Europe, or being at the right place at the right time, he might have gone to England after Operation Moonshine and then been drafted by the OSS to go to France on the plane that had been stripped—the single-engine Lysander, which was painted black and could land and take off on a dime. That was undoubtedly the expedition where he'd taught newly recruited Maquisards how to handle weapons—and the one where he'd shot the Gestapo sergeant.

From early March to mid-April 1945, there's another conspicuous absence of orders in his file. In a memo I found dated March 2, 1945, he reported he had just gotten weapons blueprints and photos and was expected to figure them out and brief the brass on them imminently. I assume he was dispatched some time later to northeastern France, in Alsace, with a division of the Sixth Army group. By February it had successfully thwarted Hitler's Operation Nordwind (put into action simultaneously with the assault on the Allied "Bulge" in Ardennes) and driven Germans from French soil. By late March, the Allies had crossed the Rhine and were penetrating deep into Germany. By then, my father would have discovered and shot the Communist double agent and raided Nazi weapons facilities as part of the T-Forces or some similar unit. A day or two after the American liberation of Ohrdruf on April 4, 1945, he was dispatched to Ohrdruf to report on the camp. (Contrary to his testimony to the Museum of Jewish Heritage, which he'd slightly altered to protect his oath of silence, he'd later admitted to me that he wasn't sent to Ohrdruf from the U.S.). Then, a week later, on April 11, when Nordhausen was discovered by American troops, he could have been sent to one of the smaller weapons sites in nearby towns to study rocket components.

His next orders for U.S. duty are dated April 20 and send him to Charleston, South Carolina, to "inspect ordnance." From the middle of May to the middle of June, there's another gap in his orders; this is probably the time when he went back to Germany to interrogate rocket scientists for what was to become Operation Paperclip.

It all fits.

I open the mail one day to find a little gift from the Navy Department: Dad's "fitness reports" from his service in the Pacific. One Joseph Lockwood, commander of Argus 13, writes that during his first four months in the southwestern Pacific, through December 1943, Tom Franks had proved to be "the best ensign I have had under my command. Although an OV(S)—Ordnance officer—he is adaptable for any duty and learns quickly. He leads by doing things better than his men . . . his duties with this unit have been varied. In all his assign-ments, he has demonstrated excellent judgment and leadership." Then, after his transfer to Argus 14, a second commander, H. L. Curtis, reports on his last five months in the Pacific: "Officer of many talents: radar, recognition, construction . . . Best recognition teacher we've met in the Navy . . . intelligent . . . thorough, conscientious, gets work done."

I'm happy to have this belated recognition of my father's talents and versatility. As glowing as these report cards are, however, I long to jump off the sterile pages.

One day, I flop down on our antique Morris recliner, pushing back the bar until I'm staring at the ceiling, something I do when I'm frus-trated. Bob comes over. "What about his war buddies?" he asks.

"I've tried! The only Ordnance buddy I know of was Jack Steele and I've already tried to find Dad's Argus mates and I came up with zilch, you know that." I close my eyes.

Then I feel the unaccustomed presence of The Scowl. "You'd bet-ter try again," Bob says, "because these guys aren't going to hang around much longer."

He's right. The history of the secret radar outfit would remain, but its people would not.

It's time to do everything I can to find the other eyes of Argus.

Chapter Twenty-two

I'd dreamed of Dad as a coast-watcher, a brave but hapless soldier parachuted into the jungle of a little island in the Pacific with a heavy, black radiotelephone set, a pair of binoculars to spot enemy aircraft, and a willingness to be left there for years. It wasn't until after the Americans engaged the Japanese that the Marines joined the valiant Australian and New Zealander coast-watchers, who by then were half-starved, with beards tickling their knees. Finally, in 1942, came Argus, with its newfangled, high-powered equipment, and it largely put the coast-watchers out of business.

After plowing through stacks of mostly impenetrable military memoranda on Argus from NARA, I'm finally able to piece together this operation's mission. Its very existence was top secret—which is the reason it's virtually unknown today—because the Japanese tracking system was at first so primitive compared to the Americans' high-level technology. The U.S. Pacific Command was desperate to keep their plans out of Japanese hands.

There was a bounty on every Argus head captured by the Japanese, and Marines guarded them around the clock. The unit received its own intelligence reports from Naval Intelligence, and its own weapons and demolitions materiel. During an island invasion, Argus would hit the beach with the first wave of Marines and set up mobile stations within an hour; the heavier, stronger ones that contained even longer-range radar came in later. The units would operate day and night to ferret out incoming enemy bombers or ships and then direct Allied fighters, as well as antiaircraft artillery, to intercept and shoot them down. In addition to the main headquarters, seven-man outposts, the kind my father periodically commanded, would be hidden away on hilltops in sometimes dangerous jungles where they could spot even more distant enemies. According to the records, Argus had complete control over all antiaircraft fire and searchlights as well as over aircraft fighters once they were airborne. It was the island's Command Information Center, and like its Greek mythological namesake, it had eyes that saw in every direction and would hold a pilot's life, and an island's safety, firmly in its hands.

There were more than twenty Argus units in the Pacific, and they were on hand for some of the fiercest battles there. All but two Argus units were decommissioned in mid-1944—Argus 14 and Argus 20. These were elected to be in the vanguard for important island invasions. It just so happened that my father was attached to each of them.

In my father's effects, I'd found two unit photos of the officers of Argus 13 and Argus 14. Dad had written the names of Argus 13ers neatly on the back, and the Argus 14 snapshot was accompanied by a next-of-kin list typed by my mother. I'd tried unsuccessfully to locate the men on both lists but now, with the help of new history websites, I'm at least able to find some men from other Argus units.

James O'Neill was a petty officer with Argus 15 at Tinian, one of the most heavily trafficked airbases in the Pacific Theater. "I'm not surprised that to this day, nobody has even heard of the Argus units," he tells me. "You weren't even allowed to speak the word 'radar' or tell anyone else what you did. Barbed wire surrounded our unit. They swore you to secrecy for life."

Gregory Barber, the son of one Argus officer, swears that his father was some kind of spy. "My father went on to become a Navy captain, and then he had a little business, which turned out to be fictitious. He had a wooden locker full of different kinds of rifles—and he had Minox cameras." Another doppelganger for my father.

By the time I'm finished calling Argus veterans, I've plowed through a 139-page stack of names and numbers and racked up a four-figure phone bill that causes my husband to display The Scowl.

Then, just when I've almost given up, I locate two veterans who miraculously recall precisely who my father was. The first is Alvin Pate, age seventy-seven, who was chief petty officer of Argus 20. He tells me he was with Dad for the invasion of Peleliu in September 1944.

But how on earth could Dad have been attached to Argus 20 for the Peleliu invasion on September 15, which his military summary sheet says he was, and then be reattached to Argus 14 only a few weeks later to set up the radar unit on Ulithi, 232 nautical miles away? I'd learned that Admiral William H. P. Blandy commanded a naval task force that landed Army troops first on Peleliu and then on Ulithi. Did Blandy finagle this strange back-and-forth swap? Did Dad travel on his ship?

In his Holocaust testimony, Dad had described Peleliu as a horrible event. When we speak by phone, Pate confirms what an understatement that was. Peleliu was a deadly miscalculation by military decision-makers. Indeed, Admiral William F. Halsey tried too late to cancel the controversial assault because he didn't consider it worth the anticipated casualties. Aerial photos of the island had indicated a gently rounded hill some distance from the landing beaches. Instead, the land was a Byzantine system of sharp coral ridges, valleys, and sinkholes.

"They were one or two miles long," Pate tells me. "Concrete bunkers with big guns pointed at us and we couldn't knock them out." The Japanese soldiers stayed well back from the beach, holed up with their machine-gun nests and mortars, all interconnected by a honeycomb of tunnels and caves, immune to the U.S. naval and air strikes that were concentrated on the beaches. Deployed in oncoming waves, the Marines were like ducks in a shooting gallery; the water turned red as thousands of American fighting men were killed or wounded over the ten weeks the battle raged. The Americans finally prevailed on this tiny island, but at the cost of nearly 7,000 American lives and 12,000 Japanese.

Pate remembers Dad running up the beach at Peleliu with the second invasion echelon. "He went in right behind the Marines, carrying a piece of mobile radar equipment, I think. They needed men with a lot of experience and smarts, and your Dad had that. I'm pretty sure he was in command of something, acted as an executive officer. He was probably sent to secure the radar because he could do the job better than anyone else. As soon as it was secured, he could be whisked out.

"But then as a liaison officer to the Marines, he could have been doing something else again. Those were hush-hush jobs. Not too many people would know what he was really doing. He could have been working the radar, while also doing something very secret.

"I remember, he was a tall, skinny man, right? He had somebody with him; they worked very close together." I'm guessing that was Jack Steele. "Your dad was a good fellow," Pate continues. "He was reasonable and down to earth, not like a lot of the other officers. The enlisted men didn't care much for them, you know. But your dad would talk to anyone; he didn't judge a person by his rank."

I smile. That was Dad.

To my excitement, I find that the other Argus veteran who served with Dad knew him even better than Alvin Pate. Jack Hessey, a retired engineer, spent more than a year with Dad when he was a lieutenant on Argus 13, the outfit that had been stationed on Guadalcanal and then had invaded Emirau.

I travel to the retirement development in Matawan, New Jersey, where Hessey lives. I'm supposed to meet him in the parking lot, but he isn't there. I back up and nearly crash into a gold car that seems to have appeared out of nowhere. Jack Hessey steps out, comes over, and leans into the window.

I am looking at my father. The same long upper lip, the thin mouth, the high cheekbones, and that familiar shadow of pain passing over his face. Jack is short and his ears stick out, but otherwise the resemblance is startling.

We stare at each other, forgetting to exchange introductions. "You look like your dad," he says finally.

"I look like my dad?"

"Pretty much," he says. I don't know who is more astonished. Jack motions me into the car. Then this slight octogenarian guns the motor and screeches round curves until we arrive at a sedate, rose-colored cottage.

Inside his home, Jack's wife, Elaine, has a big smile and a cup of coffee ready for me. She sits down to listen in on my interview of Jack, who carefully brings out a big Navy book with photos of various battles. Iron is in his voice as he talks of all the men he knew who died. Then he spreads out a big war map over a card table. He smoothes the creases from it and places a little pointer first on Guadalcanal, then Bougainville, Emirau, Ulithi. He explains the significance of each island where Dad had been, with a meticulousness like my father's. "We'd train, and we'd practice setting up the Argus equipment over and over in Guadalcanal," he tells me. "We were getting ready for the invasion of Emirau. That was in, let me see, March of '44."

Jack pauses, then studies my face. "Your smile," he says suddenly. "That's what reminds me of Tom."

"It does?" The smiles I knew were more winning for their rarity, for the fact that they didn't come from a happy person.

Jack turns back to the map. "He was someone who went off on his own a lot. For instance, one time after we had been on Emirau for a while, he told me he'd talked his way into a trip on a PT boat. They were going to go to New Ireland, to Kavieng, about fifty miles away at the tip of the island." Jack moves the pointer. "See on the map, here it is. Kavieng was still held by the Japanese, but we had isolated it. He said they were going to patrol along the shore and if they saw Japanese trucks or other military vehicles, they were going to shoot them out. When your dad came back, I could see him come in and there was a big flow of light on the water. A hole had been shot in the bow of the boat."

"What was the point?" I ask.

"You know, the more I think about it, the more I think the trip on the PT boat was an intelligence detail. Maybe they were looking to see if any of the larger Jap ships had been brought there; maybe they went in close to look for shore batteries, other kinds of defense."

"Jack, what do you remember about the invasion of Emirau?" I ask. That move had put the Allies closer to bombing range of Truk, the base of Japanese operations in the Solomon Islands and New Guinea. It was General McArthur's first step toward the retaking of the Philippines. The American brass had decided, in accordance with their island-hopping strategy, to bypass Kavieng for the relatively undefended and tiny island of Emirau.

Jack raises his head, closes his eyes. "We went in with the Marines, and we would have been dead ducks if the Japs had been there, because the landing crafts hit the coral reef and we had to wade ashore up to our knees.

"I think your father was a fighter-director officer—the enlisted men would follow the concentric circles of the radar screen, and if they saw a suspicious blip, they would call the fighter-director, who would hustle over and decide whether the blip signified an enemy reconnaissance plane or a bogey [enemy bomber], in which case he might scramble our air defenses.

"We would kid around with the headquarters, the CIC [Combat Information Center], calling them 'Christ, I'm Confused.' But they—we—were good—spotted every Jap reconnaissance plane that flew over. But the Japs didn't bother sending any Bettys to bomb us. Charles Lindbergh flew in to visit us, but that was about it. We spent a quiet three or four months on the island."

His description of Emirau reminds me of how my father described the miniature island to Amy: "It was so small that on the airstrip you had to rev up fast and go around a curve and hope you got the wheels up fast enough so you wouldn't roll into the drink."

The last island my father was on, Ulithi, was a staging area for the invasion of Okinawa, where many thousands perished. My father was saved by his sudden December 1944 orders to return to the States, but Jack Hessey got orders for the doomed island near the Japanese mainland.

It's a long day as memories of grueling battles swim to the surface. As I'm getting ready to leave, Elaine takes my hand. "You've been quite an experience for us," she says. She is teary. "You've brought back all those days. Made us remember."

But Jack is more subdued. "Well, I assume you got what you wanted," he says stiffly.

I look at him. "I think I just wanted to be closer to my father," I say.

His face softens. "That's what I was hoping," he replies.

Chapter Twenty-three

I drive out of the parking lot and onto the highway. This is the end of the line. No more people to interview, no more records to pore through. I thought I would feel elated, but instead I'm disgruntled.

What had I expected Jack to say? "Yes, I knew your father was a spy—and he was the best damn spy the war ever had!" I know of course that I'll never hear those words; this is a generation honor-bound to keep promises. But I wish I had just one more piece of circumstantial evidence. Had the war really turned my father's personality around? How will I ever be able to find out unless I know what he had been like before?

Then I remember Marajen Stevick. If my father's temperament had darkened because of his war activities, she would know it, for she knew him before it all happened. Marajen had been my father's best childhood friend in Champaign, Illinois. Later, she left her family, who owned a chain of newpapers, and married an Italian count named Chinigo.

Now a widow, she lives in Ravello, above the Amalfi Coast, amid lemon, fig, and kumquat trees. Her home has become a salon of sorts for luminaries from Gore Vidal to various European royals. The Countess has alert eyes, is sharp and vibrant, and has long thick hair twirled into a comb in the back.

I talk to her over the phone. "Tom was a happy boy," she recalls. "Terribly cute. He gave me so many laughs. He loved adventure but he just wouldn't lie, even to avoid getting punished. He didn't gossip or tell tales and he was very even-tempered, not depressed or lonely or anything in spite of being an only child. When he became a young man, we had this group, you know, and he was very open and carefree, but I'd say he was somewhat naive. I never saw him get mad though he had this irresistible power—he sort of lorded it over me because I was a girl. He had a lot of friends, probably because he was so much fun—a happy-go-lucky guy."

Then I telephone someone who knew my father after the war: Barb Mustard. She paints a very different picture. "He was an odd man, your father," she says. "He clammed up, you know, especially at any social function. He was a stylish dancer but you'd dance with him and he wouldn't say a word, he wouldn't even crack a smile. He seemed pent-up. If there was an open bar, he'd be the first one there. That would loosen him up a bit. His personality? Well he certainly wasn't a happy man. In fact I think he felt blue a lot of the time."

Minutes later, Penny calls, as if by some mystical design, with new information about our father. It turns out that during all those long afternoon conversations he'd shared more with Penny, then a teenager, than I'd ever known.

In the tropics, he told her, the men under his command were so desperate for boots he'd been forced to pry them off Japanese corpses, sometimes actually digging out rotting flesh. "I thought to myself, 'Who is this man?' He had this ability to stay completely emotionally detached," Penny says. "It was scary. I was thinking, if he could do that, he could do anything during the war, and I think they knew it. Later, it obviously tore him up." She'd sometimes come upon him staring off into space in broad daylight, moaning, "Ohhhh, no, no, oh no."

Dad told Penny how he'd been dropped by parachute onto a Japanese-occupied island in what he called "a suicide mission." He said, "I landed on top of a mountain, then radioed back which planes were going overhead, which installations the Japanese had there."

This was possibly one of his Argus operations. "There was a high probability of my not coming back," he'd told Penny.

"But, Daddy," Penny said, "if you hadn't come back, there wouldn't be a Cindy or a Penny." He looked away.

"That's when I realized that a hero not only has to sacrifice himself but also the people he loves . . . Daddy had to make himself become cold and cruel."

I think of the young soldier who wrote those first letters to his bride at the beginning of the war. A man who loved life—advising her on which dinner-dance clubs to visit, scouting dresses for her, lustily envisioning reunions between her and Junior, entertaining her with funny anecdotes, wistfully describing the romance of the South Pacific without her by his side, longing to come home and begin a family.

I put my hand under the desk drawer in my study, which is stuck so fast that only I know how to budge it. The last in the pack of letters from the Pacific is dated Christmas Eve 1944. In it, my father is frantic about not hearing from his wife, though the sporadic wartime mail delivery has delayed her letters before:

> . . . *I have been the most unhappy little boy lately that you ever saw. The last letter I have received from you was mailed Nov. 27. I thought sure I would hear from you around Xmas . . . If you don't love me any more please write and tell me. It would be infinitely better for me to know than to sit and brood about just what the situation is . . . I love you, darling, and I want to be with you so badly. I can't express myself adequately enough to even start to tell you how much I love you and how miserable I am away from you. If you don't love me any more and think you are doing me a favor by not telling me you are terribly mistaken. I never have been as miserable as this before . . . I hope to God the next Xmas isn't like this one. I love you darling, more than I can ever tell you and I am so unhappy right now. I love you, Tom.*

In that mood, he would have been sent directly to Sweden for Operation Moonshine, then perhaps to Denmark and France to aid the Resistance, to shoot a Gestapo guard, to assassinate his friend, and to witness the terrors of Ohrdruf and Nordhausen. He would have come home in a state of shock, a spy and a killer.

There is a gap in his letters of three months from early March to late May, and when he returns, his letters to my mother are noticeably subdued, with no more effusive language or gushy terms of endearment. One is signed simply: "All my love, Tom."

In late May 1945, he talks about "going overseas with this group," and days later, my mother gets a cryptic note from an army captain in St. Petersburg, who explains to her that her husband had to leave suddenly before he'd even had the chance to send a letter. He's probably in the middle of Operation Paperclip.

There are a few more letters before he's discharged in November 1945. But these infrequent letters are cursory, robbed of the richly described anecdotes of his frequent letters from the Pacific. Perhaps it's because he's no longer far from home (surely he sees his wife more often), and certainly their marriage is experiencing problems. But there's a lack of his former verve, a certain tone of defeat. Even when he's out of the service and his letters are sent from a Cleveland business trip, they're flat, gloomy. "The unhappy little boy" has turned into a hardened husband.

Tucked inside one of these letters is an undated note on lined paper: a note from Mom written to Grandma Leavitt:

Dear Mother,

. . . Tom is still sour and acts as if it's a chore to even speak to me. He sloshed down I don't know how many martinis at the Country Club and had to be helped to the car and we don't even belong to the club yet! What would you imagine our chances are now? I know, he saw those awful camps, but Denny saw his best friend die and he's not that way, . . . and Mary Huckin's husband is in fine fettle, thrilled to be back home with his wife. It's been almost a year since V Day! I've tried and tried. I don't

know what I did to deserve this. Can I come home? I could take
a train to Chicago and Daddee could pick me up.

My father's secret war has stolen from the killing fields to the home front. He has moved in on himself, and even the wife he adores hasn't the least idea what he's become.

I can see her. Wigs: fine champagne bobs, honey streaked with starlight, mahogany pageboys, any guise that might arouse his interest. Lacy corsets that run from hip to breast. Undulating satin nightwear, spreading over her like the colors of a sunset. How can he resist? Rich pork roasts with crackling, corn roasted under the broiler, sensuous shortcake with mounds of lavender Chantilly. Anything. But his eyes gloss over. Her hunger for him, her anxiousness to know what has happened, only drives him deeper into the void.

She gets desperate. She gets fatter. She gets spiteful. She nags, she treats him shabbily in front of others. "You will pay for this," he writes, on the back of a place card at a public dinner. This is their endgame. The nerves have crossed and what seemed like their endless reserve of love has turned to cruelty.

It is undeniable. My father's character had been a casualty of war. And the war he'd brought home had caused collateral damage: to his own daughters.

One day long ago, my father and I took a walk through the woods. "Look up, Cindy, see how big these trees are. Guess what made them grow that tall?" He looked down at me. "Fire," he said. "The seeds can only grow when they're scorched. Sometimes a lightning storm will burn the forest, but it'll grow up again, because the fire cracks the seeds open."

We had been seeds in the fire, my father and I. And I saw the chance for us to begin again. I glimpsed layers of a new, old life, secrets that could reinvent my childhood, that could bring me together again with the man who should have been my father. The operation to extract these secrets had necessarily employed clandestine methods, but how cathartic the end would be. How noble, how redeeming for us both.

Altruism, alas, seldom exists alone. When had I begun to enjoy, even glory in this venture that caused him so much pain? Dreaded patterns are passed on from generation to generation, no matter how we try to reverse them. Was I as vengeful as my mother; had the means become the end?

You start by loving someone, searching out their love for you, but what happens when it doesn't come freely? Then you must squeeze it out, bend it, stretch it, shout at it, punch it, bruise it, until finally, loving and hurting have intertwined.

I had wanted to hurt my father as much as he had hurt me. I'd nagged him, manipulated him into confessions, then shamelessly condemned him. Little by little, I'd forced him to give up every shred of camouflage, until he was utterly exposed. Now, sitting in the wheelchair, staring up at me with his whole heart, he was finally mine.

The price for this gift had been clear. Just as he had unquestioningly done his duty, it was time for me to do mine: to care for him, to love him, to abide with him for the balance of his days.

But what of this love rooted in dependence? Was it really love? Or its antithesis?

My father's dependence on me, at first stifling, in time became cleansing. He appreciated me at last. My resentment faded. We stopped demanding from each other. No more giving and taking as the measure of our love. No more counting the number of times I visited, and the number I didn't. Miraculously, we had stepped off the battlefield.

The stillness between us at the end wasn't an imposition of will. We were beyond any sense of expectation or duty. All our debts had been paid. Perhaps we only truly love our parents when we've given up the gnarled ties with them, stopped keeping score. I think of the words of the Sufi poet Rumi: "Outside ideas of right doing and wrong doing, there is a field. I'll meet you there."

Chapter Twenty-four

I've taken the best room available at the Colony Hotel, near Pat's home in the little town of Gardner, Massachusetts. It happens to be the bridal suite, and that's where we are, curled up on a king-sized sleigh bed whose tapestry coverlet is threaded with gold. With its palatial marble floors and dappled antique armoire, it looks like the bedchamber where Queen Victoria might have ensconced Prince Albert. We're mellow from the martinis Pat ordered for us at dinner "with the ice chopped very fine, and cold . . . that's the way Tom made them."

I've grown thoroughly comfortable with Pat since Dad's death and I've readily accepted her invitation to visit for the weekend. She's wearing a blue silk blouse with ruffles down the breast. Her eyes retain their Irish sparkle. Her tawny hair is casual, but styled. At eighty years old, she's grown slighter and often rubs her fingers, knobby with arthritis, yet she is still beautiful, more so than I've ever seen her. She's been flying around the room, opening and shutting the curtains, fluffing the pillows, and talking a mile a minute. She flops back against the cushions at last.

"Your father was the great love of my life, you know, the only real love I had." She runs a finger across her eye. "He was so tender, he was the only man who could comfort me. Sometimes we would just lie together, holding each other, not speaking but just being close.

"Cindy, Dad and I connected emotionally. We were empathetic and empathic. He didn't have very much of that in his life. Oh, he didn't exactly pour out his heart, but he could find peace with me. You see, he really thought that your mother never loved him. He thought that there was only one woman who did."

I knew, of course, the outline of their romance. Dad and Pat had met before I was born, at General Alloys, where she was a secretary. With Daddy's support, she'd fled to Florida with her young son and divorced her first husband. Daddy wouldn't leave Mother, so Pat had married someone else. She'd had another son and then her husband got rich and left her for a younger woman. In time, Daddy became a widower, old and broke, and now he wanted to marry her. But yet again, Pat had wed someone else.

"Why didn't you marry him then, Pat?" I ask.

"I thought Dad didn't care about me anymore. He kept backing out of seeing me. I had idealized him so much; I didn't know it was the first signs of dementia. I would say, 'Tom, I've put the dogs in the kennel. I've arranged everything. Don't do this to me.' But he canceled anyway. And I couldn't endure it. I needed to be supported, and taken care of. So I married David Cosentino."

So Dad pushed the great love of his life away just as vigorously as he'd pushed the rest of us. For so long, I'd thought that Pat had abandoned Dad when he most needed her.

"Even after David, we still saw each other," Pat says, looking down. She sighs. "Poor thing, he needed cash badly and so we went through his attic, gathering up anything that I thought worth selling. I had gotten to know antiques and was somewhat of a dealer by then, Cindy."

He sold our valuable heirlooms, and didn't even tell me? Was he getting back at me for not providing him with a living? "What did he sell, Pat?"

"There was a big, hand-painted Victorian fish platter and matching plates. And, Cindy, a rare Eskimo bag with a little note from your grandmother inside—one of you had labeled it for the trash. We pulled out this huge crystal basket, but there was too much of a shock going from the heat of the attic to the cool air. It shimmered in the sun for a moment and then it just disintegrated."

The gorgeous basket that overflowed with homemade caramels every Christmas? My grandmother's most precious possession, shattered into a million pieces? But then again, could I blame Pat for coming to my father's rescue, this old broken man?

Pat picks up a red sateen pillow with yellow tassels and hugs it to her. It turns different colors in the beams of light coming through the heavy velvet curtains. "You see, through everything, through our respective marriages, through the absences from each other, we were the only constant in each other's lives. He had a sixth sense about when I was in trouble. If I was in turmoil about my husbands or my children, I knew to expect a call from him. I also understood his spirit. I felt when he was in a depression too. We were passionate soul mates. We should have been together all the time. He just couldn't leave your mother. It just wasn't meant to be.

"When we met, I was demoralized, brainwashed. Your dad began spending time with my son Peter. He taught him to fly fish, to swim. I felt protected with Tom, we all did.

"Did he ever tell you the story of how he saved my life? A terrible storm came up. Tom was up on the flying bridge trying desperately to keep the boat from capsizing and I was holding onto the edge with all my might, but the wind was tossing me around and I thought I was going to be catapulted into the sea. Tom put one hand on the wheel, grabbed me with the other and pulled me to him. He held onto me until he made it back to the harbor."

Pat sighs. "He was a hero. But Peter needed a full-time father, so I married a fellow who owned a corner deli—that was Ken. Oh, but he was nothing like Tom. The day I told your father I was marrying him, he got up and started to walk out of the hotel room. I made him come back so I could explain why I was doing it. He sat there; his face had gone absolutely gray, Cindy, and I knew what he was going through. I hugged him and told him I understood why he couldn't marry me. He wouldn't leave you kids, you know, especially not to her. He finally accepted what I had to do, but he never liked it."

I take out a long, dog-eared letter from Pat's second child, Noah, and give it to her. The meticulously written letter thanked my father for the Civil War books he'd sent and told in detail about the thesis he was writing on postwar construction.

Pat is surprised: "Tom was like a father to my kids. They loved him. He taught Noah how to run a big boat. But I didn't know about the letter. I didn't know they had their own private thing. I guess it's better that way, better than me saying, 'Tom, have a relationship with Noah' and 'Noah, have a relationship with Tom.'"

The next day Pat helps me pack to leave. When we're finished, she says, "Come here, I have something to show you." She picks up her tote bag and motions for me to sit down beside her on the bountiful mahogany bed. "Do you want to hear the history of your life?" she smiles.

She takes out an album of pictures of Penny and me as children, teens, adults. Each photo is meticulously mounted, a labor of love. And she has a bulging folder of my published stories. I page through it; she's even collected reviews and quotes from my pieces on blogs and websites I've never seen. I'm amazed.

"Your father brought me the pictures. We used to look at them together." She pats the cushion next to her, opening the album. "Look here. When you were three, you were so happy and content." There, pasted on creamy linen, is a snapshot of me in a little wool coat and matching hat, laughing at whoever was taking the picture. Pat and I smile at a parade of photos of Penny and me at varying ages. When we get to me at age nine, however, I'm far from happy: I look sad and subdued, undoubtedly sobered by my domineering mother.

"But never mind," she says, quickly closing the album when she sees my distressed face. "He got such a chuckle out of peeping into the attic and watching you dance around in your grandmother's old flapper dresses. Listen to this: he knew how much you loved the Bobbsey Twins—remember how he used to bring back the next in the series for you?—and later *The Secret Garden* and the *Anne of Green Gables* books. He'd tell me, 'Pat, she is such a reader. I can hardly keep her in books!'" Pat smiles shyly. "I was the one who bought you *The Black Stallion*.

"Oh yes, and he marveled at the fact that when you were seven, you got up in the night and took your own asthma medicine. He would listen sometimes all night for the sound of your wheezing. It scared him. He stood behind the bathroom door and watched you to make sure you were doing it right."

"You *have* to be kidding!"

"No, I'm *not* kidding, Cindy."

I struggle to keep my face composed. How could I have known he was there? He was, as always, the outsider looking in, the observer behind glass. Watching me, watching over me.

Steam rushes by the window from some heating system outside. It reminds me of the globe-shaped asthma vaporizer that sat on the chair next to my bed. When I was four or five, my mother used to turn it on, then leave the room. I was scared, the noose around my neck tightening, choking the air out of me. Was I going to die? Would the bogeyman that made my chest tighten finally come for me? Faintly, I saw Daddy step into the room. He calmed my panic by telling me a story, holding the vaporizer near my mouth, waiting until the steam loosened my congested bronchial tubes.

And now I realize that there's always been another watcher, one standing even farther back in the shadows. For all these years, Pat, the one I thought had stalked me, had actually been standing guard over me too, settling for the crumbs of my life: secondhand reports from my father, photos passed and pasted into an album no one else would ever see. I picture them on a couch, heads together, proudly reviewing the accomplishments of my sister and me. Pat roaming the aisle of a bookstore, pressing gifts for me into his hand, imagining my delight.

Pat shakes her head. "When that girl in sixth grade knocked your

front tooth out, he wanted to kill her. And when your stories got published in the lit magazine of Beaver Country Day School, he was
pleased as punch. And, oh, the way he talked about how you shopped
for a dress for your mother at Christmas! He said, 'Pat, she examines
every hem and seam,' and I told him, 'She's like you, Tom. Punctilious.'"

"He noticed how I *shopped*?"

She nodded. "And how he loved your sister! He could really talk
to her. He thought it was hilarious when she painted that vicious
neighborhood cat green when she was four or five, how mischievous
and smart she was, how her love of animals revealed her true character. He was very, very proud of her."

"If Penny and I were so special, why didn't he ever tell us?" Once,
when I was about ten, I'd written a poem that I thought was pure
greatness. I gave it to him. "Is it as good as Shakespeare?" I'd asked,
hopefully.

"Well . . . not really," he'd replied, ending the conversation.

"I don't think he knew how to tell people what they meant to him,"
Pat says. "The three girls in his life that meant so much to him—you,
Penny, and Amy—he just could never tell them he loved them. When
you graduated from Vassar, I would have given anything to be there. I
made him tell me all about it. But he was depressed. You had told him
you were going to leave and live in England. He was so upset, he cried."

"He *cried*?" I'd waited until close to my father's death to see
him cry.

She nods. "Tears. Real tears. When your folks waved you off on the
ship in New York, you said, 'I'll probably never see you again.'"

"I said that? Oh no."

"But that was all right. I told him, 'You should be happy. She's
flying off. Let her have wings.' Then you won the Pulitzer for the
Diana Oughton stories. You were my poetic inspiration. My muse.
I was sitting on a bench and I read your story in the *Boston Globe*. I
was all agitated, and I grabbed for my notebook and pencil and
wrote my Diana poem. I didn't even realize until I'd finished that
you were the author."

And I had thrown that poem away.

She looks at me wistfully. "I didn't have a daughter, you see, I didn't have a daughter to nurture with my own aspirations."

I look down. I'd always longed for a gentle mother's love and acceptance. It seems I'd always had it. If only I had known it.

"You know, your father would talk to me about your achievements, your problems, as though I *was* your mother," Pat tells me. "I'd ask him, 'Where's Cindy today?' And he would say, 'She could be anywhere, Pat. For all I know, she could be at Buckingham Palace, or she could be passing the time with the Pope.' He was so proud of you. I internalized you, Cindy. I had never met you, but I knew you.

"When you were born, it was a kind of salvation for him," Pat says. "You see, when he was in the camps, he saw this pit and in the pit was this little girl, this baby girl with her eyes open. Her hands were frozen, held up as though she was defending herself. She was only about two years old. The body was covered with lime. He could never get her out of his mind. Having you and Penny was very redemptive, very emotional for him. It took away some of the horror of that moment."

A little girl? Dad had told me about the boy wandering around the camp in a dirty flour sack. But he'd never mentioned a little girl. Was that the thing he couldn't bear to tell me, that propelled him out of the kitchen that morning after he gave his testimony?

"He adored you, Cindy. He had something on his wall, it wasn't even properly framed, but he wouldn't let me sell it. It was a gold knight on black paper, a brass rubbing. A gorgeous brass rubbing from Westminster Abbey. You'd gotten down on your hands and knees and rubbed that knight's tomb with a chunk of gold wax. Dad said the wax alone was worth twenty dollars or something like that. He said, 'Cindy did that for me, Pat. Not her mother and I, just me.'"

It had been a birthday present I'd made for him when I was living in London, working for UPI. I had rubbed and rubbed the brass knight, who stood with one foot on a dog or wolf, until it was perfectly solid gold, no black showing. And I had sung extra sets at the Tip to buy the gold wax.

My father. The man who couldn't wait to brag about me to Pat. Who apparently knew every little thing I had done.

It doesn't matter that he took Pat to Stella's, that he'd stopped caring about anything I'd written. He'd really seen me. He'd known me all along.

I look at Pat. The breeze from the window ruffles her blouse. She stands still and white, like a statue.

We get up. It's time for me to leave for New York. And Pat must teach a poetry course. She's designed a college-sponsored program for older writers, founded a literary magazine called *Tapestries*, and is treasurer of the New England Poetry Club. "And to think I'd barely gone through high school when I met Dad," she says. "In a sense, he made me."

"Well, in a sense, you made him. I think you saved his life," I say.

"No, you were the one, Cindy. His love for you and Penny kept him functioning long after he had any right to function. He didn't want to let go and he knew you didn't either."

I have a lump in my throat. It's cold and windy outside and the leaves are rolling about like lost hats.

I'd been dabbling in alchemy, calling my father's childhood friends, poring over his letters, visiting Pat, trying to transform the dead. But Pat was the true alchemist; she had transformed the living. She'd taken my father's love for me, increased it with her own, and given it back to him tenfold: the perfect mother.

I shift painfully on the bed. "Oh, Cindy, your knee hurts you, doesn't it?" Pat says, rubbing my sore muscles. She makes me promise to buy Icy Hot and Tiger Balm. Then she gives me a bag full of presents: books, scarves, a scented candle labeled "Love," a jewelry box that reminds me of a childhood treasure, and a Tupperware container of fruit and nut cookies she baked herself.

"Do you know how pretty you are, Cindy," she says, putting her arms around me. "My angel," she whispers, standing on tiptoes so she can reach my ear. I've never heard those words before. From anyone. I see this flash of blue silk, pale skin, and freckled hands. "You," she says, her cool hands holding my cheeks, "were always our girl."

Epilogue

When summertime comes and the tiger swallowtails tremble on the bush, their wings transparent gold, striped with ebony like the keys of a piano, this is when I think of Dad. I think of him watching as they float from branch to branch, stopping to sip nectar from each lavender flower on my moon shadow shrub.

Sometimes, if I lose myself in the rhythm of their graceful motions, my father seems to inhabit me; his body, my body; my mind, his. Then, as quickly as he comes, he will be gone.

And I will have to be content with the part of him that endures in me. He has taught me how to rest in silence. I cradle my chin in my fingers, watch others closely, consider what I will say before I say it. I even hear myself occasionally mumbling, "Hell's bells."

Josh has opened the glass collecting boxes now, weeded out the crumbling moths, faithfully sprinkled naphthalene flakes over the velvety wings and glassy black eyes of the surviving specimens. He found an old butterfly identification book and treasures it. My father had taken a fountain pen and in tiny, neat script, written in the Latin name of each species. Eastern tiger swallowtail? *Papilio glaucus.* Great spangled frittillary? *Speyeria cybele.*

Recently Amy spotted her camp counselor wearing a pink "Princess" button. "My Grandpop used to call me that," Amy told her sadly. The counselor took the button off and pinned it on her collar.

I like to close my eyes and picture him in a moment a few weeks before he died. It was a Saturday in September:

I enter his room at Mary Manning Walsh. He is lying curled up, a pilling blue blanket tucked under his chin. "Daddy," I say softly. His eyes are stuck together, but he knows my voice.

"So," he drawls, "so nice to see you." Those are the only words now that he ever says, and he says them only to me. I smooth down the spikes of his fine hair.

He hasn't been out of bed for weeks, but today I'm determined to change that. It is brilliantly sunny, and outside his stuffy room autumn seems borne on a breeze. Perhaps some fresh air will jog his brain, awaken his brilliant intellect. I call an orderly and we lift him up. He's so light, it's so easy, and we maneuver him into His Chair.

"No, no!" he protests, but I shake my head. "Yes, Daddy, we're going outside to see the trees and the birds. It's beautiful."

Holding onto his IV stand, I wheel him through the hall to the terrace, attempting as I go to lure him back into the world. "There, in that corner, see, it's the rubber tree plant. Remember the rubber trees Mom had, she used to say they were having babies."

"Ba-bies." he slurs.

"Yes, Daddy! Babies! Oh yes," I say excitedly. "Remember how they multiplied, I mean, how new plants would sprout from the old? Grow up through the pot, the soil, right up from nothing! There were so many of them, we would clip them off, you know, cut them, and put them in a glass of water. And then they would grow!"

He looks into space.

"Or maybe that was avocados. Of course, stupid me, it was avocados." I kneel down in front of him and try to meet his eyes, but I don't think they see me. "We put a toothpick through the avocado pit, the seed that grows very big and becomes a big hard pit, and we balanced it on a glass so it wouldn't fall into the water. And soon roots would dangle down into the water. You remember, Daddy? You remember that? Babies, soon there would be avocado ba-bies."

Now he looks up at me, his blue eyes tinged with yellow. "Ba-bies!" I say, "Babies. You would plant the pit and before you knew it, up would come an avocado. A baby."

"Bay . . ." he whispers, looking at his knees.

"—bies! Yes, Dad. Babies!" He understands me, I know it. Once he took me by the hands and whirled me around through the air. In a burst of foolish pleasure, I run his wheelchair round in a circle, crying, "Whee!"

"What do think you're doing?" snaps an older woman on her way to the terrace. "That's elder abuse," she mutters to her friend.

I bring the chair to a halt. My father is grimacing. But his eyes are glazed, distant.

I wheel him past some prints. I take his hand and point it at the wall. "Look at the nice picture of the sailboat. The green sea, the red hull. Someday we'll sail in a boat like that, Dad."

We go onto the terrace and sit, looking over the wall. "The trees are losing their leaves already," I say. I look for a bird, but none roost in the trees nearby. We sit in silence. I don't know what he sees, what he knows—very little, I imagine. But I feel that he's happy with me here. It's so comfortable, so relaxing. I don't have to gather myself up to make small talk. I can simply behold the face I've known all my life, take his hand and feel him softly squeeze mine. He wants nothing from me but my presence, the essence of perfect love.

Now, when there's finally nothing left, the silence is at last enough. We can just be. This time is completely empty, yet completely full. The sweetest time is sometimes the end time.

I will be an orphan soon. But right here, right now, I am free, we are free. Everything else has fallen away. My father was my first hero, and now he is my last.

The tinkle of ragtime travels down the terrace. Someone has broken the rules and turned on a radio. I feel a sense of longing for my childhood, full of this music that he loved and cannot now remember. I look at my father, disappearing in his wheelchair, his face gray and drawn, his frog-like upper lip etched sweetly on his face. His swollen feet swallowed up by oversized slippers. I close my eyes and remember a man leaning over the record player, snapping his fingers and stamping his heel to the sound of Knuckles O'Toole.

I hear a steady little thump and I open my eyes. Then I open them wider. My father's foot is just barely tapping out the beat. He nods his head in rhythm. He lifts his finger off his lap and swings it back and forth, conducting the empty air. Then he gives me that knowing smile that lights up his face like a sliver of the moon.

Acknowledgments

Thank you to my rare and excellent editor and publisher, Rob Weisbach, always available, always ready to invigorate this project with his creativity and vision. To Betsy Rapoport for tirelessly and gracefully helping sculpt the book; Laura Pancucci, whose fine instincts helped guide me; Blair Brown Hoyt, for her literary expertise; Joshua Morgenthau, my brainstorming and editing companion; and Bob and Amy Morgenthau, whose wisdom helped turn memory into history.

To Penelope Franks, for lovingly sharing insight and information; Elaine Markson, my faithful agent and friend; Pat Cosentino, who imparted so much of her life; Lt. Col. Joe McNamara, for his steady help, encouragement and advice; Jill Comins, for her tough love; and Thomas Ensminger, fellow author and explorer of wartime regions unknown.

My gratitude to gunner's mate Benny Montenegro for his aid to me and his caring friendship to my father, and to Lou Golden, the man who thankfully spilled the secret.

In Washington, thanks to Congressman Charlie Rangel; historian Richard Breitman; archivists Marc Masurovsky and Kathy Lloyd, and Bernard Cavalcante at the Naval Historical Center; and to Michael Kurtz, Barry Zerby, Tim Nenninger, and John Taylor at NARA.

Thanks to the invaluable contributions of my international helpers—Al Jensen in Scandinavia, Richard Robinson, and Steven Kippax in England, and Sam Roberts and Charles and Daniel Pinck.

To Kate Medina; Jonathan Burnham; Ida Van Lindt; Bonnie Gurewitsch; David Marwell; Wendy Loehrs; Victor Navasky; Ed Marolda; Tom Blankton; Marilyn Bauza; Troy Sacquety; Judah Gribbetz; Kenneth Smith; Noah Rosenfield; George Sinclair; Harold P. Katz; Bob Sargent; Randy Belano; Steve Smith; John Chambers; Pam Distefano; Larry Hayes; Nerrisa Roberts; Renia Hylton; Ivy Barsky, and James Mintz.

And to these men, quiet heroes of WWII: Jack Hessey; Alvin Pate; Dr. Alan Roberts; James O'Neill; Craig Carmichael; Jack Sjobring; A.T. Barber; Charles Hinzey; Otto Linsenmeyer; Adm. Robert L.J. Long; Jack Steele; Adm.William H. P. Blandy; and to their wives and children, Gregory Barber; Christine and Lee Steele; Catherine Blandy Donich; Mary Sjobring; Irma Linsenmeyer; Mike Pate; and Jack Hessey.

Thanks to Judy Hottensen; Kristin Powers; Katie Finch; JillEllyn Riley; Camille March; Richard Florest; and the devoted team of professionals at Miramax Books. And to Harvey Weinstein, whose sharp eye and enthusiasm helped bring my father's story to the page.